Inside Jobs
A Realistic Guide to
Criminal Justice Careers
for College Graduates

Edited by
Stuart Henry

Eastern Michigan University

Sheffield Publishing Company

Salem, Wisconsin

For information about this book, write or call:
    Sheffield Publishing Company
    P.O. Box 359
    Salem, Wisconsin 53168
    (414) 843-2281

ISBN 1-879215-21-7

Printed in the United States of America

7 6 5 4

To Studs Terkel for his compassionate commitment to the appreciation of working people's lives.

CONTENTS

PREFACE

As a criminology instructor for the past 15 years both in England and the United States, I have found that one of the major weaknesses of many undergraduate criminal justice programs is the lack of attention they place on outcome. What do our students do when they graduate? Where do they go? How useful do they find the information and problem-solving skills that we provide for them? Do they like what they do? How would they have done it differently knowing what they know now? As an instructor I had been unable to answer these questions beyond the superficial suggestion that they "go to the careers center" or, "you should do an internship" or "there are several books on careers in the library!" This never-satisfying "passing of the buck" was revealed as a major weakness following our 1990 survey of students who had graduated from our criminology and criminal justice program.[1] As a result we began several attempts to correct and improve the transition of our students from college to their profession. This book is the outcome of one of these.[2]

Inside Jobs is a no-nonsense guide to careers in the criminal justice system. It is direct, concise and written in simple English by college-educated criminal justice professionals. It is sometimes amusing, occasionally shocking, and if nothing else, informative. It is designed to go beyond the mundane; to delve beneath the TV hype; to peek behind the badge; and to give the current criminal justice student a real feel for the careers that they may wish to enter.

---

[1] Stuart Henry, *Jobs: A Realistic Look at the Possibilities*, mimeo. Ypsilanti: Department of Sociology, Anthropology and Criminology, Eastern Michigan University, 1990.

[2] To address the question "what comes after graduation?" Eastern Michigan University's Department of Sociology, Anthropology and Criminology developed a multi-faceted career dimension which included expanded internship/coop possibilities, concentrations in applied fields of legal studies, law enforcement, corrections and management and administration, a class in criminal justice careers, a visiting speaker program and a bi-weekly jobs newsletter, *The Criminal Justice Employment Digest* (CJED), which senior students themselves compiled from area newspaper advertisements, and "published" for the benefit of their fellow students. *Inside Jobs* is the latest dimension of our effort to provide better informed, better educated graduates to the criminal justice field.

While a number of career texts provide information about criminal justice occupations, these are typically written from the perspective of a formal job description. Little information is available from an insider's view of criminal justice jobs. Moreover, nothing exists that gives such a view from the perspective of former criminal justice students. I believe that former students now working as criminal justice professionals are in an ideal position to describe the content of their jobs to students currently considering entering those professions. They know what it is like to *be* a student in search of a career and what their criminal justice career is like, beyond the basic job description, salary and prospects.

Inside Jobs contains the personal accounts of criminal justice professionals, ranging from private security and law enforcement officers through court personnel, corrections officers and human service workers. It describes what someone entering the profession will do on the job; what it is really like to be a police or corrections officer, a social worker or a lawyer. If you are currently looking for a career in a criminal justice or related field you will find this collection of original articles and the accompanying information invaluable. Each account covers several related themes including a description of how these professionals got their job, what qualifications are needed, the actual content of their work, their likes and dislikes, what is boring and what is fun, and the current prospects for promotion and career moves. *Inside Jobs* includes several accounts on the most numerous positions, such as law enforcement, and a few on others, such as Immigration Inspector. The balance of articles is designed to reflect the extent of interest in and demand for the different positions within the criminal justice field.

In addition, each section begins with an overview containing recent data on such things as hiring trends, typical job ads, entry-level qualifications and salaries,[3] and where to obtain further information, including position announcements.[4] Finally, a concluding section on criminal justice careers with the federal government includes a

---

[3] The salaries listed should be used as a rough guide, since there is considerable variation between states and even between different departments within the same state.

[4] The prices quoted for subscriptions to various jobs newsletters and information services were correct at the time of publication.

description of the various positions available, how to apply for these and what salary levels to expect. In addition, the names and addresses of federal job information centers, federal agencies, and the location of FBI field offices are contained in the appendices.

Because of the no-nonsense, "warts and all" nature of the articles, some of the contributors have elected not to use their real names for fear that this might jeopardize their current and future job prospects. These authors are shown with an asterisk by their name (*), which indicates that this name is fictional. Also, while the place and company/agency names on the illustrative job advertisements contained in the introductions to each section are fictional, their substance is taken from genuine published advertisements.

In such a book there are many to thank, not the least being the current graduating students, who have shown such enthusiasm for this work! I wish to thank colleague Dr. Ron Westrum for inspiring me to do something about the dearth of career information for criminal justice students. Mr. Horace Thomas, Eastern Michigan University Careers Services Center liaison deserves my sincere thanks for his commitment to equipping our students for their criminal justice careers, and for his cooperation in providing a source of speakers for our program. An invaluable resource for us and for this book has been the Michigan Occupational Information Service (MOIS) data base, with its outstanding peer-reviewed job descriptions and up-to-date career information.

In the various introductory sections of this book I have drawn on several sources. The invisible guide for these sections was the research papers of current and former students taking my criminal justice careers class and I wish to thank them for helping me stay in touch with the realities of today's criminal justice job prospects. I thank Michelle Kaminske, Rebeccalynn Staples, Christopher Jacobson, Joseph LaLonde, Melissa Rajewski, David Szlezyngier, and Vanessa May for their exemplary effort. For her able, organized assistance that went "beyond the call of duty" in producing our Criminal Justice Employment Digest, my warmest thanks go to Rita Urben. A special commendation must go to the founding student editorial team of Wanda Angel, Tami Brake, Dave Nagy, Gena Vilums, Keith Jones and Mark Ellis who came up with its title and contributed a vigorous effort toward its early development. These students along with Daniel Alder and Rick Erickson also took the idea on to public acclaimed success and have each themselves taken up positions as criminal justice practitioners.

xiii

I particularly wish to thank the various former students and speakers who gave enthusiasm, advice and cooperation in the preparation of this book, especially Tracy Tillman-Diroff, John Stakoe, Linda Peck, Jim Robertson, Robin Bahling, DJ Culkar, Samuel D. Garcia, Vickie Kopcak, and Erik Mayernik. I appreciate their patience and their help. My most heartfelt thanks goes to these and the other contributors to this volume who took valuable time out of their hectic professional lives to describe and reflect on what they do and to share with us the inside of their jobs. Without their voluntary efforts we would all be a lot less informed and our criminal justice students would certainly not be as well-prepared.

Stuart Henry
Manchester, Michigan

xiv

SECTION ONE:
LAW ENFORCEMENT

Of all the criminal justice careers, the most popular remains the publicly hired police officer. There are approximately 600,000 police officers in the nation employed by over 15,000 local municipal departments, ranging from the largest which is New York City, employing around 27,000 sworn officers, to many rural departments employing just one officer. The average department size is 40 officers, but this is meaningless given the polarization between large urban departments with around 1000 officers and small rural departments with under 5.[1]

Although the 1980s saw considerable efforts to hire more women and minority officers, the largest departments still average only 10% women, 14% African-American and 8% Latino. This, too, depends on location. Detroit has a 19% female force compared to Newark, New Jersey's 1%. Similarly, Washington DC has a 55% African-American police force compared to Phoenix's 4.3%. San Antonio's force is 38% Latino compared with many other cities such as Pittsburgh, Columbus and St. Louis, that have less than 1% Latino officers. Problems exist for some female officers who may be challenged more frequently by male suspects, or who may draw disdain from male officers who feel insecure about having females as partners. As part of an effort to encourage female recruits, some police departments offer the Crime Prevention Assistant Program (CPA). The eight-week program is targeted specifically at females to help them with their academic and physical training needs and any areas of weakness, before they enter police academy. A former African-American student of ours, Marilyn Horace-Moore, demonstrates that it is possible to break through the traditional racist and sexist bias of traditional police hiring and promotion practices. She went on from her undergraduate degree to become a police officer, then a police sergeant and, after obtaining her master's in criminology and criminal justice in 1989, she was appointed to Lieutenant of the

---

[1] On average there are 2.3 police officers per 1000 of the population in metropolitan areas but this can vary, from 1.5 per 1000 in San Diego and San Antonio, to 4.7 in Detroit and 6.2 in Washington DC.

1 LAW ENFORCEMENT
Typical ads

PROPERTY OFFICER: Evanston, IL. **Job Description:** A variety of police work related to property and evidence necessary for police business in prosecutions. **Qualifications:** 2 yrs. experience in property control, records inventory or related field, high school diploma preferably supplemented by 2 yrs. college with a concentration in criminal justice. **Salary:** $26,928 to $33,108/yr. plus benefits.

PATROL OFFICER: Saginaw, MI. **Job Description:** Community-oriented crime prevention. **Qualifications:** Must be certified or certifiable. **Salary:** Up to $30,699.

PUBLIC SAFETY OFFICER: Oklahoma City, OK. **Job Description:** Perform duties of police officer & firefighter. **Qualifications:** Minimum of BS/BA degree with police academy training preferred. **Salary:** Starting $23,442 to $35,413 after 4 yrs.

PUBLIC SAFETY OFFICER: Durham, NC. **Qualifications:** 60 semester/90 term hours of college credit, written and physical pre-employment tests. **Salary:** $28,823 to $41,175 plus benefits.

POLICE OFFICER: Ann Arbor, MI. **Job Description:** Basic police work. **Qualifications:** Must have passed the MLEOTC; related course work and/or experience is a plus but not required. **Salary:** Starts at $24,232, after one year $30,222 plus 3% with a 4-yr. degree.

POLICE OFFICER: Aurora, CO. **Qualifications:** 3 yrs. police experience in past 4 yrs. Minimum age 21, high school graduate or GED.

PUBLIC SAFETY OFFICER: Toledo, OH. **Job Description:** Must serve as police officer and firefighter, as required. **Qualifications:** Must be certified or certifiable.

POLICE CHIEFS: Farley, WI. **Qualifications:** Associates Degree in law enforcement, 2-5 yrs. experience as supervisor in law enforcement. Certification is required. **Salary:** $21,000-$35,000 plus benefits.

POLICE OFFICER FIRST YEAR: Pittsburgh, PA. **Qualifications:** Must become a city of Pittsburgh resident before appointment and remain a resident throughout employment, excellent physical condition, must have a valid Class C (or Class 1) drivers license at time of application. **Salary:** $24,553/yr.

Ypsilanti Police Department.

Police officers and detectives function to protect life and property, preserve the peace, detect and prevent crimes, and maintain public order through application of the law. The duties of police officers and detectives are highly diverse and may include: patrolling an assigned area known as a beat, preventing crime and making arrests, preventing and investigating crime, examining crime scenes for clues and evidence, arresting suspects and criminals, investigating accidents and giving first aid to victims and assisting others in need of emergency services, issuing traffic tickets, resolving conflicts and disputes, doing community relations work, preparing cases for court, appearing in court to give evidence at hearings or trials, writing and filing daily activity reports, and testifying before a court or grand jury. For example, a former criminal justice major, who is employed by the Dallas Police Department as a patrol officer, answers 911 calls, runs warrants, investigates gang-related activity, and gives court testimony, whereas another who is a Los Angeles County Deputy Sheriff is involved in routine patrol and also works with prisoners in the county jails. She points out that "After patrol there are various specialized fields offered, all within the department, such as special enforcement, vice, narcotics, child abuse, and community prevention."

A third alternative, beyond municipal police departments and county sheriff departments, is to be employed as a State Trooper. The work of a State Trooper is much more diverse than the public's stereotypical view of it seen from the freeway. Some State Troopers work in drug enforcement, others are members of specialist diving teams. One of our former students, for example, is a Canine Specialist for the Michigan State Police where he "handles two departmental canines, which includes care, maintenance, training."

In spite of traditional media images of police as primarily crime-fighters, most research reveals that the majority of police time is spent maintaining order through peace-keeping/dispute-settlement activities. A number of police departments have recently adopted this as official policy, which means adopting a more "problem-oriented" approach to police work under the umbrella concept of "community policing." This policy directs police toward preventing incidents by becoming more visible in problem areas. By working cooperatively with members of the community to solve problems, the police reduce both the fear and the risk of incidents and thereby improve the quality of life of neighborhoods. This community approach to policing is part of a general trend that has emerged since 1980 and which the Director of the National Institute of Justice has called "better, smarter law enforcement."[2] Although police work has always involved interpersonal and problem-solving skills, these are likely to become even more important in the future. As Lieutenant Horace-Moore says, "The classes you take today, that you feel are useless, will certainly help you in your job tomorrow." She points out, for example, that classes on the sociology of the family have been an enormous help to her in understanding the context of domestic disturbances and have enabled her to better manage such incidents. Another officer points out the importance of psychology and sociology, and advises prospective officers to "learn as much as you can about human behavior and human prejudices."

Requirements to become a police officer vary by state but typical qualifications are that officers must be a U.S. citizen; have no felony convictions; have a clean driving record; and have a high school diploma. While minimal entry-level requirements may be at associate's level in recent years, bachelor's degrees are becoming increasingly important in order to actually get a position and most departments give special consideration to college education when considering promotion and special assignments. While students are convinced criminal justice or a related field is desired, most departments do not mind what discipline a student majors in. The 1978 Sherman Report on Higher Education for Police Officers was critical of narrow, hands-on training programs and generally recommended the broader liberal arts curriculum.[3] Part of the reason that police departments are wary of hands-on programs is that they believe their own department is the best qualified to give training for their particular needs. Most departments mandate officers to take around 440 hours of approved on-the-job training in law enforcement, which includes passing written and performance examinations, including eyesight and physical fitness tests. Eyesight requirements vary considerably, and each year several students

---

[2] Charles B. DeWitt, in "Community Policing in Seattle: A Model Partnership Between Citizens and Police" NIJ *Research in Brief*, August 1992, p. 1.

[3] Lawrence Sherman, et al., *The Quality of Police Education*. San Francisco: Jossey Bass, 1978.

are disappointed to find that they do not qualify, so an early vision test is recommended. Also, be very careful before undertaking eye surgery to correct vision impairments such as myopia. Some states and police departments consider this "experimental surgery" and disqualify you from employment if you have undergone it. At $2,400 for the treatment, this can be a very expensive way to discover that you are ineligible for a career in law enforcement.

Training, typically at various community college "police academies" for 12 to 16 weeks, is taught by acting police officers. Increasingly, departments are expecting interested candidates to pay for their own academy training, which can cost around $2500.

Another important and often neglected informal qualification for police work is a demonstration that the candidate has developed awareness of the problems confronting policing. These include the shift work, the stress, the burn-out and cynicism of older officers, and the difficulty of dealing with people who have problems. Not least of these problems is "the public" who are often demanding and dissatisfied with the reality of police work and particularly with the inability of police to recover stolen property or to provide adequate protection. Working in a police department as a civilian employee, as a police dispatcher or in another service capacity, can provide this insight and can be accomplished through an internship. This also gets you into a network of officers and other contacts who can provide valuable advice. A former student points out that because of the complex selection process, those intending to become an officer, at minimum, should "make contact with departments ahead of time and participate in some type of internship, reserve, or auxiliary program."

The salary of police officers varies widely based on years of service, rank, and location of the community in which they work. The national median annual income for police officers was $27,648 in 1989 and ranged from $32,577 in the West to $23,589 in the South. Entry-level salaries averaged $21,096 but this ranged from $25,000 in the West to $17,654 in the South. Typical annual salaries of detectives ranged from $27,582 to $38,712 (1990). Most departments provide educational allowances and pay overtime for night-shift work as well as paying cost-of-living allowances.

While it is difficult to assess the future prospects for recruitment for the nation as a whole, some indication can be given by considering the employment outlook for police officers in a particular state. For the State of Michigan, for example, there is expected to be an average growth through 1995. There will be an estimated 280 annual openings, with 170 openings due to growth and 110 due to replacement of officers who retire or leave the labor force. However, government spending and policy does influence hiring trends, and the Clinton administration has said it will increase the number of police nationwide by 100,000 over the 1993-1996 period.

We have five articles in this section. The first two are by female officers. The article by Meredith Orloff describes a common experience of many who enter law enforcement: a life-long desire to become an officer. She recounts the many difficulties associated with being a female police officer, especially in a previously all-male department. She also indicates some of the advantages and disadvantages of being in a small rural police department. Melanie Pierson documents in detail the long and arduous process of applying for a city police officer position and of going through police academy. She describes the waiting and the frustrations, and the endless weeding out process that accompanies what can be an assaultive regime of testing and hurdle-jumping. She also discusses some of the unseen informal pressures of social control on the job.

Not all those who enter police work do so intentionally. This was the case with John Stakoe, who describes how he drifted into it. His article examines the varying problems that arise for police officers, many stemming not so much from offenders as from the general public, lawyers, and the inequities of the criminal justice system. From John's insightful reflection we see the roots of the stress, alienation, cynicism and burnout experienced by so many officers with years in the profession. John also illustrates his personal method of survival, which is to invest considerable energy into community policing. In the article he, too, weighs the advantages of working in a small department over that of a large one. In his contribution, Bill Wise talks about how the idealistic and altruistic motives of young police officers can both be undermined by the realities of police work, by an officer's own departmental administration, and by the politics within the job. Bill highlights some of the less known but vital skills necessary to make police officers successful in their daily interaction with society, such as mediation, negotiation and empathy. He documents how police discretion, career and political interests can affect the way police work is actually done. Finally, in the article by Edward Dudas we see how working in private security kindled a desire to go into police work. Edward reaffirms that bachelor's students should stay away from courses that are police training oriented and go for a liberal arts degree. He discusses the benefits of working in a small, rather than large department, not least of these being the greater likelihood of involvement in many different tasks and greater opportunity for training in various specialties. However, he also describes the political pressures that can affect small departments and that can detract from ideals of professionalism and justice, undermining the department's operation. Overall, each of these contributions adds a different and intriguing dimension to our knowledge of police careers.

For more on police careers:

Cohen, Paul and Shari. *Careers in Law Enforcement and Security*. New York: Rosen Publishing, 1990.

Coleman, Joseph. *Your Career in Law Enforcement*. New York: Arco Publishing, 1979.

Good, Stephen M. *How to Get a Job with a Police Department*. New York: Barnes and Noble, 1985.

Lunneborg, Patricia W. *Women Police Officers*. Springfield, IL: C.C. Thomas, 1989.

Mahoney, Thomas E. *Law Enforcement Career Planning: A Handbook*. Springfield, IL: C.C. Thomas, 1989.

Martin, Molly, ed. "Police Officer" in *Hard Hatted Women: Stories of Struggle and Success in the Trades*. Seattle, WA: Seal Press, pp. 71-80.

Panzarella, Robert. *Police Officer*. Englewood Cliffs, NJ: Prentice Hall, 1989.

Pickens, Frank. *So You Want to be a Cop*. Royal Palm Beach, FL: EES Publications.

Rachlin, Harvey. *The Making of a Cop*. New York: Pocket Books, 1991.

Stern, Ron. *Law Enforcement Careers: A Complete Guide From Application to Employment*. Mt. Shasta, CA: Lawman Press, 1988.

_____. *Law Enforcement Employment Guide*. 2nd ed. Mt. Shasta, CA: Lawman Press, 1990.

Stinchcomb, James D. *Opportunities in Law Enforcement and Criminal Justice Careers*. Skokie, IL: VGM Career Horizons, 1990.

Vincent, Claude L. *Police Officer*. Ottawa, Canada: Carleton University Press, 1990.

Yentes, Nancy A. and Meagher, M. Steven. "Choosing a Career in Policing: A Comparison of Male and Female Perceptions." *Journal of Police Science and Administration* 14. Dec. 1986, pp. 320-27.

For the latest information on developments in policing:

Crime Control Digest
   Washington Crime News Service, 3918 Prosperity Ave, Suite 318, Fairfax, VA 22031 or call (703) 573-1600.
   Weekly—$295.00 for the first year subscription.

Criminal Justice Newsletter
   Pace Publications, 443 Park Avenue South, New York, NY 10016 or call (212) 685-5450.
   24 issues/year—$198 annual subscription.

FBI Law Enforcement Bulletin
   U.S. Department of Justice, Federal Bureau of Investigation.
   Monthly.

Law Enforcement News
   John Jay College of Criminal Justice/CUNY, 899 Tenth Avenue, Suite 43B, New York, NY 10019 or call (212) 237-8442.

24 issues/year—$18.00 annual subscription.

Police Times Magazine
American Police Hall of Fame, 3801 Biscayne Blvd., Miami, FL 33137 or call (305) 573-0070.
Quarterly—$36.00 annual membership.

For position announcements:

National Employment Listing Service (NELS)
NELS, Criminal Justice Center, Sam Houston University, Huntsville, TX 77341 or call (409) 294-1692.
This is a monthly listing from Sam Houston State University's Department of Criminal Justice. Positions in policing, private security, probation and parole, corrections, government. It includes jobs nationwide but most jobs are in the south and west. $17.50/ 6-month subscription.

Police Career Digest (includes *Express Jobs Newsletter*)
Harvest, P.O. Box 1672, Eaton Park, FL 33840.
This is a bi-monthly (6 issues/year) publication out of Florida. It is a good source of police jobs nationwide but many are above entry level. $23.00 for 6 months or $32.00 per year.

Law Enforcement Employment Monthly
C & R Enterprises, P.O. Box 155, Clawson, MI 48017.
Despite its title, this monthly includes positions nationwide in private security, probation and parole, corrections, government as well as police. It is only available on a monthly basis at $3.75/issue.

Knight Line USA
Knight Writer Publications, Knight Line USA, P.O. Box 38331, Tallahassee, FL 32315-8331 or call (800) 264-8448.
A bi-monthly forum for police officers which includes some police agency hiring information. $19.95—annual subscription.

CHAPTER 1:

Realizing a Dream: Being Female and a Police Officer

by *Meredith Orloff*

I wanted to be a police officer since I was about 12-years-old. At that time I visited the FBI building in Washington D.C. and was absolutely entranced with what I saw. I envisioned myself as the first female mounted patrol officer on the Metropolitan Toronto Police force.

By the time I graduated from high school, I knew that I could not be a police officer in Canada due to the fact that I was an American citizen! I had spent most of my life in Toronto and wanted to become Canadian, but my parents were adamantly opposed and warned me that career opportunities were more abundant in the United States.

I decided to move to the United States and work towards a bachelor of science degree in criminal justice and psychology. I went to a midwest university close to the Canadian border and received my degree after 3 1/2 years of hard work and many headaches.

I was fortunate to get my feet wet in the law enforcement field during college. I worked in several related jobs: as a marine safety officer for the sheriff's department, a parking enforcement officer, a dorm security guard, and as a dispatcher for two years with two university public safety departments. While with one of these I worked full-time on the midnight shift and went to classes during the day. I enjoyed my work but found some resistance from my supervisors who felt that my job should be my first priority, whereas I felt that school should be. They frowned when I brought my books to work so I could study during the quiet early morning hours.

By the time I received my degree, I knew that law enforcement was for me. It's hard to explain why I was so drawn towards it. I wanted to help people and try to make a difference in their lives. I thought it would be an exciting career and felt that I could handle putting my life on the line for other people. Police work was challenging and I saw myself excelling in it. I'm a people-oriented person and I figured that being a police officer would afford me the opportunity to meet new people and make many contacts. I felt that I would be looked up to and supported by the

11

community. I now know that the reality of police work is very different from these ideals, as I shall explain later.

The first obstacle I had to overcome was a written and physical test administered by the Michigan Law Enforcement Officers Training Council (MLEOTC). The physical test consisted of six parts: pushups, grip strength, a 160 lbs backwards dummy drag, an obstacle course, a 95 lb. carry, and a 1/2 mile run. Each event was timed and women were given more time than men. Many of the people who took the test with me failed, and I overheard some of the men complaining that the women had it easy and should have to get the same scores as them. Fortunately I knew what to expect and started training for the test months in advance.

Once I had my scores in hand, I began applying to departments all over southeastern Michigan. I put hundreds of miles on my car driving to tests, oral boards, and physical and psychological exams. I was hoping to be hired by a department who would put me through the police academy. I figured that with my education and experience, I wouldn't have a problem finding a job. I couldn't have been more wrong.

Many departments that I applied to were small and didn't have **any** female officers. I got the impression from many of the older officers who conducted the interviews that they didn't think women belonged in police work and that they couldn't handle the job. I was ill-prepared for many of the questions that were thrown at me. Oral boards are different from regular interviews in that the panel attempts to stress you out with scenario-type questioning and questions which are difficult to answer. Many of the questions don't have a right or wrong answer. The interviewers try to get you frustrated so you will change your answer. The best advice I can give is to stick with your original answer and don't back down. Most of all, don't talk back to the interviewers and don't let them get you riled up.

After many months of fruitless efforts at being hired, I decided to put myself through the Police Academy. I resigned from my position at the university, borrowed money from my father, and entered the Police Academy in April of 1990. I also took a part-time job on the weekends working at a gas station to help pay for my living expenses.

I was lucky when I entered the Police Academy in that I knew exactly what to expect. Many of my friends had been through the same academy and told me what it would be like. I put in 14 weeks of extremely hard work. I would come home in tears some nights because every muscle in my body ached and I knew I would have to return the next morning and do it all over again. I lived, breathed, ate, and slept the academy. On Friday evenings a group of us would go out to let off steam. We would take out all of our frustrations and aggressions from the previous week on each other. It was one of the only things that kept some of us going during those long grueling weeks.

It was particularly hard for those of us who put ourselves through the academy. We had no way of knowing whether we would find jobs when we graduated. The women were expected to do everything the men did, including hundreds of push-ups, rope climbing, and even boxing.

The academy taught me discipline and how not to be a quitter. I learned to be a team player and to support even those I did not particularly like or get along with. Many of the men teased the women and gave us a hard time. We learned to stick together and not to back down. I matured a lot in the academy and credit our excellent instructors and the director for making it a great educational experience.

Shortly after graduating from the Police Academy, I was hired in Northville City as a part-time police officer responsible for race track security! I also filled in as a dispatcher when needed and worked part-time as a Security Officer for a nearby shopping mall. I continued to look for a permanent police position and felt much more confident at the oral boards. The problem now was that very few departments were hiring and the competition was fierce. Sometimes, over 200 people would apply for only one or two positions. Due to budget cuts and the end of the race track season, I was laid off from Northville. I accepted a temporary full-time position with Plymouth City, responsible for handling the "cruisers" on Main Street. In both departments I was the only female officer. Luckily, the departments had employed female officers previously and didn't treat me any differently from the other officers. I didn't feel as if I had something to prove and didn't run into any problems.

A few weeks after starting with Plymouth, I was offered full-time positions with Carlton (fictional name) and Oak Park. It was a tough decision to make, but I chose Carlton. I felt that Oak Park only wanted me because I was a woman. I didn't think I had done well on the oral board and knew there was a big push to hire women and minorities.

It was a big deal in the community when I first came to Carlton because I was the first full-time female police officer. The station didn't even have a women's locker room and converted a bathroom into one just for me! The local newspaper did an article about me and I seemed to get support from the community. Unfortunately, I didn't feel as if I was getting the support I so desperately needed from the officers in my department. There seemed to be some resistance from the older officers who weren't used to women in law enforcement. To make things worse, I was young, single, educated, and slightly arrogant! I was also very aggressive in my patrols. During my first year, I pulled over every vehicle I could and wrote hundreds of tickets and arrested many drunk drivers.

I tried to get along with my co-workers as best I could and figured that it would take some time for all of us to get adjusted. In some instances this was true, but in others it was all I could do to keep myself from bursting into tears. There was one officer who, when called for backup, would take his time getting to my location and then sit in his patrol car and watch me. For weeks at a time he would completely ignore me. On one particular night, he was scheduled to leave on vacation and five minutes prior to the end of his shift, I requested a back up. I had three intoxicated subjects and a German Shepherd in a battered old pick-up truck and I could sense that things might go sour at any minute. This officer responded and proceeded to chastise me for making a traffic stop right when he was scheduled to get off duty! This personal unwarranted attack was done in front of my subject who I ended up arresting for drunk driving, driving while on a suspended license, and having four outstanding warrants from four different departments. His total bond was over six thousand dollars.

Another problem I encountered was the lack of a field training officer (FTO) program. I spent my first two weeks on the day shift, riding shotgun with a senior officer who showed me the 36 square miles which make up the Village of Carlton and Carlton Township. I then advanced to the midnight shift and spent a few nights riding with the Sergeant. From there I was on my own. I relied on a map and common sense to get me through the long nights. The other midnight officer was very patient with me and always very helpful. We had some minor tiffs but, for the most part, he was the most supportive officer in the department.

Working for a small department definitely has its advantages and disadvantages. Our department is made up of six patrol officers: three Sergeants, two Lieutenants, and a Chief. Many times backup is not nearby and occasionally, there is only one midnight car between the hours of four and seven in the morning. We don't have the luxury of having evidence technicians, detectives, etc., at our beck and call. We handle most of our own follow-up and many of the investigations. We prepare our own warrant requests and when there isn't a day shift officer available, we arraign our prisoners. I have worked fifteen or more straight hours to secure a felony warrant and handle a weekend arraignment. Overtime is plentiful whether I want it or not, but scheduling time off is difficult because only two people in the department can be off at the same time and not more than one person per shift.

There are many advantages, however, to working for a small department. I am able to get more involved in the cases I handle and get more experience when I follow a case from start to finish. Carlton has a mounted division in which I am very active. I am able to meet and get to know many people in the community as well as many officers from the area departments upon whom I depend for backup from time to time. Our officers attend specialized training schools in areas such as arson investigation, CSC investigation, accident reconstruction and many others. Each officer has many specialties.

Being a police officer is not a career one can wake up one morning and decide to do. Police work isn't just the badge and the gun and the lights and siren. I experienced this first-hand when I was brand new in Carlton and had to stand by helplessly as two young children perished in a fire. There was no way to save them and I will never forget the horrifying feeling and painful expressions on the parents' faces as we stood waiting for the fire department to respond. Another incident which sticks in my mind is the night I had to shoot an injured dog that had been hit by a car. It was late at night and there was no emergency veterinarian clinic close by. The dog didn't have a collar. It broke my heart when she looked at me with her big brown eyes and I cried out loud when I pulled the trigger. It was days before I was able to drive past the spot without tears rolling down my cheeks. Or the medical I responded to where a three-month-old baby died. The other midnight officer performed infant CPR but it was too late. And a traffic fatality where I had to notify the parents that their son had been killed.

Police work is not all fame and glory. Supervisors and the general public alike are quicker to reprimand you for doing something wrong than to pat you on the back for a job well done. But this is not to say outstanding achievement goes unnoticed. I had only been with the department for five months when I was awarded the Distinguished Service Award for apprehending my arson suspect who was later found guilty and sent to prison. During my first full year in the department I received the M.A.D.D. life-saving award for having the most drunk driving arrests in the department. Overtime and time spent in court takes you away from your family and friends. Many dates have been broken and parties left unattended because duty calls. I have lost friends who could not understand the complexities of law enforcement and boyfriends who felt intimidated by the fact that I was a police officer.

The best advice I can offer anyone who is interested in making police work their career is to get a college degree first. Good writing skills are a necessity in law enforcement. A degree is also something to fall back on if you decide to leave police work or are badly injured on the job. Many departments only take applicants who have degrees and are stressing education more and more. Another piece of advice is to either intern with a police department or spend some time in a ride-along program. This will give you some first-hand experience and insight into what police work is all about. And I don't mean simply spending a couple of days on the day shift. Try riding with a midnight officer for a week or on afternoons. Also, most importantly, don't wait until you graduate to start looking for a job. Hiring processes take months and competition is fierce. Prepare yourself both mentally and physically for the police academy.

I love my job and all that it stands for. I have seen many older officers become cold, hard, and cynical. We deal with the dregs of society, day in and day out. Police officers tend to stick together because they understand each other. Fortunately, I have many friends outside of law enforcement who help me forget about work. I am sure that in five years or so I will start to feel the strain and displeasure that the older guys feel but right now I am happy with what I'm doing and look forward to a long career as a law enforcement officer.

CHAPTER 2:

Becoming a Law Enforcement Officer: The Application Ordeal

by *Melanie Pierson*

I am a police officer in a midwestern city police department. I decided to pursue this career during my senior year of college while obtaining my bachelor's degree in sociology. In my junior year I took a course in criminology. The instructor had a lot of practical experience. Because of this he really stimulated me to learn more about the subject. When I started taking criminal justice courses I had no idea where I wanted the schooling to lead me. I have an uncle in law enforcement and I was able to speak to him about being a police officer and about the criminal justice field in general. He encouraged me to do an internship with a law enforcement agency. Eventually, in my senior year, I interned with the State Police. I became very attracted to the job, but of course I was only seeing a few hours of the whole picture. I didn't realize what it would be like to do this day in and day out. I was convinced that being a State Trooper was the best career in the field and started thinking about becoming a cop. Where else was I going to find a job where I could drive another person's car fast, see the excitement of shoot-outs and be a part of an elite club!?

After graduating I applied to the police department where I was eventually employed. I had heard positive things about the department from some of the State Police Troopers with whom I had ridden. I had wanted to become a State Trooper but didn't meet the vision requirements, which in this state are very stringent. I decided on this city because I was raised here. I didn't want to move to unfamiliar territory while trying to learn a new job.

The application process turned out to be frustrating and intimidating for me. It proved to be a very lengthy affair. I started my application in the fall and did not complete it until the following spring (about 6 months later!). Let me take you through the process to show you what to expect.

The first step was to fill out a "blue card" showing interest. This card has just the basics—name, age, address, etc. Then I had to complete two tests required by the state, called the MLEOTC tests. (This stands for Michigan Law Enforcement Officers Training Counsel.) These tests consist of a physical agility test comprising push-ups, hand grip, obstacle course, lifting and carrying a weighted duffle bag, dragging a "dummy" and then running. The second part is a written test much like the English sections of the ACT and SAT. These tests can be taken on the same day or at different times, but both must be passed and valid at the time of hire. If you don't pass one or both, there are several testing dates each year to allow chances to retake them.

After passing the MLEOTC tests, I was invited to attend a "packet meeting." This is open to anyone who has filled out a card and completed the MLEOTC tests. At this meeting I met literally hundreds of other applicants. This can be quite depressing since there are only a few who can be hired each recruiting round. The recruiter explains the benefits and basic design of the department and several officers are available to take questions after the presentation. Then, if you are still interested in a position, you are given a very thick "background packet" which has to be completed. It is designed to reveal all there is to know about you. There is a deadline set for returning this packet with both high school and college grades. After returning this packet I waited...

After waiting over a month I was lucky enough to be invited to attend what's called an "Oral Board." This consisted of me facing a panel of officers and personnel staff. They asked me questions about my "packet responses" and a few hypothetical situations to help verify my honesty, and then threw in a surprise physical test. After the interview I was sent out of the room while the members of the panel discussed how I did. I was lucky and was told that same day that I had passed. I've since heard from others that they had to wait for a letter.

I wasn't done yet! The next step was a written psychological exam that took place several weeks later. The exam consisted of two thick packets containing a series of questions, worded differently to determine honesty and consistency, and supposedly to establish an applicant's personality traits. These two packets took a few hours to complete. After the psychological exam I had to schedule an appointment with the psychologist to talk with him one-on-one. By this time in the application process I found that the field of applicants had been narrowed from hundreds competing for 5 positions to about thirty. The oral portion of the interview consisted of explaining why I wanted to join the police force, my expectations, why I thought I should be hired, what my weaknesses were, and, of course, responding to questions about what I put in the written exam, along with probing into my family life. Then the worst part—more waiting...

Finally, after what seemed like an inordinately long period of time, I received a phone call asking me to come to the station. Upon arrival I was advised that, as long as I got a clean bill of health from the doctor, I was going to be hired and would start training in a few weeks. I was ecstatic. The ordeal had been worth it. I was sent to the doctor and released ready to start my 14 weeks of training. Having thought I was "in", now came the really tough part; training at the police academy.

During police academy training I very quickly found out that I was not prepared, either mentally or physically, for what was to come. We were an experimental class with physical training 5 days a week, and several hours of classroom work.[1] I was especially not mentally prepared for the psychological atmosphere associated with the paramilitary organization, which is typical of most police departments and has to be experienced to be believed. For example, I was told that I was lower than anything on earth. It actually made me begin to doubt my own abilities to do the job. I found myself concentrating on just succeeding in finishing the program as a personal goal. Several people dropped out and the temptation to do so was high. I wondered why I was taking mental abuse from people I thought were supposed to be co-workers helping me learn how to do the job. I understood the idea that this was supposed to help me become a stronger person, but I disagreed with the method.[2]

After graduating from police academy I had to attend another academy put on by the city department for their employees. This academy also consisted of some physical training, but in a much more relaxed atmosphere. Here the classroom training focused on local ordinances, attitudes and expectations. This lasted another 9 weeks!

The next step was my "on-the-road" training. This consisted of being partnered with a senior officer who was supposed to help orient me into

---

[1] After our class was completed, the system reverted to physical training 2-3 times a week because they realized the experimental regime was causing too much strain, injuries, illnesses etc.

[2] The intensity and abuse in police academy training varies depending upon the state and the personalities involved, but intending trainees should expect at least the military-style training and rigorous discipline.

the job. I was graded daily on my abilities, and towards the end of the program there was a lot of pressure to perform well, since you were constantly being watched and assessed. The problem with this training is that the grading is subjective and the recruit is transferred several times to different trainers. Each officer has his or her own style and pet peeves which the recruit must accommodate. As a result the training can become inconsistent, if for no other reason than individual personality differences. In spite of this, the program is the best anyone has yet been able to establish and it is better than just putting a new recruit on the road right out of the classroom.

After finally being allowed to be on my own, I then had to establish myself and prove to the department that I could handle the job. I had to decide on the kind of officer I wanted to be and to develop my own style and way of doing things that would be acceptable to the department. I also had to come to terms with the idea that some people are going to have personality clashes with me and others who may like me, may not agree on how things should be done. The idea that this is a club and that we are an "all for one and one for all" organization is unfortunately not true. For our safety it is necessary to present a public image that we are 100% behind each other. But that image is quickly lost within the department. There is a lot of gossip and no one is safe from "locker room" talk. This both surprised and disappointed me. I guess I thought police officers would be different than other work places due the nature of the job. I was sadly mistaken. If anything, I found that people were a lot more critical of each other in the police force than in any of my other jobs.

The job itself didn't disappoint me. It was as I had expected. There was a little bit of excitement to make up for the daily grind. Most rewarding for me are the good things we have the power to accomplish; seeing a thief caught and successfully prosecuted, sending a rapist to jail, or putting a beaten child somewhere safe. I can always draw on this feeling of accomplishing something good during the down times. The diversity of people that I have encountered in this job has been very interesting and a little unexpected. I have learned never to take anything for granted. Just when I think I've met the strangest person or had an unbelievable encounter, something else will come along to make me think again.

Becoming a police officer will probably be whatever you make it. If you dwell on the bad, that is what you will see; if you look for the good, it's there too. But don't expect to change the world. We aren't going to stop crime in one lifetime. There's job security in knowing that! I happen to be a person who likes dealing with people, which makes this job work for me. I get to deal with lots of different people every day. It's a job that allows me to work in several different professions each shift. Almost any profession someone can name is a role that an officer must play at some point in their career. We are whatever an individual or society needs us to be in a given situation.

A lot of people see police officers as people on some sort of power trip because of the amount of control we have over others' lives. What is often forgotten is that we are servants of society and are supposed to uphold the laws of our government. The problem is that we get ridiculed for doing just that. For example, I am a part of a community policing program. I am told by the community I patrol what they see as a problem and then I enforce that particular complaint. The people in my area requested that I patrol a stop sign that has a lot of violators. After doing as I was asked, I found that a good number of those violators were the same people that wanted me to patrol it. But they don't want me to enforce the law against them. It's always the other guy who needs controlling.

The biggest pressure of the job, perhaps surprisingly, comes from wearing the uniform. Not only is it cumbersome to chase someone who is wearing shorts and tennis shoes when I am wearing long wool blend pants, a vest, and a utility belt, but everywhere I go and everything I do is being observed by the always curious public. At lunch, more often than not, I am approached by someone with a question or problem. On breaks many times I end up entertaining a curious child, etc. The uniform represents power that makes people nervous and when another officer anywhere in the world abuses that power we all answer for it. Our department has a policy of investigating any complaint issued against an officer. This is a good policy as it provides a necessary check and balance. But it can be bad when the people complaining are making false accusations to try and force the charges against them to be dropped. Often the media will publish the charges but fail to mention that the officer accused was completely exonerated. On the other hand, there are occasions where officers over-step their authority and it is important that those involved be held responsible.

It is imperative for anyone considering law enforcement as a career to realize that the "thank you's" are few and far between and the complaints are many. The rewards of this job come mostly from within. You have to know that what you are doing is worthwhile and that people do appreciate you even though they don't usually verbalize it. It's easy to lose focus of the big picture. Everyday we deal with people who are venting anger towards us and we aren't supposed to show any emotion or reaction. It is so easy to take the anger out on our families, which can make for a lot of stress. There are many frustrating circumstances that we encounter in a day and an officer's patience can run thin at times. It is important to be aware of this and find some way to not take the pressures of the job home or it could destroy your family and social life.

The job has many obvious negatives and many hidden positives. Once you find and focus on these positives, the job can be filled with fun. Our department, along with a lot of other departments, has started to explore the new type of "problem- oriented" policing that allows us to have positive contacts within the community rather than always negative. It's a community oriented approach much like that of the old "beat officer" who had an intimate knowledge of the neighborhood and the people that live there. I've had the opportunity to participate in the program and have found it incredibly rewarding. The public doesn't fear us as much. The kids get used to us and play with us. Once they get older this may make a world of difference in how they treat us. Rather than being a deliverer of bad news I can be greeted positively when I knock on the door of a house in the neighborhood. The first thought is no longer a bad feeling of "What's wrong?" I have seen a remarkable change in the worst area of town. Here the people are helping us clean out the area rather than standing mute.

I think the key to good law enforcement is good communication skills. There are several other very important skills to master, but if you can't tell someone what it is you are asking of them, or can't listen to what it is they need, this job will be much harder for you. Police work involves a lot of excitement also. It is not as exciting as one might hope but it still provides the chases, the shootings, and putting the "bad guy" away. There is still no other job like it and nothing I'd rather be doing at this point in my career. You have to want to learn. Learn as much as you can in school about other cultures and be ready to learn every day on the job. Things keep changing in the field and we have to be ready to change with them. I am happy to say that I think this field is changing for the better and I hope it keeps moving in a positive direction and that I can be a part of it as it does.

CHAPTER 3:

The Frustrations of Police Work:
The Idealism and Realism of Being a Police Officer

by *William C. Wise*

I decided to become a police officer in my junior year at Michigan State University while studying for my bachelor's in sociology. As part of that program I began taking criminal justice courses which piqued my interest.

I was attracted to police work for a number of reasons. Like many who become police officers, I am somewhat altruistic. I wanted to provide a service and to see that justice was done. I wanted to protect people and their values and to make the world a safer place. I was willing to put my life on the line so that innocent, law-abiding people could live and move about without fear.

At the time I had high ideals. I felt that police work was a noble profession. I enjoyed the idea that I would be admired and trusted by others. I felt I would be doing something worthwhile and rewarding, to which society would respond favorably. I expected support from the majority of people.

I enjoyed being outdoors, moving about, meeting different people and encountering new challenges every day. The excitement of the job, the uniform, and the marked patrol car made for an attractive prospect. I envisioned myself as a "crime fighter" engaged in street fights, shoot-outs and high speed chases. Police work promised to provide all these things. This was Hollywood and the popular media's influence on my decision to become a police officer.

Upon graduation from Michigan State with my bachelor's in sociology I applied for the entry-level position of police patrol officer with a number of large cities in Michigan, Ohio, Indiana and Illinois. I also applied to become a State Trooper. I possessed all the necessary qualifications: a high school diploma, good health and physical condition, and good character. I passed the background check, was a U.S. citizen and had no prior arrests. My choices were quickly narrowed to a handful of departments due to local residency requirements and my eyesight. Most departments require eyesight to be no less than 20/40 correctable to 20/20. Mine was 20/100 correctable to 20/20. The Ann Arbor Police Department had rather liberal eye requirements and accepted applicants with eyesight correctable to 20/20. After passing an oral and written exam, I was hired by the city of Ann Arbor. I was sent to a 440-hour police academy administered by the Michigan Law Enforcement Officers Training Council (MLEOTC), followed by a 160-hour training academy at the Ann Arbor Police Department (AAPD). I was assigned to uniform patrol duty in September 1972, three months after being hired, and remained in uniform patrol for thirteen years until 1985 when I left to head the criminal justice program at Siena Heights College. During the eight years from 1977-1985, I was trained and served as an advanced accident investigator.

Although I knew police work would be difficult, I felt the day-to-day decision making processes with the public and the offender would be easy. Conduct is either legal or illegal. A person is either right or wrong. There would be no gray area, no room for interpretation and, most important, no politics or special favors. I would be able to enforce the law equally for everyone. These ideals were reinforced in my classes and again by the police academy.

I was to learn early in my career that things are rarely black and white but mostly gray, and politics is very much a part of law enforcement. As a new recruit I failed to see this. I also had a media-distorted view of the duties of a police officer. Any posted job description for an officer will include a range of activities such as: protecting life and property, preserving the peace, detecting and preventing crime and maintaining order through the application of the law. The officer's duties might be listed as: patrolling, crime prevention, making arrests, investigating, inspecting, issuing tickets, writing reports, reporting hazards, and appearing in court. Certainly these duties are a part of the job and, to the outsider or even the new recruit, they might be seen as the totality of the job. But these descriptions leave out the crucial social service function of police work which consumes as much as eighty to ninety percent of the officer's time!

I found that problem solving and social service networking were used far more frequently than the power of arrest or other means of official disposition, such as tickets or code violations. Officers' abilities to mediate situations and to provide alternative solutions for family, neighborhood, and personal problems are far more important and frequently used than their knowledge of the penal code. Often police are called in to handle situations that could be more appropriately handled by another social service agency. The officers must know which agencies are best suited to intervene and then be able to work and communicate with agency professionals. I was not prepared for this. It was not emphasized in the criminal justice classes nor in the police academy. Empathy and communications skills to deal with all types of people outside the context of official action are also very important. For example, I would have benefitted enormously from having taken courses in counselling, family therapy, interviewing and social work services, as well as having had practical experience working with problem populations. Officers must also be socially aware and respect cultural differences. Training that emphasizes the cultural diversity of American society would be enormously valuable in enabling police officers to more effectively perform their duties.

My preconceived ideas on the police use of technology were also seriously revised. Official job descriptions for police officers include the stipulation that they master the use of firearms, handcuffs, motorcycles, radios, radar, nightsticks, rescue and emergency equipment. These are very important tools of the profession and much emphasis is placed on proper training in their use. However, during my thirteen years as an officer I came to realize that other, more abstract "tools" are of equal importance. For instance, the ability to reason with people, the ability to empathize and the ability to negotiate are extremely important. A police officer's job revolves around people and human situations. Because of this much emphasis must be placed on training officers to manage people in different situations. Officers need to know effective ways of dealing with difficult people, violent people, angry people, frightened people and grief stricken people. For example, in the course of my career I had to deliver many death messages to relatives and respond to many ambulance requests in which people died. Beyond providing various ways of telling a person that a loved one had died, the academy provided no direction. There was no training on how to deal with the survivor or how to assist the survivor in beginning the process of making arrangements or how to deal with your own emotions in these circumstances. Situations such as these are regularly faced by police officers, yet very little time is spent on training an officer to deal with such incidents. Of the six hundred hours of initial officer training, only twelve hours focussed on these issues.

Another underemphasized tool that I discovered to be invaluable was the ability to write with detail, clarity and organization. Not only does writing ability help officers make and prove cases to judges, juries and attorneys, but if officers can logically and clearly state their reasons for action in writing, to justify and argue the case, this serves as a protection against the increasingly encountered possibility of criminal and civil litigation.

A practical example of how good writing skills might help is in the use of affidavits for search warrants. Here a clearly articulated, logical narrative will easily show a judge the probable cause for requesting the warrant and the officer's expertise in the area being discussed. All too often warrants can be denied where good cause is present because of an officer's inability to argue the case. Good writing skills will also help the officer to document all the events leading up to an arrest, thus making it easier to obtain arrest warrant authorization from the prosecutor.

As I have said, many reasons, hopes and expectations accompanied my decision to become a police officer. I think every one of my expectations was somewhat modified as I worked in the field. I wanted to provide a service, see justice was done, and help everyone feel safe. It was soon obvious that these ideals were not achievable from my role as an officer. I could not make a significant difference to the conditions in Ann Arbor, much less the world! I was forced to move from a global set of ideals to a more localized, personally focussed set of goals. Instead of changing the whole system, I had to focus on the specific incidents in which I became involved, and to do the best I could to solve problems and correct the wrongs in specific situations. I was forced to realize that I could only impact situations over a narrow time frame: from the point at which I became involved to when I had to turn the case over to someone else. There was little I could do to prevent situations from occurring and I had no control over dispositions, criminal or otherwise, once they were passed on to the next stage of the process. Police officers often become disenchanted with their jobs when they feel they are individually responsible for the entire criminal justice process. Yet no one had trained us how to detach our emotions and to let go. In order to survive I learned to rationalize: "It is only possible to influence people and events in a small way, and I should not despair about the large issues over which I have no control."

Nor was the decision-making system as easy and clear cut as I had imagined. Even though procedural law and department policy mandated uniform, consistent enforcement, the criminal law was not equally enforced towards all people, at all times. There were more gray issues than black or white ones, more ambiguity and circumstantial considerations than could ever be imagined. Individual officer discretion was a far greater determinant of who was arrested and of what laws were enforced. Arrests were made, tickets issued and alternative actions were taken based more on career considerations of individual officers than on legal mandates. Police action or inaction was influenced most by pressure groups and powerful individuals. Community sentiment influenced the types of laws enforced, not what was written in the penal code. What is more, any action taken by police was open to a vast amount of interpretation and scrutiny by the public, the courts and other police officers. Making decisions became one of the most difficult components of the job.

Regarding public "support," I found to my great surprise that the most vocal comments came from people who did not approve of police actions. Moreover, this negative view was carried over and reinforced by the police administration, who were quick to respond to a complaint against an officer, assuming the officer guilty until proven otherwise. In contrast, most of the people who were satisfied with police services said nothing. Commendations from citizens for officers were few and were not handled with the same degree of zeal as complaints. This distorted exposure to the negative gave me the feeling that there was little support from the public and that most people did not understand police officers, their job or their frustrations. One thing that I really had to work on was the idea that the public did support the police even though this support was typically silent.

Finally, the hectic, action-packed *Starsky and Hutch* image of police work is largely a myth for the typical middle-America police officer. Even the recently popular realistic police shows like *Cops* and *American Detective* and *FBI—The Untold Stories* are distortions since they are incident-driven, otherwise they would make poor television. Actual police work, the day-to-day kind, can be very routine and boring with long periods of uneventful patrol. Many menial tasks such as writing parking tickets, handling noise complaints and transporting prisoners, serve to frustrate officers, especially those who anticipate bigger, faster and more exciting things. Working overtime was a common and unexpected occurrence and the resulting fatigue of working fifteen hour shifts was not something that I had anticipated. Just as waiters and waitresses cannot go home until all their "side-work" is completed, so it is with police officers who can't go home until all the reports are written and the evidence is logged. This is especially a problem if a major crime occurs near the end of an 8 or 10-hour shift. The officer may have to stay 8 to 10 more hours to finish the reports! This can have an unanticipated and destructive effect on family life and social relationships.

Then there are systemic problems of the organization of police work. In fact my greatest disappointment came with the officer evaluation system instituted by the Ann Arbor Police Department. This was a productivity-based system that measured officer performance by the number of tickets issued, traffic stops, arrests made, and incidents investigated. On the surface it might seem appropriate to measure the number of tickets and arrests each officer makes as a gauge of his effectiveness. However, in Ann Arbor this became the **sole** basis for evaluation upon which depended whether an officer would receive promotion and special duty assignments. As a result officers began competing with one another. Quantity was valued over quality. Many marginal tickets were written and questionable arrests were made. The teamwork so necessary for successful law enforcement was compromised as officers refused to cooperate with one another in attempts to hoard arrests. Moreover, the easier traffic arrests would sometimes take precedence over the serious felony. Not without justification, the public saw the police as primarily traffic enforcers and not surprisingly, police/community relations suffered. The problem-solving, social networking approach, which is necessary to community vitality, became nonexistent. In fact it was precisely my frustration with the numbers-oriented police evaluation system that led to my career change in 1985.

In spite of these disappointments there was considerable satisfaction in some aspects of the profession. I enjoyed my job the most when I was investigating a complicated case. It was especially enjoyable to start with very little information and to put the pieces of the puzzle together to develop a case on suspects. During my career I was awarded a number of professional excellence citations for developing a case, writing a complete report and bringing the case forward for successful prosecution. It was also very rewarding and exciting to make an apprehension on an in-progress felony or to render first-aid or CPR to save a life.

I think anyone entering law enforcement today needs to be flexible, open-minded and tolerant of alternative lifestyles. Certainly one must be thoughtful and have the ability to empathize with others. A college education is a must, increasingly with a bachelor's degree as a minimum starting point. The apparent classroom redundancy of learning various aspects of social and societal relations, learning about families and about social problems will prove enormously valuable later in the job. It might be compared to learning to read and write, only here you are learning to read and write people and society. I am sure that many people will eventually find, as I did, that a master's degree is desirable and may eventually become the standard as police work becomes more specialized and more professionalized. Perhaps one of the most misunderstood aspects of police work is that it requires using one's intellectual capacity and not physical power.

I don't think I would have played my career any differently, although I could have been better prepared. I was an independent thinker who often questioned department policy and procedure. I believe that the paramilitary structure, common in many police departments, serves to stifle individual thought in favor of strict adherence to sometimes inflexible and unworkable rules and regulations. To be successful in a paramilitary police agency and to advance through the ranks, one must compromise; one must sell one's soul to the police administration. I had to put the police department above family, friends and personal life. This served to further alienate me, as a police officer, from the community I served. Hopefully, this will begin to change as the criminal justice system realizes the need for greater involvement between the police and community.

William C. Wise is currently Assistant Professor of Criminal Justice, Chair of the Division of Human Services and Director of Campus Security at Siena Heights College in Adrian, Michigan.

CHAPTER 4:

The Politics of Small Town Policing

by *Edward Dudas**

I never planned a career in law enforcement. I just fell into it. In 1981 I received a bachelor's degree in biology. Job openings were limited. 1981 was a recessionary year. I had a couple of friends who were working security at a local shopping mall. In order to pay my bills I joined them as a security guard. Here I came into contact with local police. I found that their level of professionalism was far superior to that of ours in security. Part of this resulted from the higher entry level qualifications. Whereas the police department expects a bachelor's degree, the private security company had supervisors with little or no education past high school.

I desired to be in the company of police officers. I enjoyed their stories and envied their ability to travel beyond the confines of the mall! I began applying to area police departments. I quickly learned that getting a job in law enforcement was going to be a lot harder than I first thought. While I had the required degree, I learned that I lacked one very important credential– certification. This is required by many states and means you must complete police academy training, which in this state is a 16-credit program. You are certified for one year. If you don't find a position in that time you lose your certification. Increasingly the academy, which can cost $2500, is expected to be paid for by the prospective candidate, but there is no question that you can increase your chances of being hired by putting yourself through it.

The reason this is so important is simple economics. Eighty percent of officers belong to departments with less than twenty officers. In order to save the cost of paying for the tuition, as well as the wages and benefits of the person going through the program, departments advertise for persons "certified or certifiable," so that they can put them straight to work.

*This is a fictional name used at the author's request.

In order to make myself more marketable, I began work as a reserve officer for a local police department. Then in 1984 I put myself through the police academy at my local community college. After graduating from the academy I received three offers of part-time positions in small local departments. Toward the end of 1984, while working as a part-time officer for various departments, I applied to a nearby township police department. After a series of written tests, oral boards, psychological and medical tests, I was hired by that department in 1985.

In the years since I applied, the process of becoming an officer seems to have become even more competitive. Most departments require a four year college degree, and not necessarily in criminal justice. Smaller departments look to fill special needs. Many times a candidate who has majored in social work, business, public administration, engineering, history or sociology will be accepted in preference to a student with a criminal justice degree, especially if that degree is heavily practice oriented, rather than conceptually based. This is because there are in-service classes that will train you to perform certain tasks within the department, in precisely the way the department wants them done. Also, people can be misled about the importance of internships. They are valuable for experience, but don't rely on them to get you a job. I have never seen an intern hired by a department. I have, however, seen many reserve officers hired who have proven themselves on the road, and many departments use the reserve program to get a first look at possible new recruits. So get involved and get noticed!

Policework in a small department, such as the one that hired me, is extremely different than working for a larger department. For example, detective bureaus in a small department typically consist of only one man, and road officers have to complete many aspects of the investigations. But there can also be benefits in the smallness. Unlike large departments, where getting a position in the detective bureau could take years, in the small department officers often rotate in and out of the bureau, giving experience to many who would not normally receive it. During my tour in the bureau I worked on a murder case which ended in a first degree murder conviction for the suspect. For my work on the case, I was awarded the only Certificate of Merit that the department has ever given!

Another benefit comes from specialized training. I have received hundreds of hours of training in such things as firearms, evidence technician work, and hostage negotiations. Each department develops special needs and sends officers to schools to develop the required skills. Because the resources of a small department are limited, they may link up with other departments, with each contributing manpower and equipment. The result is a specially trained unit, at reduced cost, to meet the particular needs of an area. For example, our area is close to a national border and has an international airport. I currently act as a hostage negotiator in our area's Special Response Unit. The training for this role has involved some very interesting activities such as a mock airliner hijacking which we recently staged.

The duties of the police officer in a smaller department also vary greatly. On any given day you might be asked to do such tasks as deliver packages to members of the Police Board, escort township receipts to the bank, answer complaints about barking dogs, and make sure that the police cars are maintained. It often seems like making traffic stops, writing tickets and patrolling, take a back seat to these other things.

One of the nicest things about law enforcement is that no two days are alike. The scenery and the actors are constantly changing and there can be a great deal of excitement due to armed robberies, fraud, etc. These events are not commonplace the way that television makes them appear. However, when they occur, it is these times of crisis that can be most rewarding to me. I get to observe people at their worst as well as at their finest. The bonding that occurs when two people are depending on each other to survive lasts a lifetime.

Unfortunately, with small departments comes the problem of heavy political entanglements. When this department was first formed there was a Chief of Police, a Deputy Chief and the road officers. The Chief, who is a political appointee, (there were no mid-level management positions) refused to delegate any responsibility to any officer, including the Deputy Chief. Many times we would be called into the Chief's office, not because of the seriousness of an incident but because the offenders had political connections to the Chief!

A further illustration of these political manipulations can be seen in the attempt by our township to prevent the formation of a union of police officers. When the department was formed, each officer was required by the township to sign individual contracts and agree not to form a police union. Not surprisingly the officers were making far less than neighboring police departments. After a couple of years the issue that finally brought the resulting feelings of resentment to a head was the creation of a much needed position of sergeant. The township decided to test for sergeants. The process was not well defined. It was unclear what the criteria would be. We did not know what would be measured and were uncertain how it was to be measured. In fact the test results were never fully disclosed. In spite of the contracts they had signed, the anger and frustration of this promotion process resulted in the officers forming a union. The township took them to court. Eventually the union won the right to exist but as a result of several subsequent "political" promotions, there was unending doubt in the minds of many officers about the whole process, which caused the officers to have less respect for the new sergeants. This greatly reduced their ability to function properly.

As in any career, there are real or perceived inequities in hiring and promotion. Overall one has to weigh the good and the bad. In spite of the politics which I detest, I very much enjoy working in a small department, as I indicated earlier, and I would recommend it to anyone starting out. I would also point out that police work has changed considerably in the last few years. As well as a degree and prior police academy training becoming the entry level standard, we have entered an age of "community policing." It may come as a shock to many wanting to enter law enforcement but departments aren't looking for macho, muscle-bound gun experts. Rather they are looking for college graduates, of varying races and genders, sensitive enough to be aware of cultural differences and of potential conflicts in our communities. Departments want officers who can deal with many complex problems of urban life, who are more skilled problem solvers than knuckle crushers. Departments want officers who will say that their best weapon is their mind, not their baton.

CHAPTER 5:

Tough Job:
Conflict, Contradictions and Inconsistencies in Police Work

by *John P. Stakoe*

Choosing a career is never simple. It is fraught with indecision, experimentation and, for a few, pursuit of idealistic dreams. My selection of a career in law enforcement some 16 years ago was the culmination of many different things. At the university I attended we were encouraged to take a bachelor's degree without specializing and then later come to a career decision based on trying a wide variety of classes. I eventually settled into a comfortable program as a secondary education teacher majoring in history with thoughts of long summers and professional respectability. It was a dizzying prospect: good pay, guaranteed holidays, summers off, and daylight hours. So how did I become involved in law enforcement?

I took a summer position in a large recreational and camping facility which employed a considerable security and police force. I was employed as a private security officer. Despite the fact that there is usually no love lost between private security and police officers, we maintained an amiable relationship. Possibly this was because, as summer help, we did not present a job threat and the overwhelming number of intoxicated vacationers necessitated keeping anyone around who might be able to assist. In this setting I rapidly began to obtain hands-on experience.

There is a certain feeling of awe when sitting in a police cruiser for the first few times, provided you're not in the back. You are instantly aware of the authority and responsibility which is associated with a marked and equipped vehicle. Turn the lights and sirens on and it produces a narcotic effect which can seduce the strongest of wills. I was no exception and soon found myself in the reserve training program of a large municipal police department.

Auxiliary officers are something of an enigma. They are welcomed by administrators, who see an easy and inexpensive method of augmenting the police force, yet reviled by regulars. Reserves receive cursory training in the fundamentals of the law and arrest procedures, and are then assigned a day or two a month to work with an officer.

35

Unfortunately, regular staff generally view reserves as something tantamount to a scab. Officers become derisive and extremely unpleasant. I was provided, however, with some insight into the attitude of seasoned officers. Auxiliaries are not new to law enforcement; they have played a role in policing since the Roman Empire. The mind set exhibited by regulars had nothing to do with the fear of replacement. There is simply an "us against them" attitude which officers develop. The reserves are viewed as interlopers, outsiders who do not have a place in the inner sanctum of police work. Officers, over time, become detached from the very community they are empowered to protect. Those I observed early on in their careers as sincere, sensitive, empathetic men, have become cynical and distant.

Despite the negative aspects of my exposure to the profession, none of it measured up to the shear terror I suffered in a brief stint as a school substitute teacher. So, law enforcement took over the top honors in my career quest. I settled into a position in a small department in a township largely made up of upper middle class homes and light industrial areas.

Starting my employment when I did allowed me to witness some interesting changes in the type of individuals entering the profession, as well as seeing some dramatic changes in the screening process for applicants. The pressures of civil liability had not yet become of paramount importance in recruiting. Now it seems that there are written regulations for everything. At that time my screening consisted of a written application and a cursory once-over by an amiable administrator, who checked for two legs, two eyes and conversed just enough to see that I could speak English.

Fifteen years has brought considerable changes in hiring practices. Those choosing to enter the field today can expect a serious battery of testing and background investigations. Criminal laws and procedures are constantly challenged by law violators. In addition, the public is not satisfied with a purely reactive police force. Recognizing this, our department, like many others, selects those candidates with the highest skills, education achievement, demonstrated capabilities and those who have clearly thought through their personal and professional goals. When I began my career, I was handed the keys to a patrol car and a map and given my first call. Today comprehensive written examinations are followed by physical testing, mental health screening, and oral interviews. None of this, though, ensures that the candidate will be able to function in a crisis. The police academy provides little more than a cursory introduction to the job you are expected to perform. The sad truth is that there is simply no way it can prepare you for the job. You cannot condense three years of law school into 14 weeks. Add to that arrest procedures, self-defense training, firearms, driving, civil liability, report writing, accident investigation, etc. To alleviate uncertainty, the large departments have instituted lengthy probation periods under the supervision of trained officers. In smaller departments, such as mine, this is impossible. New recruits are closely supervised but are still on their own much of the time.

When I embarked on my career I was never idealistic enough to believe that I was making any type of serious impact on society. I have always equated the patrol officer with the little boy with his finger in the dike, just barely holding back the flood. But I did maintain that the law could and should be dealt out uniformly and this was flawed thinking. To insinuate there is equality of treatment in the American criminal justice system would be a disservice to all those who have experienced it and who know better. Despite my obvious cynicism, I do believe that our system is sound. It has just been manipulated and abused by those sworn to uphold and serve. Having studied as a historian, I found the evolution of the common law system from Henry II to the present, fascinating. The duty of the defense to ensure that a fair trial is presented by the state and the provision that judgement will be by your peers, is a laudable ideal. It is unfortunate that courtroom tactics have degenerated to a game in which the quest is victory regardless of right, wrong or ethics.

One of the most intense and perhaps difficult areas in which the officer performs is the courtroom. On numerous occasions, I have had witnesses leave a trial stating they will never again become involved in any case. I have learned to cope by remembering errors, anticipating questions, and by careful preparation. There is nothing pleasant in watching an obviously unprepared officer squirm on the stand. Of course, the presence of a court appointed attorney does much to raise the spirits. The most glaring example of inequities is in the level of representation provided the defendant. The image of the public defender distorts the reality of courtroom pragmatics. Typically, the case will be bargained away in the most expeditious manner possible. Little or no regard is paid to the officer's wishes or those of the victim. Only the highest profile cases, which may provide campaign fodder for a prosecutor, are maintained within strict policy guidelines. Those who can afford a reasonable defense will equip themselves to find every loophole in the system. I have been to court with witnesses up to 7 times over the course of a year; the defense did nothing more than call in a delay. Yet let an officer fail to show up and the case will likely be summarily dismissed. The logjam in the courts has been created as much by the endless unwarranted delays by attorneys, with the blessing of the court, as any other factor that can be conceived.

One of the troubling aspects of police work is the general attitude of the public towards the street officer. Those entering the field with a high degree of skill and education will find it particularly disturbing. As noted earlier, I have witnessed a transition in the caliber of men and women entering law enforcement. Young people with 4-year degrees, many with graduate school, are seeking to achieve new levels of professionalism. The expectation exists that you will be held in a level of esteem justified by your training, wisdom and hard work. The problem is that everyone wants the police when they need help, but no one wants to be on the receiving end of enforcement. The most prevalent example exists in traffic enforcement. People frequently will stop and offer an endless number of complaints about the speeders and reckless drivers on their street. Yet, more often than not, when I increase the enforcement I catch the original complainer, who can't comprehend why they are being violated!

The love-hate relationship police receive from the community serves to alienate officers. Many men exhibit a false stoicism while festering resentment builds on the inside. The media only serves to reinforce the negative attitude with their one-sided reporting, depicting perpetrators as victims, and officers as criminals. Over the years it becomes easier to recognize the growing resentment; the difficult task is dealing with the stress that builds.

While attending to calls, I have always been concerned about the proper amount of empathy delivered to the victims. Yet, people don't want empathy, concern, or good stories. They want an immediate arrest which, those in the field will tell you, is nearly impossible to obtain. In spite of the fact that I may be called for help, very often I end up on the receiving end of anger and hostility. This only serves to produce more stress.

In order to deal with the stress I decided on a positive course of action: to use skills developed in teaching in conjunction with my knowledge and training in law enforcement to provide proactive programs. The reality of police work is that, unlike many professions, there are no tangible results to make you feel good about what you do. Tired of making excuses, I directed my energies towards finding methods to reduce the chances of victimization. Also, it's easier to put the home or business owner on the defensive when they start crying by pointing out what an unimaginative job they did on security. That's not as callous as it sounds. Most people, in particular those out in suburbia, believe they are devoid of crime and safe from violent acts and ill-mannered types.

I have found community policing or crime prevention to be an excellent outlet. I can provide positive and productive information to victims and potential victims and, in return, I receive the gratuitous thank you's on which an ego thrives. It is a pleasant relationship and I have readily exploited the media sources available today. I not only have a newspaper column but also a regular spot on cable television. A single officer can create a bond or link to his community which had never before existed. Administrators, always eyeing the political ramifications of their decisions, leap to programs like these. It has taken a long time, but departments are finally waking up to the fact that you cannot function properly if you remain an isolated element in your city.

On the downside many of the older officers find it demeaning to have patrolmen carrying teddy bears and talking to school children, rather than thumping bad guys. Although I find many of these dinosaurs are lumbering off to retirement where they can spin yarns about the old days, the trick is to avoid replacing them with similar types.

Many of the young people I meet seeking to enter police work often comment on how they would only "work for a really big department." Provided you can find a job, any goals are noble. Don't, however, overlook the advantages of a smaller setting. Over the years I have become certified as a D.A.R.E. instructor, a crime prevention specialist, a firearms instructor, and a pursuit driving instructor. In a larger department each of these tasks would be filled by a separate specialist. In addition, due to the lack of support services, I have had the opportunity to see most cases through from beginning to end. There is challenge in being your own investigator, accident reconstructionist and juvenile officer. I have spoken to numerous men in larger concerns who are frustrated because, although openings are available, they compete against scores of officers for each position. All of our personnel have an area in which they have received advanced training, from arson investigation to motor carrier enforcement.

All of this does not come without a cost. While it may make you more resilient to developing cynical attitudes, you do have a tendency to burn out somewhat more rapidly. The more calls you get, the more work you do. There is no one around to take on some of the load. It is customary to handle calls alone that would require 2 to 3 officers in a large department. Family fights, arrests, and burglar alarms get one car because most of the time others simply aren't available.

There is an inherent risk of danger in police work, no matter where a person works. Yet, in suburban and rural areas with their manpower constraints, the anxiety level of the staff may be extremely high. This is contrary to the view shared by many residents that it's quiet and safe.

It is also very frustrating to go to your community time and time again for manpower and equipment requests, only to be turned down, because they fail to comprehend the need. Our department has remained static in size for 22 years, in spite of rapid residential and commercial growth over the last decade.

Twelve years into my career, an opportunity arose for promotion. Keep in mind that getting promoted in a small department can produce several difficulties. Obviously with the intimacy under which we work, we become very familiar with each others' personal work habits. Had I chosen to adopt the work habits of a sloth, the position would have been much more difficult. As it was, I maintained a fairly respectable work ethic, so I was comfortable requesting a similar level of commitment from the officers. If you have the ambition for promotion, keep in mind that one day you may have to give orders to your "buddies." Remember to always maintain professional relationships with colleagues, otherwise the job will be much more difficult.

A line supervisor presents other difficulties too; maintaining a discreet distance, while remaining approachable and open. I have found that staring at pure statistics when evaluating can be deceiving. Productivity is affected by morale, family problems and various other personal issues. There isn't always a workable solution. Keeping an open mind and attempting to work with the officer may help. In a small department the task is easier, because you work closely and with fewer officers.

Many larger departments have the luxury of keeping the supervisory personnel away from the day-to-day road activities. They are concerned more with proper shift scheduling, discipline and proper handling of complaints. I would enjoy that, but with limited resources I am required to take care of those matters and work as a road patrolman. That's one of those things which you have to weigh when choosing a department. There can be some major differences throughout the ranks. On the top end, about the only place to go is Chief, and that is unlikely. We don't have a contingent of Lieutenants, Captains, and Inspectors, so your career pretty much ends at the rank of Sergeant.

Having spent my entire adult life in public service, it is difficult for me to compare the work ethic with the private sector. A community's resources are not based on market share, productivity or cost effectiveness. They have guaranteed income. I discount tickets as a revenue generating device. The percentage of fines returned to the municipality is so small that it would require a tremendous amount of time and effort to produce notable results. In general, it is a poor utilization of manpower since traffic officers barely pay their own wages. I firmly believe that due to the lack of competitiveness a certain lethargy develops; insidious habits that would never be tolerated in other fields.

Very much of what an officer does is discretionary. It is one of the few professions in which you can do as little as you want or as much as you want. Many arrests are dependent on how alert and attentive the officer is. The patrolmen and women with the best records are often looking, digging and checking into something. The ones with the poorest records always find an excuse to be doing something else. When careers stagnate, they find blame and justification for that also. I have witnessed bitterness raging inside men who have done little more than sit on top of the seniority pile for years. In a previous era, seniority counted for everything. Today, I am happy to say, preparation and work ethic are beginning to count for something.

Much of the reason for the slow change is that the chief administrators are still the only real vulnerable members of the organization. While the officers are protected by the union, the chief of police is still a political position. As a result, the chief is responsive to the needs of city council rather than the needs of the department and the community. Policies are often adopted to satiate the individual desires of elected officials. I have observed this phenomenon in both large and small cities. The blame lays squarely on the shoulders of the electorate, who turn out in shamefully small numbers for local elections. Citizens are concerned with only one matter: that an officer shows up when they call for one. The daily needs, policies and activity of the police force seem to be of little interest.

The reality of police work is that much of it is still a routine, with little thanks from the community and continued resentment from listless officers. Advancement comes in degrees and for many will be unobtainable. However, just because work weariness sours some officers, that does not mean it will happen to you. As I have said there are tremendous possibilities if you look for them and keep a positive attitude toward the job. It's necessary to recognize that police work is changing increasingly from crime fighting to crime prevention. The media enhanced picture depicting hard hitting, fast shooting officers is no more reality than the John Wayne image of the cowhand. Very few go one-on-one in a fight and, surprising though this may seem, 95% will never fire their gun. I have noted a number of officers caught up with projecting the irreverent image rather than the correct one, perhaps because so much of the job requires role playing. That is the real stress in law enforcement—changing your face for every situation, being something at times you are not: counselor, tough guy, parent and confessor. It's a tall order for anyone to fill. But with the right attitude it can be financially and emotionally rewarding.

SECTION TWO:
PRIVATE SECURITY AND
LOSS PREVENTION

According to a National Institute of Justice Report, "Private security is now clearly the nation's primary protective resource, outspending public law enforcement by 73 percent and employing 2½ times the workforce."[1] While public law enforcement has an annual expenditure of $30 billion and a workforce of 600,000, private security agencies spend $52 billion and employ 1.5 million. The projected average annual rate of growth in private security is 8% through the year 2000. This reflects both specialization and a privatization of policing functions.

Private security is provided either by direct hiring (proprietary security) or by hiring specific services or equipment (contract security). A typical security guard might work for one of the established private security companies such as Wells Fargo, where they engage in watch clock tours, traffic control, fire prevention, access control, and property protection. Alternatively, major transit centers, such as airports, also employ numerous security personnel. For example, one of our former students works as a supervisor for Detroit Metro Airport's security operations and is responsible for ensuring the airport's compliance with FAA regulations. She oversees a contract security guard force and manages the security clearance operation for 15,000 airport employees.

Private security services include much more than the stereotypical uniformed guard and patrols, alarm services and armored escorts. They include private investigations, security consultation and analysis, employee drug and honesty testing, forensic analysis, loss prevention, and risk management. Indeed, private security companies are one of the main agencies investigating crimes against business. Investigations

---

[1] William C. Cunningham, John J. Strauchs and Clifford W. Van Meter., "Private Security: Patterns and Trends," *NIJ Research Brief*, August, 1991, p.1. Since the 1950s there has been a continuing trend of private police outnumbering public police and since 1977 private police have also outspent them.

1 SECURITY AND LOSS PREVENTION
Typical Ads

SECURITY OFFICERS:
Flint, MI. **Job Description:**
Security, crime prevention
and crime control for
university campus.
Qualifications: Degree in
criminal justice desirable,
certified or considerable
experience as police officer.

**ANIMAL CRUELTY
INVESTIGATOR:** Detroit,
MI. **Job Description:**
Fighting animal cruelty.
Qualifications: Writing
skills, ability to deal with
public and any animal-related
experience. Criminal justice
degree or law enforcement
background.

SECURITY MANAGER:
Indianapolis, IN. **Job
Description:** Security
management for 45-store
chain in midwest.
Qualifications: 2-4 yrs.
security experience. **Salary:**
Competitive.

**DIRECTOR OF CAMPUS
SECURITY:** Toledo, OH.
Qualifications: AA or BS in
criminal justice or related
field. Minimum three yrs.
law enforcement experience.

LIBRARY SECURITY:
New York, NY. **Job
Description:** Monitor,
identify and report security
problems to public safety

dept. **Qualifications:** Good
communication skills and
maturity. Experience with
public in service capacity.

SECURITY MANAGER:
Chicago, IL. **Job
Description:** Manage 250-
bed facility. **Qualifications:**
Degree in corrections or law
enforcement and 3-5 yrs.
related experience.

**SECURITY OPERATIONS
MANAGER:** Seattle, WA.
Job Description: Manage
day-to-day operations.
Qualifications: Experience
required and degree helpful.
Must be self-motivated and
career-oriented.

**LOSS PREVENTION
MANAGER:** Norfolk, VA.
Job Description: Loss
prevention for sporting goods
company. **Qualifications:** 3-5
yrs. loss prevention
experience in retail
environment, B.S. in
criminal justice/risk
management or equivalent,
strong communication skills,
and investigative know-how.

**LOSS PREVENTION
INVESTIGATOR:**
Charlotte, NC. **Job
Description:** Loss prevention
investigation with major drug
company. **Qualifications:**
Security experience, degree.

44

2 SECURITY AND LOSS PREVENTION
Typical Ads (Continued)

LOSS PREVENTION/ SECURITY: Phoenix, AZ. **Job Description:** Loss prevention and security investigation in major retail chain. **Qualifications:** 2-3 yrs. retail loss prevention, management experience and investigation/interrogation skills.

LOSS PREVENTION AGENT: Los Angeles, CA. **Job Description:** Shoplifting prevention and loss prevention, safety training and auditing. **Qualifications:** One yr. retail loss prevention experience or related college level courses, good writing and investigative skills.

STORE INVESTIGATOR: Orlando, FL. **Job Description:** Internal/external investigations, enforcement of physical security procedures and writing related reports. **Qualifications:** Written and verbal communication skills and retail security experience.

SECURITY OFFICERS: Washington, DC. **Job Description:** Full and part-time positions available. **Qualifications:** OPOT, CPR and First Aid beneficial. **Salary:** Benefits include life and health insurance, vision care, paid vacation.

SECURITY SPECIALIST: New Orleans, LA. **Job Description:** Responsibilities include maintaining security operations, assessing and conducting training and educational programs for security personnel. **Qualifications:** Bachelor's in criminal justice or related field. **Salary:** Excellent salary and comprehensive benefit programs.

AREA LOSS CONTROL MANAGER: Portland, OR. **Job Description:** Manage security and loss prevention for a major retail chain. **Qualifications:** 2-yr. degree in criminal justice, and/or 2 yrs. work experience.

CHIEF OF HOUSING SECURITY AND INVESTIGATOR: Detroit, MI. **Job Description:** Public Housing and Drug Elimination Project. Will be performing a variety of tasks related to the provision of internal and external security in major housing operation. **Qualifications:** Bachelor's in criminal justice or related field, former police officer, knowledge in public administration, local law enforcement procedures, and investigative techniques.

45

include white-collar as well as blue-collar occupational offenses, such as computer crimes, copyright and trade mark infringements, industrial espionage, fraud, embezzlement, employee background checks and evacuation planning. For example, as an Assets Production Manager for a national discount warehouse chain, a criminology and criminal justice graduate is responsible for stock shortage and reduction, employee investigations, safety, and operational audits.

Several other former criminal justice students work for one of the large pizza corporations based in Michigan. As Security Intelligence Analysts they are involved in the collection and dissemination of information (auto accident, worker's compensation claims, robberies and security incidents) to field personnel, for policy-making, and tracking security trends and products. In addition to completing investigative reports on security incidents, they also conduct surveillance and security seminars. As one says, "I'm a liaison between the store operations and the field security directors. I work to prevent security incidents at stores and on deliveries."

Because of the nature of their employment relationship, private security personnel rarely investigate crimes by corporations or those by state or government officials. However, this does not mean that private security is restricted only to policing blue-collar employees. As a Loss Prevention Manager for a major retail group and as a Licensed Investigator responsible for corporate security across 10 stores, one former student not only investigates employee theft, but also corporate level embezzlements; and her work involves interviewing, interrogating, and making many court appearances to represent companies. She is enthusiastic about her job, pointing out that "retail has tremendous opportunity in the loss prevention field and it's becoming an established profession. You only need a bachelor's degree to start and some investigative experience." Indeed, a Loss Prevention Manager with J. C. Penney says criminology and criminal justice students should seriously "consider careers in the area of private security/loss prevention. There are lots of opportunities. The field is growing, changing and becoming more professional. The pay is good to very good, especially in management."

Another dimension of private security is to work independently as a private investigator or private detective. In 1988 there were 46,700 private investigators employed nationwide, although less than 20% of these are self-employed and roughly 50% work in loss prevention. The private investigator does a lot of research involving records and much paper work, including filing reports to businesses, clients and courts. They will be involved in interviewing, researching personal histories, conducting background checks for employment and reviewing financial records. In addition, they may stake out premises to monitor movements, examine crime scenes, do forensic tests and give testimony in court. The possibility of establishing her own private security business and of being a Licensed Investigator occurred to Kathy, who graduated in sociology, with a minor in criminology. She joined her brother to start their own company and is currently Vice-President of New Hudson Electric Company and President of Lorimar Security. New Hudson is a successful electrical contracting business which handles all business and finance as well as providing consulting services for electrical construction projects, recommending burglar alarm equipment, lighting and motion-detector placement, and/or guard service following crime area research. Kathy says that some states make it quite easy to obtain a private investigator's license and allow criminal justice education to be substituted for experience. In Michigan, for example, a person can substitute their bachelor's in criminal justice for the requirement of working in a criminal justice agency and can obtain a two-year license issued by the state police for $100.00. More typically, people enter the profession by applying to agencies that are already licensed.

Because of the variability in entry-level qualifications, training, salary, promotional possibilities and supervision; it is impossible to provide a broad indication of average salaries for careers in private security. The basic guard position pays close to minimum wage, but the managerial positions command very respectable salaries. These positions may also require additional skills such as accounting, computing, management and administration as well as the American Society for Industrial Security's professional certification—the CPPC (Certified Protection Professional Certificate). A self-employed private investigator in the midwest earns from $20 to $70 per hour and typically charges $25 per hour, depending upon the nature of the work and the competition's fees.

Because there is no national regulation of industry standards,[2] the prospective employee should be very discriminating between employers and closely examine what the job requires. Some of the most questionable contracts have been those in which an employer hires private security personnel to work plain clothes as non-unionized labor and trains them in strong-arm tactics in order to displace union sympathizers, union employees or to break strikes (known as strike-breaking goons).[3]

However, there are some very interesting and important preventative careers available in the security industry and these can serve as a useful bridge to other criminal justice careers. Students must be wary, however, of believing private security will necessarily lead to law enforcement positions. As one of our Security Analysts told us: "If you want to be a police officer—work for a police department, not a security guard agency. Be specific in your desires and what you want for yourself. Weigh the options and then go for it. There is no better job than the one you enjoy doing and no worse job than one to which you dread going. Be careful not to trap yourself into a corner."

To give a greater insight into the work of private security and loss prevention professionals we have four contributions. The first is from Jan Collins who is employed in-house in a major national pizza chain and is responsible for supervising investigative field security. The second is by Thomas Jazdzewski who is employed as a Loss Prevention Investigator by a nationally recognized department store. The third is from Bill Wise, the director of security for a private college campus. The final paper describes the work of a private investigator through an interview by Joe LaLonde, a former student interested in entering the private detective business.

---

[2] 35 states license guard and patrol firms and 37 states license private investigators according to Bureau of Justice Statistics, *Report to the Nation on Crime and Justice*, 2nd edition, Washington DC: BJS, 1988, p. 66.

[3] A notorious example is the use of private security as "scab labor" in the New York newspaper industry.

For more insight into private investigator or private security careers:

Cohen, Paul and Shari. *Careers in Law Enforcement and Security.* New York: Rosen Publishing, 1990.

DeLucia, Robert C. and Doyle, Thomas J. "Careers in Private Security" in *Career Planning in Criminal Justice.* Cincinnati, OH: Anderson Publishing, pp. 91-95.

Orion Agency. *Obtaining Your Private Investigator's License.* Boulder, CO: Paladin Press, 1986.

Thomas, Barbara L. *Successful Private Eyes and Private Spies.* Gettysburg, PA: Thomas Publications, 1986.

For the latest information on developments in private security:

Police and Security News
Days Communication, 1690 Quarry Road, P.O. Box 330, Kulpsville, PA 19443 or call (215) 538-1240.
Six issues/year—$12 per year or $20 for two years.

Campus Crime
Business Publication Inc., Pershing Drive, Silver Spring, MD 20910 or call (800) 274-0122.
Monthly—$240/year subscription.

For further information on private security contact:

American Society for Industrial Security (ASIS)
1655 North F. Myer Drive, Suite 1200, Arlington, VA 22209.
ASIS is a world-wide organization that publishes a directory of its 23,000 members annually. This is a great source of names and a wealth of contacts to whom you may send resumes. Student dues are inexpensive ($30).

International Foundation for Protection Officers (IFPO)
7327 Horne St., Mission, British Columbia, Canada V2V 3Y5.
IFPO is concerned with providing education, training and certification
for security officers and property protection officers.

International Security Management Association
400 Atlantic Avenue, Boston, MA 02110.

Also consider applying for Detective Agency License. Contact your State
Police for details of licensing.

One of the best sources of jobs is:

The PSIC Listing
Protective Services Information Center, P.O. Box 1562, Decatur, IL
62525.
PSIC collects and disseminates information on jobs in policing and
private security. It costs $21.95 for four monthly issues or $57.95 per
year.

See also:

National Employment Listing Service (NELS)
Criminal Justice Center, Sam Houston State University, Huntsville,
TX 77341 or phone (409) 294-1692
This is a monthly covering all areas of criminal justice. Positions in
private security are listed under the section: "Law Enforcement and
Security." $17.50 for a six-month subscription.

CHAPTER 6:

Securing the Corporation: Private Security Analyst

by *Jan Collins**

I graduated from college in December 1987. While visiting the university's Career Placement Center I saw a job posting for a big-name pizza company which we will call "The Big Cheese." The posting listed some unusual requirements and my first thought was that it was for a security guard: "Ability to do shift work; typing at approximately 45 words per minute; a degree in criminal justice; computer experience; and physical fitness standard." I met most of the requirements but completely lacked the computer experience. The high school I attended did not have computers then and I did not take any computer classes in college. I applied anyway and was interviewed by the supervisor who turned out to have graduated from my college, and used our Career Placement Center when she needed people. I was hired in March 1988. Since then I have been promoted to her job of supervisor and recently changed jobs within the organization.

When I first joined The Big Cheese I worked on a 24-hour communication link between the stores and head office. All security-related incidents that occur at store level are called into the 1-800 (Hotline) number. Whether it was a driver that was being robbed, or a store clerk being assaulted, or a store broken into, or missing money, we would take a police-type report so that our Field Security Directors could begin to investigate the incident.

Two things quickly became apparent in the early years. First, as the number of stores grew so did the amount of crime and violence, which meant that it was futile to keep investigating these incidents **after** they had happened. We had to start preventing them from happening. Second, the efficiency and acceptance of the hotline led the company to use this device for other things such as taking first reports of injury. This occurred because many of our employees were being injured in security related incidents. We also took reports of auto accidents, general liabilities, and any safety or security related violation and product

*This is a fictional name used at the author's request.

51

complaints. Our food warehouses that supply the stores also began to call in their semi-truck accidents.

The job proved to be a very good entry job into the company, although the responsibilities are not anywhere near entry level. For example, the semi-truck industry is regulated by the Department of Transportation. Therefore, if one of our semi-trucks that supplies the stores with food is in an accident, the DOT has to be notified within a certain time frame; failure to do so results in monetary fines. Since we are the first people to be contacted when a semi-truck is in an accident, we have to contact the appropriate DOT people, regardless of the time!

There is no sense in collecting all this information if you aren't going to use it to make the stores safer and more secure. All of our reports are taken on a computer. This enables the data to be readily analyzed so it can form the basis of operational policies and procedures. For example, after making a delivery, all drivers are required to drop their money into a locked box. We have found that if these policies are followed the chances of an incident happening are greatly reduced. There was some initial resistance to these policies because employees thought that the extra precautions hindered store operations. In the case of the "DROP," drivers think that the extra time taken to use the box is not worth it. We point out that if a driver gets robbed of $60, this puts all other drivers into jeopardy because the robber comes to expect that kind of money from robbing pizza drivers, and may become violent if the next driver only has $13. It is important to stress to the employees that their actions or lack of actions can contribute to serious injury to their co-workers. Also, a lot of crime in the fast food industry has been shown to be committed by current or ex-employees; people who know the system. Based upon the analysis of our information we are able to minimize these incidents and prevent many before they actually happen.

There are several things to consider if you are thinking about obtaining a position in loss prevention, security or police work. First, you must be "customer service" oriented. The people working in our stores are our customers. Our job depends upon their job. Therefore, you must always be polite and helpful. We never say "I don't know" to any employee who calls in. If we do not have the answer we tell them we will find out and get back to them.

Second, you have to be able to work with diverse groups of people. The workforce is changing to include more women and minorities. As an employee you must be sensitive to different cultures and to the language barriers that exist. We deal with people in shock and distress. They may have had a gun put to their head and thought that they would not live to see another day. These same people may not speak English well, especially when they are upset, so you need a great deal of patience when taking their information. The phone also reduces the quality of voice reproduction, so it takes considerable concentration to maintain accuracy.

Third, it is important that you are a responsible, dependable person who can work under stress and do so at irregular hours. In security work the hours are rarely 9 to 5. Someone has to be on 24 hours a day, 7 days a week, with no breaks for holidays. At first you may think that shift work will not cause you any problems but it's ten times harder than you can imagine. People who call in sick or show up late will not last long because this forces someone else to work "a double." Not only are you part of a team, with co-workers depending upon you to cover your shift, but the people in the field expect and depend upon you to be there to assist them.

Also, the job can be depressing because we see a concentration of all that is wrong with society. It is difficult to take reports day after day about our employees being robbed, stabbed, shot or kidnapped just for a pizza and $13! It is hard to understand why these criminals do these things to people who are working hard and just trying to make a living.

On the up side, one of the best things about this job is that the people working on the hotline have the ability to help others. The store managers that call in are experts in store operations, but not in crisis situations. The managers need advice and assistance in dealing with situations ranging from a driver being shot on a delivery to a customer slipping inside the store and breaking an ankle. The managers appreciate the fact that there is a real person at the head office to assist them 24 hours a day. Therefore, you learn a lot about the company because you get asked all types of questions that are not related to safety or security. Another positive aspect is that no two days are the same. Like police work, you never know what to expect when the phone rings.

In short, private security of this sort is not a job to be taken lightly as most people imagine, but it is a job which is helpful to others and very satisfying when viewed from the prevention perspective.

CHAPTER 7:

Minding the Store: Loss Prevention Investigator

by *Thomas R. Jazdzewski*

I can remember the beginning of my junior year at college. I asked myself, "What can I do to get a job that is related to my field of study?" I thought about a lot of jobs, but the one that came to mind was that of a Loss Prevention Investigator. The first step I took to get this job was to look at the newspaper classified ads. I responded to an advertisement in the newspaper but nothing came of it. I then applied directly to the personnel departments of several retail department stores that I knew had such a position. (I had discovered this through research and asking people questions). From some stores I received a response; from others I did not. I was very fortunate to eventually get an interview with two major retail department stores. I thought I did well at the interviews. I bought a book, "How To Make an Interview into a Job," and I applied all of the techniques to the initial interview. I thought that it really did help. It was a good investment. Some stores I interviewed with several times and some of the interviews went better than others. I have been employed with Juno's Department Store for a little over two years now. I am responsible for all of the alarm systems inside and outside the building. Once a month I have to perform alarm tests to insure building security is maintained, and I turn in my report and it is logged. All of Juno's buildings are equipped with sophisticated alarm systems which include: fire alarms, motion detectors, burglar alarms, and hold-up alarms. I am also responsible for weekly auditing of cash terminals, the cash office, and the high shortage department areas.

The content of the Loss Prevention Investigator's job includes more than I expected when I first interviewed for the position. The Loss Prevention mission is to protect the company assets, which includes its customers and employees, merchandise, equipment, money and media, supplies, properties, information and reputation. The Loss Prevention Division of Juno's strives to achieve professional interaction with others. We execute this professionalism in all of our activities without regard to race, color, creed, religion, age, or sex; with a particular emphasis in the following areas:

A. The protection of company merchandise from theft (internal and external) through the maintenance of merchandise protection standards, the identification of thieves and the investigation of losses.

B. The prevention of customer and employee accidents through the maintenance of safe working and shopping environments, prompt response to calls for first-aid and the immediate correction of accident causes. This is important because considerable money can be saved by prevention before problems arise which incur health costs or injury law suits.

C. The formulation of reasonable rules, regulations, policies and procedures, monitoring for compliance and the identification of violators, and/or dishonest employees.

D. The development and installation of reasonable safeguards and controls to prevent frauds with checks, credit cards, refunds and gift certificates, and the investigation of fraud activity.

There really is no part of my job that I dislike. The work changes from week to week. Retail working hours in my company are from 9:45 a.m. to 9:45 p.m. There is no boring part of the job because you always have to be on your toes, and be ready for the unexpected. At one minute you could be dispatched to a "charge card fraud" in progress, or to a suspicious person in an area that a sales consultant wants watched closely. The next minute you could be dispatched to a customer "slip and fall" which calls for the administration of first-aid. The exciting part of the job is arresting shoplifters or people who commit "charge fraud;" stopping or preventing a shoplifter from taking merchandise; and cutting store shortage statistics, whether it results from internal or external causes.

In this job the external theft or shoplifters that we see includes both professionals and amateurs. I have arrested both types. After an arrest is made, the subject is escorted, usually in handcuffs, back to the loss prevention office where the processing takes place. A report is made of the incident. The city police are notified and an officer is dispatched to our location. If the incident involves merchandise under $100 this is known as "Retail Fraud 2," which is a misdemeanor. Any merchandise in excess of $100 is considered "Retail Fraud I," which is a felony. If the subject has no outstanding warrants for his/her arrest, and has a valid picture identification, a ticket to appear in court is usually issued and they are released on their own recognizance. In the Retail Fraud I cases, the subject is automatically taken to the city police department for booking. After they appear in court, usually 1-10 days after the incident, a pre-trial is scheduled and the arresting investigator will appear in court through a subpoena.

Perhaps surprisingly, many subjects admit responsibility for the crime they have committed. There are some cases in which the arresting investigator has to testify in court in an exam or a bench trial. This is another part of the job that I thoroughly enjoy. Going to court to testify against these offenders, some of whom are habitual, is extremely interesting, as well as useful, when they are guilty of the crime and dealt with appropriately by the court.

The rewards of this job that I most like are the fringe benefits. I have medical insurance, dental insurance, and I am vested in the company's 401K retirement program. I am a plain-clothes investigator. The company has a dress code that I do have to follow. I have the freedom to go anywhere inside the store. The aspect of the work that I most enjoy is investigating dishonest employees, interviewing or interrogating them, and terminating their employment with our company. Reasons for termination include embezzlement, excessive crediting to one's own account(s) or an acquaintance's account without the merchandise being purchased, creating fictitious cash refunds, policy and procedure violations, and creating NSF (Non-Sufficient Funds) BAD CHECKS to the company.

So what qualifications do you need to become a Loss Prevention Investigator? These vary in detail but basically are much the same. The following are the most important:

1.   Any prior experience in security or in retail.

2.   A bachelor's degree. Criminal justice majors have an advantage here but not in all stores.

3.   Good communication skills are crucial and you must be able to demonstrate these with examples, starting with a professionally prepared resume and a practiced and pleasant telephone manner.

4.   A customer service orientation is important. You will be dealing with customers and cannot be someone who is easily offended or offensive. If you are and know that under stress you flair up, Loss Prevention is not for you. Try hockey or coaching!

5.   Knowledge of how to administer first-aid and CPR are important job skills but they can be acquired later.

If you've got the basics then this is the next step. Suppose you have sent your resume around, you've hit some major stores, and you have read the book on how to get invited to an interview. The day comes when you have to put all this into practice. That is really what you need: practice. You may want to "write off" the first one or two interviews as you formulate your approach in the real situation. If you get hired anyway, great. If not, it will be excellent experience for the job you really want. The best position to get initially is with a large corporation with a well-established system of loss prevention that will train you in the various aspects of the business.

Do not get frustrated or disappointed if you feel the interview did not go well. At the interview, ask them when they plan to make their decision and tell them that you will contact them after that date to find out the outcome. Alternatively, after the interview, contact the person with whom you interviewed right away and do a follow-up. Ask that person if they have filled the position. Never feel that you are inconveniencing the interviewer by doing a follow-up. Keep bugging them about the position for which you are applying. This shows initiative. When you get hired as a Loss Prevention Investigator, the work really starts and the possibilities are limited only by your imagination.

CHAPTER 8:

Policing the Campus: Director of Campus Security

by *William C. Wise*

There are a wide variety of responsibilities and services provided by campus security agencies nationwide. Their function can range from simple watchman services to providing full police and fire service. As Director of Campus Security I am responsible for the overall management of the department of public safety. The Director must ensure that everyone adheres to all the policies, programs, and procedures so as to contribute to a safe and well-ordered campus environment. The Director of Campus Security at my college oversees a staff of twenty-five student guards who provide twenty-four-hour-per-day service to the campus. I am aided by one graduate assistant who serves as the Assistant Director of Security.

Campus security officers lock and unlock campus buildings, patrol parking lots, provide escort service and emergency first aid, screen persons entering campus, enforce parking regulations and provide crime and fire prevention instruction.

As Director of Campus Security I interact regularly with local police and fire officials on law enforcement and fire prevention concerns. I work with the city fire department in establishing a fire response plan for the campus and conduct fire inspections of all college buildings. I also do investigative follow-up on serious crimes occurring on campus, such as rapes, violent assaults, robbery, and embezzlement, supplying my information to the local police. For example, during the 1991/92 academic year two sexual assaults occurred within the residence hall. One male student sexually assaulted two female students. I conducted the investigation of these two incidents and took an active role in the administrative disposition of both incidents. On another occasion a suspect in an area drive-by shooting entered our residence hall and hid in a resident's room until campus security officers and the local police department located him. We also deal with white collar crimes. Some students have used ingenious methods to steal from the college. For example, one student took forms from the financial aid office, forged authorizing signatures, and used the forged documents to obtain books from the college bookstore. I conducted the investigation which led to the student's apprehension.

In such cases of serious campus crime, the local police incorporate my information with their data to obtain warrants for suspects. For example, larceny from vehicles is a common problem. In a recent case our officers observed the crime on a video surveillance camera, obtained a license number of the suspect's vehicle and called the local police. The police apprehended the suspects and cleared up a number of county-wide cases of breaking and entering of autos.

Given the full spectrum of services offered, anyone entering the campus security field in a supervisory capacity would benefit from having a social science or criminal justice degree, preferably at the master's level. Law enforcement experience is also very helpful since a large part of the job requires working with state and local law enforcement officials. Some experience in fire safety and service would be helpful as well. Clearly, someone with a degree in public safety administration and experience working as a security officer on a college campus would be well qualified to obtain a position as director of campus security. Also, because campus security is a senior supervisory position, at least three or more years experience may be necessary. I had just the right combination of experience. A position became available after I was employed to teach at a local college.

Before joining the college I had worked for thirteen years as a police officer for the City of Ann Arbor Police Department. During this time Ann Arbor provided police protection for the University of Michigan, a top state research university with some 35,000 students. The campus is intermeshed with the city, itself having a population of around 105,000. There were seven officers assigned to the University detail from the Ann Arbor department. I was one of them. I spent nearly ten of my thirteen years on the campus beat. In that capacity I was the first responder to all U of M calls. But I was also expected to handle a large number of city calls, since the City and the University were interwoven. The University of Michigan campus had five separate security forces besides the Ann Arbor Police. These were: campus security, which handled campus-wide security functions; housing security; hospital security; parking enforcement; and state security. State security locked the buildings and patrolled for fires and maintenance problems. I interacted daily with all of these separate security forces and became well versed in the multifaceted world of policing the campus. My involvement went beyond answering criminal complaints and enforcing the law. It included crowd control, building security, university rules and regulations, social dynamics of life in the residence halls and dealing with unique and diverse populations. This included students, athletes, administrators, and professors as well as an ethnically and racially diverse population which was not averse to experimenting with drugs and exploring diverse and occasionally perverse sexual preferences.

In 1985, after completing thirteen years in this position, I joined the faculty of Siena Heights College in Adrian, Michigan. My initial assignment was as Chairperson of the Criminal Justice Department and Assistant Professor of Criminal Justice. I had earned a B.A. in sociology, an M.A. in education, guidance and counseling, and a second master's in criminology and criminal justice from Eastern Michigan University.

Aware of my experience in Ann Arbor, the dean of students at Siena Heights College requested my help as a "consultant" on campus security. In October 1989, I was asked to review the security department and made a number of suggestions as to how to improve the operation. In February 1990, with the departure of the director of campus security, I was asked to assume the directorship along with my other duties. A separate contract was drawn up covering this aspect of my job.

At Siena Heights the director of campus security reports to the dean of students and is part of the student development staff. In addition to the dean and two associate deans of students, the student development staff includes the directors of campus security, counseling, residence life, student activities, non-traditional student services, health services, upward bound, campus ministry, food services and athletics. My broad based education and past work experience served me well in working with this very diverse student development staff.

Another part of the job of Campus Security Director includes developing and maintaining a policy and procedure manual. The manual I developed for Siena Heights was totally inclusive, covering all aspects of the campus security function. Once completed, the manual must be reviewed and updated to meet changing needs. For example, in 1990 the United States Senate and House of Representatives passed the Student Right-to-Know and Campus Security Act. This Act requires colleges receiving federal aid to compile campus crime statistics and report these to the FBI's Uniform Crime Report and to the college's students, faculty, and staff. As a result of the changing legislative context I had to develop a report form and establish a records system to monitor and report incidents on campus. Other changes might include being able to deputize your own campus police officers, as has happened in the State of Michigan. This, of course, brings added responsibilities and problems. For example, part of the State's Public Act establishing the independence of campus police requires the establishment of a Public Safety Oversight Committee. On some campuses this has served as a conduit for complaints, previously relatively non-existent, to suddenly appear. These may range from "discourtesy" during parking incidents to racial harassment while trying to intercede during noise complaints at campus parties. The hearings and investigations can take time away from an already demanding job and can be complicated when officers are members of a union.

One of my biggest concerns as Director of Campus Security is the safety and security of the residence halls. Ninety percent of the incidents occurring on campus, that involve campus security, occur there. I am faced with two conflicting needs. One is to provide safe and secure living accommodations and the other is to honor the students' right to come and go freely without being inconvenienced by locked doors, and unnecessary intrusions into what should be a relatively open time for learning independent living, emotional growth and social experimentation. The most difficult part of my job is satisfying the diverse populations on campus: administrators, professors, students, and staff. All of these persons have different needs and concerns which are often in conflict. I often find myself in the middle of some very touchy issues.

One of the most volatile issues concerns campus parking. Everyone feels they have a God-given right to a parking place next to the door that they most frequently use. Faculty have been known to refuse to teach at certain times because they claim they cannot find a parking place! Alternatively, if there are no available parking spaces, innovative drivers often create a space of their own. Cars double park, jump curbs, block entrances and fire lanes; some people will even park on the lawn. The security officers then ticket and tow these vehicles and the faculty or student becomes indignant about the disappearance of their car. They typically claim that "it wasn't my fault. If those other cars hadn't been taking **my** space I would not have **had** to..." I find myself in the middle. The difficulty with this position is further aggravated by the fact that I am part faculty, part staff and part administration and at times I am alienated from all three.

Overall, in spite of these recurring problems, policing a campus can be a rewarding job. It demands more tolerance than is typical of regular policing, and involves creating preventative policies and being able to see these through. Feedback from the university community with whom you are in daily contact makes the job of Director of Campus Security very satisfying.

William C. Wise is Assistant Professor of Criminal Justice, Chair of the Division of Human Services and Director of Campus Security at Siena Heights College, Adrlun, Michigan.

CHAPTER 9:

"Private Eye": An Interview with Kirk Bruchnak, P.I.

by *Joseph T. LaLonde*

Maybe it was the guile and charm of "Columbo," or the intrigue of the "Rockford Files," but since being a child I have always been fascinated by the work of private detectives, "sleuths," and others in the business of private investigation. I find the idea of helping people through private investigation an exciting prospect. So for my careers project I chose to interview one of the nation's fifty thousand private investigators to find out what their work world was really like. I was fortunate enough to obtain an interview with Kirk Bruchnak, a local private investigator who graduated five years ago with a bachelor's in criminal justice and has owned and operated his own detective agency ever since.

Kirk had evaluated the prospects of going into police work and federal jobs, and finally decided on private investigation. He told me the first stage is to apply for a pre-licensing application and to do this about six months before you graduate. This will considerably shorten the licensure process.

A P.I. may either be self-employed or work for a licensed agency such as an insurance company. Private investigation is still a career in which a person can strike out alone, with expectations of success for those willing to work hard. Over half of all PI's work is in loss prevention. Often self-employed P.I.'s are one person operations. Kirk informed me that being self-employed is difficult and sometimes lonely. Income can be very tight until you are well established.

The usual way people start their career is by being hired to assist an established investigator or investigation company. This is useful in providing experience in investigative work, and in keeping costs down. The earlier you decide on your career objective, the better. Some agencies will be willing to work around a student's class schedule and provide them with close supervision and may even be prepared to offer the student an internship. Then, after graduation, and with some experience built up you may consider either going into partnership or starting your own business.

There are P.I. schools which offer 2 to 6 week specialty courses. The costs vary, but are around $5,000. These are very helpful but cost more than most people can afford. Typically participants are employees of large corporations and insurance companies, who pay to train their workforce. It is far cheaper, therefore, to attempt to work for such a company and to seize every opportunity they provide to gain licensure and training.

If you work for someone else, Kirk explains, the most likely thing you will be doing is serving summonses as you become familiarized with other techniques of investigation. Doing basic investigative work will introduce you to various ways to find information. Beginning with the traditional "phone book," you will move on to learn about more high tech investigative techniques such as computer searches, and about how to examine public information documents held by various state agencies like the Department of Motor Vehicles, Voter Registration or Employment Licensing. This will lead you to the more complex and sensitive areas of investigative work such as interviewing people, examining crime scenes for forensic evidence, and the use of video cameras, tape recorders, and listening devices used in undercover surveillance operations. It will also expose you to considerable report-writing and form-filling as well as how to provide effective courtroom testimony.

Like most professions the training for investigators never really stops. Apart from the expensive training schools, the experienced professional can improve skills and research techniques by attending junior college seminars which cost around $50.00 each. Seminar topics might include surveillance, data base searching or any of the countless new techniques promising greater efficiency and success.

Kirk said that a typical day is primarily spent locating missing people. Common reasons clients want to find people are to: establish the identities of their real parents in cases of adoptees; serve lawsuits; or simply to locate a missing relative. Other daily activities might include research and surveillance to establish whether a spouse is having an affair, background inquiries on individuals, and business and insurance surveillance. Private citizens and business organizations are the primary clients for most private investigation companies. In rare cases the police may contact a private investigator for help to supplement their own investigative efforts.

The first stage in looking for missing people is to obtain as much information from your client as possible. Next you go to the phone book. Kirk says, "From there it's anybody's guess. You do whatever time, money and your own personal research skills and experience dictate." Kirk believes that 75% of missing people can be located within 48 hours.

The work of a P.I. is creative, interesting and varied. "You meet and work with a wide variety of people. Helping people is rewarding. You get to work indoors and out, and you make your own hours," says Kirk. He points out that interviewing people, working around police, and the constant interaction with all sorts of characters, keeps a person alert and informed. The process results in a continual broadening of one's interpersonal network, which often proves both personally and professionally rewarding.

There are some disadvantages to PI work also. Kirk dislikes the administrative headaches of running his own business, including the heavy amount of paperwork, report writing and bill collecting. He also dislikes having to deal with employee problems. Surveillance over the long term becomes "boring and very tiring." He says, "Hour after hour spent in a car alone becomes a drag. Often I sit without a radio, newspaper or other distraction in order to stay focussed." Stress and burnout is a factor in any job and P.I. work is no exception. If you work for someone else there will likely be more stress because you will get the worst jobs, especially until you prove your worth.

Owning your own business, Kirk explains, also provides a number of advantages. For example, you can try to vary your cases to keep interest keen. You can pick and choose cases, take time off if needed and, if you have employees, you can pass on a portion of the drudgery to them.

Kirk sees a future with considerable growth in private investigative work. He believes accident reconstruction, loss prevention, background searches, and workman compensation cases as the areas most likely to grow. Consistent with this he plans to expand his own company and to move his office to a larger city where work will be more plentiful and where higher fees may be charged.

SECTION THREE:
LAW SCHOOL, LAWYERS
AND THE COURTS

There are basically two types of law work in the courts: the work of lawyers and the work of those who support them such as court administrators and legal assistants. While there are other court workers, such as bailiff, court reporter, stenographers, security personnel, research analysts and interviewers, these positions will not be considered here.[1] Moreover, the court probation officer and parole officer will be considered in Section Five.

There are three academic stages to becoming an attorney. The first of those consists of obtaining a bachelor's degree with an above average G.P.A., at least a 3.0 and preferably 3.5 or above. A prospective law school candidate can choose any area for the bachelor's degree, though many select political science or criminal justice, believing this will better prepare them. However, the better training is to attend an undergraduate program that provides adequate preparation for law school education, which is typically intense, rigorous and often intimidating. One former student of ours, for example, was disappointed with his undergraduate degree, feeling that it was not sufficiently demanding for preparation for law school and did not provide the practical experience necessary for legal work. He maintains that unless you want to teach, "change your major to a field that has some practical application to law!"

The form taken by legal education has not changed much since the 1870s. It involves the humiliating question and answer "Socratic" method founded by Christopher Langdell, then dean of Harvard Law School. The concept is to teach specific reasoning skills rather than the substance of law: "It is good for teaching students how to think like a lawyer, but not good at training students in the various specialties within law, nor in

---

[1] For an excellent summary of these and related positions see Chapter 3, "Careers in the Courts" in Robert C. DeLucia and Thomas J. Doyle, *Career Planning in Criminal Justice*, Cincinnati, OH: Anderson Publishing Company, 1990.

1 LAW AND COURTS
Typical ads

LEGAL COORDINATOR:
Maumee, OH. **Job
Description:** Coordinate legal
resources with agency's needs.
Qualifications: JD preferred,
MSW, Master's in public
administration or related field,
3 yrs. experience in children's
services and legal issues.
Salary: $35,071-$54,709.

PARALEGAL: Newport
News, VA. **Job Description:**
Coordinating court proceedings, litigation support and
client responsibilities.

**LEGAL ASST./ PARA-
LEGAL:** Detroit, MI. **Job
Description:** Prepare summary
plan descriptions, planned
amendments, resolutions, trust
agreements, and IRS sub-
missions. **Qualifications:** BS,
some computer experience.
Legal asst. training a plus.
Will consider law school grad.

LEGAL ASSISTANT:
Baltimore, MD. **Description:**
Assist attorneys in collection,
litigation and other legal work.
Qualifications: ABA-
accredited paralegal program
or equivalent, word processing.
Salary: $24,128 plus benefits.

PRE-TRIAL OFFICER:
Chicago, IL. **Job Description:**
Court-related work.
Qualifications: 4-yr. degree
with 2 yrs. experience.

LEGAL ASSISTANT:
Toledo, OH. **Job Description:**
Working with general civil
litigations, personal injury,
medical litigation, and
collections. **Qualifications:**
Legal assistant degree/
certificate preferred and
computer skills required.

LEGAL ASSISTANT:
Madison, WI. **Job
Description:** Litigation work
with Madison law firm.
Qualifications: B.A. and
2-3 yrs. litigation experience.

**JUVENILE COURT
REGISTER:** Macon, GA.
Qualifications: 5 yrs.
experience in legal
environment (juvenile court
preferred), 4 yrs. supervisory,
and computer literate.

COURT DEPUTY:
Manchester, NH. **Job
Description:** Provide security
for judges, court personnel,
jurors, and public. Serve
warrants for arrests, assist in
placement, security and
transportation of criminals.
Qualifications: Peace officer
training certificate, 3 yrs. law
enforcement experience,
familiarity with court system
and/or degree in law
enforcement or criminal
justice. **Salary:** $21,830 with
full benefits.

preparing students for modern cases or the new technology of law work."[2] This results in legal education producing generalist lawyers.

Before being allowed to submit to this onslaught of humiliation, it is necessary to pass the LSAT (Law School Admissions Test) with an acceptable score and to select an appropriate law school. This test is the critical second step to becoming an attorney. It will also determine which law school accepts you. The top rated schools are highly selective and use LSAT scores along with extra-curricular activities and undergraduate G.P.A. to rate and select applicants. The LSAT examines you on: (1) facts and rules, (2) argument, in which you need to distinguish between assumptions and conclusions, (3) reading passages, to determine how well you can identify core ideas, and (4) problem-solving through various exercises. Each of these test sections is scored separately and each must be completed in 35 minutes. A fifth area of the LSAT assesses writing skills (also 35 minutes). Since law school applications must typically be completed a year in advance, it is important to take the LSAT in one of its four possible test times at sites throughout the U.S. (February, June, September or December) in the year preceding your intended fall start date.

The selection of law school is important and may have a lasting impact on your future career direction. Key issues beyond obvious cost and location include the staff/student ratio, American Bar Association accreditation and job placement rates. Also important is the law school's prestige rating; its reputation in the legal community. The third and last stage of the preparatory process is to pass the state "bar exam." Most graduates are successful on the first attempt. If unsuccessful, successive attempts are usually allowed; however, significant gaps in time often exist between retakes.

Suppose you have completed all these hurdles and finally want to begin practicing law. What do lawyers actually do? They conduct research and gather evidence, interview and advise clients, prepare and write legal briefs, plan and devise courtroom strategies, appear in court, and file appeals. In addition they may advertise, market and manage their law practice similarly to other businesses. Some even teach college courses. The newly practicing attorney may choose to stay a generalist

---

[2] James D. Gordon, III, "The Trials of Reforming Legal Education," *The Chronicle of Higher Education*, January 22, 1992, pp. B1, B3.

or to specialize in one of the many sub-fields of law including: criminal, contract, real estate, divorce, personal injury, corporate, tax, copyright and patent, immigration, and estates and trusts.

The motivations for choosing a law career seem to be a mix of materialism and altruism. The desire to accumulate wealth has become synonymous with lawyers' tarnished public image. The thought of lawyers as public servants helping those in need, serving to uphold the principles of justice and the Bill of Rights are less acknowledged but no less present. Certainly the entry level salary for lawyers is excellent. It generally ranges from $30,000 to $70,000 a year. The federal government generally pays around $5,000 less per year than private industry for beginning attorneys but that gap widens to as much as $50,000 per year for experienced attorneys working for private industry who make upwards of $100,000. However, many lawyers are concerned as much with upholding the rights of victims and changing the parts of society that do not seem to best serve its citizens. While these are laudable ideals, the reality of law work is that, like other professions, the amount of impact one can have on the system is limited and the cost, in terms of energy and eventual burn out, is high.

An alternative route for those who desire to work on legal matters in a court context is an assisting capacity. Some of our students go into court administration. For example, Gina Roediger, who graduated with a major in sociology and a minor in psychology, works in the Oakland County District Court as a Certified Electronic Operator and Magistrate's Assistant. Her work involves conducting informal hearings, examining documents and recording swearing-ins and arraignments. The possibility of transferring into probation, or of becoming a court clerk exists. Another graduate is working temporarily as a law clerk for a firm in Pittsburgh doing legal research, interviewing clients, and filing papers. Being a paralegal requires a degree of specialized training in paralegal studies together with certification. Legal assisting, however, requires a less specialized training and is open to criminal justice students. Legal assistants and paralegals work under the supervision of a lawyer but do many of the lawyer's tasks, especially the background legal research to establish whether a client's case is viable. Paralegals begin at an average salary of $22,000 and rarely earn more than $30,000.

In this section we have three accounts of law work. The first two are from Richard Priehs, who has practiced law on the prosecution and defense sides and shares his experiences. The third paper by Donna

Aynessazian describes the jobs of a paralegal and a legal assistant working with or for an immigration lawyer.

For information on LSAT call (215) 968-1001; for an application (215) 968-1188.

Career books on law abound:

American Bar Foundation. *Law as a Career*. Chicago: ABF, 1987.

Barron's *Guide to Law Schools*. 9th ed. New York: Barron's Educational, 1990.

Corkery, Jim. *Career in Law*. Holmes Beach, FL.: W. W. Gaunt, 1989.

Graham, Lawrence. *Your Ticket to Law School: Getting In and Staying In*. New York: Bantam Books, 1985.

Kunen, James S. *How Can You Defend Those People?: The Making of a Criminal Lawyer*. New York: Random House, 1983.

Munneke, Gary. *Careers in Law*. Lincolnwood, IL: VGM Career Horizons, 1991.

Rakoff, Dena. *Choosing a Career in Law*. Cambridge, MA: Harvard University Press, 1990.

Stuart, Bruce S. and Kim D. *Top Law Schools*. New York: Arco, 1990.

Utley, Frances. *From Law Student to Lawyer: A Career Planning Manual*. Chicago: American Bar Association, 1984.

For career information on paralegals and legal assisting:

Fins, Alice. *Opportunities in Paralegal Careers*. Lincolnwood, IL: National Textbook Company, 1985.

Fry, William R. and Hoopes, Roy. *Paralegal Careers*. Hillside, NJ: Enslow, 1986.

Johnstone, Quinton and Wenglinsky, Martin. *Paralegals: Progress and Prospects of a Satellite Occupation*. Westport, CT: Greenwood Press.

National Association of Legal Assistants. *What is a Legal Assistant?* Tulsa, OK: NALA.

National Association of Paralegals. *What is a Paralegal?* Skokie, IL: NFPA.

For current information on issues affecting the legal profession:

The American Lawyer
600 3rd Avenue, New York, NY 10016 or call (212) 973-2800.
Monthly magazine.

Inside Litigation
Prentice Hall, Law and Business, 270 Sylvan, Englewood Cliffs, NJ 07632 or call (800) 223-0231.
Monthly news magazine, $295.00/year subscription.

Legal Times
1730 M St. NW, Washington, DC 20036 or call (202) 457-0686.
Weekly—$175 annual subscription.

The National Law Journal
111 8th Ave., New York, NY 10011 or call (212) 741-8300.
Weekly newspaper, $98 annual subscription.

National Paralegal Reporter
National Federation of Paralegal Associations, 104 Wilmot Road,
Suite 201, Deerfield, IL 60015 or call (708) 940-8800.
Quarterly journal that includes news.

The Paralegal
National Paralegal Association, 6186 Honey Hollow Road,
Solebury, PA 18963 or call (215) 297-8333.
Bimonthly.

Student Lawyer
American Bar Association, 750 N. Lake Shore Drive, Chicago,
IL 60611 or call (312) 988-5000.
9 issues per year, $22/year.

From the State Capitals: Public Safety and Justice Policies
Wakeman-Walworth Inc., 300 N. Washington St., Suite 204,
Alexandria, VA 22314 or call (703) 549-8606.
Weekly—$130/six-month subscription.

For information on internships in legal settings:
Summer Legal Employment Guide
Federal Reports Inc., Suite 408, 1010 Vermont Ave. NW,
Washington, DC 20005 or call (202) 393-3311.
Annual publication available mid-fall listing clerks & legal
assists—$18.

For attorney and legal assistant positions:
Clearinghouse Review
National Clearinghouse for Legal Services, 407 S. Dearborn,
Chicago, IL 60605 or call (800) 621-3256.
Monthly—$75/annual subscription. Also publish *Job Market
Preview*, a monthly at $20/six-month subscription.

For positions in the courts:
National Employment Listing Service (NELS)
>   Criminal Justice Center, Sam Houston State University, Huntsville, TX 77341 or phone (409) 294-1692.
>   Monthly—$17.50/six-month subscription.

CHAPTER 10:

Criminal Prosecution: The Action and the Burden

by *Richard E. Priehs*

Almost all law schools require applicants to possess a bachelor's degree to be considered for admission. The Law School Admissions Test (LSAT) is the second universal criteria. Since law school admission policies differ markedly, potential applicants should contact desired schools directly. Undergraduate curricula and grades, LSAT scores, graduate degrees and professional work experience are considerations which are assigned varying weight by respective schools when making their admissions decisions.

Like many students I enrolled in law school without having specific career plans. The thought of becoming a lawyer was sufficient motivation to propel me into and through law school. The type of law I might like to practice was secondary and of little concern at the time. However, legal professions differ dramatically; advance planning and preparation can be helpful.

Prosecuting attorneys, for example, may engage in daily adversarial courtroom proceedings while other lawyers rarely see the courthouse. Although possessing many common skills, and similar training in analytical abilities, their respective educational backgrounds and work environments may be as dissimilar as policing and accounting. In law school I sat next to a biologist who left medical school in his second year, intent on eventually specializing in medical malpractice. Another student with whom I occasionally commuted was a policeman intent on practicing criminal law. His undergraduate degree was in Criminal Justice and he eventually became a top-notch defense attorney. Others had their undergraduate degrees, but no career direction. I was one of them.

Students who are able to at least generally plan their legal careers in advance have two distinct advantages. First, they can tailor their undergraduate preparation. A perspective corporate lawyer may, for example, select a pre-law business program. Second, they can obtain some specialization in law school in selecting their non-required courses. The law school I attended required only one course in Criminal Law; by itself this was not much preparation for prosecution. Several applicable electives can certainly augment one's skills. However, not everyone plans their career in a model fashion, yet they still succeed.

Upon graduation from law school I had a non-legal position and was asking myself, "What now?" Shortly thereafter I obtained an appointment as Research Clerk for a local circuit court judge; a "temporary" position allowing the recipient to obtain exposure to the legal system while preparing for the State Bar Examination and awaiting the results. I was soon able to familiarize myself with the courthouse personnel, particularly the prosecuting and defense attorneys. Within six months, I was offered a job as Assistant County Prosecutor, a position I accepted and retained for eight years.

The first day
Prior to commencing my first day as Assistant Prosecuting Attorney, I was assured by the Chief Prosecutor that the first several weeks would be devoted to "orientation." I would essentially assist the various attorneys with trial preparations and observe trials to "get a feel" for the nature of the position. Since I had the proverbial "weak-knees" regarding conducting my first trial, this on-the-job training for a few weeks seemed ideal. Unfortunately, it never happened.

Upon reporting for work bright and early on day one, the Chief Assistant Prosecutor informed me that one of the attorneys called in sick. The Assistant had been scheduled to conduct a felony trial that morning in Circuit Court; I was informed it was now my case! After the initial shock subsided, I asked how I could be expected to handle a case for which I was totally unprepared. The Chief responded by stating, "Ask the judge for an adjournment." Meekly, I walked into the judge's chambers where the defense attorney was already seated. I explained my predicament and requested the adjournment. The defense balked and, to my utter amazement, the Court insisted the trial go forward. As a conciliatory gesture the court delayed the beginning for one whole hour so I could prepare.

Needless to say, law school had not prepared me for such real life trial-under-fire. I ran back to the office and quickly read the case file which was totally foreign to me. I only had time to briefly acquaint myself with the elements of the crime (burglary) but lacked the opportunity to conduct other research. Since the prosecutor always carries the burden of proof this necessitates knowledge of precisely what has to be proven and how you intend to accomplish that end. Barely having time to speak with one of the investigating officers I grabbed the file, several law books, a note pad and rushed into the courtroom. Mistakenly, I sat at the wrong table—the one reserved for the defense.

In retrospect it seems like I bumbled my way through the entire trial, even though we won. It was an uncomfortable feeling from the onset. Never having selected a jury I was uncertain as to what questions to ask during *voir dire*. Again, law school had not prepared me for the experience. Further uncertainties abounded. I didn't know the best order in which to present my witnesses, let alone the form or substance of the questions to be asked of them. Many of my questions were "leading" and defense objections to them were sustained. Much of what I attempted to do was objected to on the grounds that it violated numerous restrictions under our Rules of Evidence. In retrospect, I am certain that the defense gained repeated advantages because of my failure to raise appropriate objections to his offerings. The axiom "experience is the best teacher" certainly rings true regarding trial proficiency.

Even with experience, however, trials rarely become commonplace or second nature. Because they all differ, adequate preparation is the cardinal rule. At a minimum, I would outline the questions and anticipated answers for each witness. Frequently I would write each question in narrative form in advance of a trial, particularly in preparation for the more crucial witnesses. The same process applied to the questions and probable answers during jury selection. Vincent Bugliosi, who prosecuted Charles Manson and authored *Helter Skelter*, wrote another excellent non-fiction work entitled *And the Sea Will Tell*. Although now on the defense side, his book illustrates the importance of thorough trial preparation. By the time his case went to court, Bugliosi literally had piles of indexed yellow legal pads which included: detailed prepared questions for all witnesses, their anticipated responses, counter-questions, precisely-worded legal arguments, anticipated defense positions, and a system of cross-references for quick location.

Because prosecutors carry the "burden of proof" i.e., they must prove guilt beyond a reasonable doubt, their job is typically more arduous than that of the defense. This doubt requires the studied preparation of witnesses, evidence, and legal arguments. In theory, the defense need do nothing except, in conclusion, argue that the government has failed to meet its "burden." Because of that "burden" and the accompanying ethical obligations, prosecution requires responsible, hard-working attorneys. The rewards may include a deep sense of job satisfaction and a salary that is often competitive to those of private practitioners. There is one guarantee, however: you will rarely be bored!

Nature of the position
Prosecutors are government attorneys employed to represent "the people" in criminal proceedings against alleged criminal defendants. The vast majority work at the local county level, where the bulk of criminal legal action occurs. At the federal level, and in some states, prosecutors are referred to as district attorneys; the titles are used interchangeably.

At the county level, the Chief Prosecutor is elected. Unlike judges, they typically run on a partisan ticket. Once elected they appoint their assistant prosecutors. In the federal system, the head District Attorney is appointed by the President of the United States and serves at the will of the sitting President. In turn, the D.A. then typically selects the remainder of his or her staff.

I have never known a prosecutor uninspired with their position. It is often exciting and fast-paced. It's where the action is! At times it can be very demanding, requiring extended hours in preparation. It may be particularly stressful when there is insufficient time to adequately ready a case. Frequently, however, anticipated trials are resolved prior to commencement, creating breaks in the schedule which allow time to unwind or prepare for future proceedings.

Contrary to popular belief, prosecution is not an endless succession of trials. The overwhelming majority of cases are resolved before that stage. Some are dismissed because of insufficient evidence, witness problems, or a variety of lesser reasons. Most cases result in settlements, often referred to as plea-bargains. The heavy reliance on these non-trial resolutions requires the development of negotiation skills. These are vital since the criminal justice system is not equipped with the resources to take every case to trial, nor is that necessary.

However, even before guilty pleas can be accepted by the court, a formal arraignment procedure is required. On a given day a prosecutor may devote the majority of his or her time to a series of arraignments. Similarly, some courts specify certain days or time frames for sentencing those previously convicted. A typical felony sentencing hearing may require a minimum of 30 minutes to several hours if pertinent sentencing issues are being contested.

Motion practice is another important aspect of prosecution. A variety of motions, often raised by the defense (e.g., motion to suppress evidence premised on an alleged illegal search), entail hearings before the judge, usually well in advance of trial. Preparation often includes interviewing witnesses, research, and written briefs. Frequently these motions also require witness testimony and in-court oral arguments.

Prosecutors spend considerable time contemplating "charging" decisions. By reviewing police reports and interviewing witnesses/investigators, determinations are made regarding appropriate crimes to be charged. Where insufficient evidence exists prosecution is denied. The magnitude of their ethical obligation is first evidenced here. Prosecutors, with their broad discretion, do not desire to charge or convict innocent people. Therefore, a careful consideration of the evidence is always in order.

Other non-trial responsibilities include conducting grand-jury proceedings or preliminary examinations (depending on the system), bond hearings, advising and directing the legal aspects of police investigations, interviewing/preparing witnesses, drafting search warrants and creating trial strategies. Following trial, most prosecutors have the obligation to continue arguing cases to the appellate courts when a claim of appeal is filed. Appellate work is essentially researching and submitting written legal briefs to the higher courts. Sometimes limited oral arguments are required before the appellate court. Larger prosecution offices often have appellate specialists for this purpose.

Unlike Hamilton Burger and Perry Mason, prosecutors typically carry a caseload requiring work on numerous cases somewhat simultaneously. One has to look at the long-range schedule and allocate time accordingly. Trial preparation is often interspersed with many of the responsibilities mentioned above. Procrastination is difficult because court schedules and legal deadlines are somewhat rigid. At a minimum delays/adjournments usually require judicial blessing. Like my first day experiences on the job, adjournments may be difficult to obtain even with valid reasons.

In addition to a working knowledge of the law and the ability to reason, other helpful prosecutorial skills include organization, persuasion, and accommodation.

Like defense attorneys, prosecutors are salespeople, in a sense. To win their case, they must convince the trier-of-fact (e.g., 12 jurors) to accept their reasoning and arguments unanimously, while the defense only has to create reasonable doubt. Persuasion is a skill which can be developed.

It's the ability to influence the mind by argument and reason. Learning to articulate one's position requires thought and practice; the better attorneys have refined this skill.

A final noteworthy ingredient for success in prosecution is the ability to work with a diverse spectrum of personalities and socioeconomic contingents. Personal contacts often occur under strained circumstances. Regular encounters with police, judges, defense attorneys, victims, witnesses, and the general public often require a certain amount of accommodation or give-and-take. These various entities may view the resolution of particular criminal matters differently. There is an old axiom in law which states, "reasonable minds can differ." Longevity in the position of prosecutor often requires a certain open-mindedness and a willingness to compromise—so long as it is "reasonable." Too much rigidity can have damaging affects on an already overloaded system, as well as on perceived notions of fairness. These can eventually have negative political repercussions.

Historically, prosection was considered a stepping-stone to more lucrative or prestigious legal positions. Today, many prosecutors have a career orientation or aspire to continue in their capacity as long as possible. Assistant prosecutors who lose their positions due to "political fallout" can often obtain similar work in other jurisdictions. Certainly prosecution is still a potential springboard to other ambitions. The notoriety and exposure can frequently propel one toward elected ranks in the judiciary or legislature. The daily contact with other attorneys can also lead to other offers or the formation of new private partnerships or associations.

Several reasons have contributed to the enhanced preference for prosecutorial career choices. Salaries in many locales have increased markedly in the last 15 years or so. However, pay still varies widely among jurisdictions. Since the vast majority of prosecutors work for local governments, levels of pay are not uniform. Salaries vary in relation to county resources and various other local economic/political considerations.

Another factor affecting career choice is the somewhat recent influx of attorneys. Competition is keener for the more lucrative positions and the prestigious firms are continually more selective. And certainly there are other considerations besides money. Prosecutors often feel a sense of accomplishment as an incentive to continue their efforts. I always carried the notion that somehow my efforts improved the quality of life in my community.

Whether elected or appointed however, a prosecutor's tenure on the job is never guaranteed. Job security depends on the electorate or the individual making the appointment. For example, upon taking office President Clinton asked for the resignation of all federal District Attorneys. Then, he appointed new DA's.

The benefits of prosecution are many and varied. The advantage of trial "experience" is even more advantageous than might be apparent. Law schools supply the basic groundwork in substantive and procedural law; however, they do not adequately train attorneys to readily apply the law to the facts in a courtroom setting, to become familiar with the application of the "rules of evidence" in real-life adversarial proceedings, or to responsibly and credibly articulate arguments to judges and juries. Law schools do have course offerings in advocacy, typically allowing each student only sufficient time to prepare and argue limited issues in a mock setting. Becoming proficient and comfortable in the courtroom however, requires repeated experiences in "real" proceedings.

Richard E. Priehs is an Assistant Professor of Criminal Justice, at Saginaw Valley State University.

CHAPTER 11:

Criminal Defense Attorneys: Guardians of the Constitution

by *Richard E. Priehs*

Criminal law always fascinated me and after eight years as a prosecutor I decided to venture into private practice as a defense attorney. The decision was difficult, but I felt I needed a change. Initially I felt somewhat uncomfortable making the transition to the defense side. The feeling only lasted until I obtained my first client. There are a multitude of ways in which an attorney can be of assistance and the satisfactions can be extensive. The experience derived from criminal defense practice is immense. It may be wise to initially work for less compensation to gain trial experience. One of the first decisions I had to make was whether to practice alone or in association with others.

Associating with an existing firm generally guarantees immediate clientele and a regular paycheck. Firms typically assume all overhead expenses which can be extensive. There are trade-offs for the necessities supplied by the firm. They make their profit by retaining a portion of the income generated by the attorneys.

I chose to be a sole practitioner, not associated with any partnership or firm. This decision had notable economic consequences. Generally, "going it on your own" carries a greater financial risk. It is sometimes referred to as "high risk, high reward." Sole practitioners bear the entire responsibility for obtaining work. As I was about to embark, an attorney friend reminded me, "You'll wake up every morning unemployed." Sole practitioners are responsible for their own secretarial, rent or mortgage, office supplies, equipment, phone, advertising, and professional liability insurance costs. These are significant as they can approach fifty percent of the attorney's gross income. This might be of particular importance to a new attorney with limited resources as these costs typically precede obtaining clientele. However, careful scrutiny can often reduce expenses, i.e., begin with a part-time secretary and answer your own phone. Sometimes two or more attorneys reduce overhead by sharing expenses for office and clerical without forming a legal association. Someone with proper preparation and a willingness to work hard will typically be successful. Fortunately, for the sole practitioner attorney there are ways

86   LAW SCHOOL, LAWYERS AND THE COURTS

to generate instant clientele. I was able to keep my financial head above water by obtaining some immediate clients via court appointments.

CRIMINAL DEFENSE SYSTEMS

Ninety percent of all criminal cases in the United States are handled by government- appointed, rather than privately retained, counsel and about three million defendants are provided government supported legal services annually, the vast majority at the state and local level.[1] The methods of service delivery to the poor vary markedly in form and prospective attorneys should be alert to the differences, particularly if they will be dependent on court-assigned clients. Unless you take a position with an established firm offering "retained" clients, most defense attorneys need these assignments.

Programs providing for legal assistance to the accused who are unable to afford to hire counsel can be divided into three major systems: public defender, assigned or appointed, and contract. In some jurisdictions these exist in combination and/or varying forms.

The Public Defender System

These programs may be either statewide or local. In a statewide system, the governor typically appoints the "chief defender" who then selects a staff, establishing branch offices or, in some cases, contracting with local attorneys. Local defender systems typically are staffed by judicial appointments. Once selected the Chief Defender selects assistants.

Large cities and major jurisdictions most often use the public defender system.[2] Generally public defenders serve full-time and are paid a salary

---

[1] This is a result of *Gideon v. Wainright*, 372 US 335 in (1963), where the United States Supreme Court ruled that the financially disadvantaged are entitled to court-appointed counsel, funded by local or state jurisdictions. See F. Randall Karfonta, "Balancing the Scales of Justice: Training and Support Services for Appointed Criminal Defense Lawyers," *Michigan Bar Journal, 71*. (February 1992), pp. 164-168., 1992. See also L. Territo, J.B. Halstead, and M.L. Bremley, *Crime and Justice in America*. St. Paul, MN: West Publishing Co., 1992, p. 276.

[2] Twenty-three states have adopted this arrangement state-wide and other states use it only in certain jurisdictions or counties. Local offices may vary in size from one attorney to several hundred. See Y. Kamisar, W.R. LaFave, and G. Israel, *Basic Criminal Procedure*, St. Paul, MN: West Publishing Company, 1986.

plus appropriate benefits, regardless of caseload. They typically have clerical support and, in some cases, investigators to assist them.

The Assigned (or Appointed) Counsel System *- declining in prevalence*

This is the most widely used method of indigent criminal representation in the United States and the easiest system in which a beginning attorney can obtain work. Once adversarial proceedings are to commence, the judge appoints counsel for the defendant who requests assistance, assuming he/she qualifies as indigent. Typically the selection is made from an existing list of local attorneys who have agreed to serve if called upon. The agreement is generally performed under a "set-fee" schedule (i.e. paid per type of case) or a pre-determined hourly rate.

Attorneys accepting such appointments are also generally involved in the private practice of law, handling other legal matters which are not necessarily criminal in nature. Other than a willingness to serve, no other qualifications are usually necessary. Unlike public defenders, their practice is "mixed" and they generally receive their assignments piecemeal or one at a time. Other than their agreed upon compensation, they do not receive the benefits (e.g., retirement, vacation, etc.) of a typical government employee. Their service is more in the nature of an independent contractor. This system lends itself well to small and medium-size jurisdictions where a manageable number of private attorneys can handle relatively smaller caseloads.

The Contract System

Contract systems are a relatively recent innovation and their presence is increasing.[3] Although public defender and assigned counsel systems are still dominant, the contract system offers some advantages which make it appealing, at least from the courts' perspective.

Under this method individual attorneys or associations of attorneys join in contracting with the government entity to provide necessary legal services for a specified dollar amount. Contracts are usually awarded based upon competitive bidding. Essentially the entire defense operation is thereby privatized. Like the public defender offices, these contractors normally assume responsibility for all the criminal offenders in that

---

[3] Currently six states use this as the most prevalent form of indigent representation. See Territo, *op. cit.* 1992, p. 281.

jurisdiction for a fee determined by the bid; like assigned counsel they are not government employees and do not receive the customary "benefits" from their employer.

Again, the contract system is sometimes mixed with other systems within jurisdictions. For example, conflicts of interest may arise when there are multiple defendants charged with the same crime(s). Thus, a given public defender office may only be permitted to represent one of the defendants even though numerous attorneys work in that office. This necessitates a backup system, usually consisting of a listing of those willing to be appointed. So attorneys who are not part of the contract can still obtain appointments.

The choice of which form of indigent services to provide ordinarily rests with the governing entity bearing the cost. In our state, for example, each of the 83 counties has the separate responsibility for providing and paying for these mandated services. Expenditures obviously vary significantly among these jurisdictions based on numerous factors, the most significant being the number of criminal prosecutions. In fact, county-level funding is the primary fiscal method employed nationwide. As a prospective defense attorney you are advised to scrutinize the systems in effect where you intend to practice. In addition, the various courts within the same local system may use different methods of assigning and compensating counsel. Besides the misdemeanor and felony state courts, the juvenile and federal systems also appoint counsel.

Nature of the position: The principles and the "practice"

Defense attorneys are accustomed to hearing questions such as "How can you defend criminals?" I certainly heard my share, particularly coming from prosecution. After a little thought however, the answer becomes clear and the questions seem naive. The theory of American justice is based on the concept of "the presumption of innocence." Determinations of guilt are made only by the trier-of-fact, usually a jury. Jurors must not only abide by that presumption, they cannot enter into any discussions with others or begin deliberations among themselves until all the evidence has been presented and the judge instructs them on the law. Those unwilling to accept that concept are legally disqualified from serving as jurors.

Thus, asking how one can defend a criminal presupposes knowledge of the defendant's guilt. It further assumes that the defense attorney knows "the truth." Truth is an elusive concept. I once had a client accused of first degree murder who admitted to me that he shot the victim. He later told me his brother was actually responsible and he originally lied to protect his sibling. Which version was the truth? At trial his brother was convicted by a jury and my client totally exonerated. I believe the verdict was proper but I'm not absolutely certain. Jurors use their best judgment. The point is that it's a mistake for the public to assume defense attorneys always learn the truth from their clients, thereby seeking legal loopholes to evade justice. Many criminal defendants lie; unfortunately, its difficult to ascertain the "who" and "when." The lawyer's assessment of his client's veracity is often speculative at best.

A related concept concerns the "burden" of proof. Our system requires the prosecutor to present sufficient evidence which convinces a jury, usually unanimously, of the defendant's guilt. This entails the highest standard of required proof: "beyond a reasonable doubt." Since defendants typically need not prove anything, an essential role for the defense attorney is to make certain the client receives a fair trial, one in which the prosecution does not abuse the rules of evidence or established Constitutional rights. This differs markedly from the concept of "trying to get a guilty person acquitted."

Remember the prosecutor and police combine as a team. Their mission is to obtain convictions against those they charge. As with defense attorneys, the law enforcement team does not necessarily know "the truth," often relying on witnesses who may be biased or deficient in perception, veracity, or memory. The Bill of Rights to the United States Constitution clearly recognized that law enforcement, if unchecked, may be overzealous in their efforts to apprehend and convict.[4] The defense bar maintains the various amendments are the only protection for the accused and truly are the "Guardians of the Constitution." So being a defense lawyer is based on highly justifiable principles. However,

---

[4] The Fourth, Fifth, and Sixth Amendments protect individuals from inappropriate governmental intrusions specifically. The Fourth protects privacy rights from unreasonable searches and seizures. The Fifth protects one's right not to incriminate themselves. Finally, the Sixth guarantees the assistance of counsel and the right to a fair trial, including confrontation of all relevant witnesses.

positioning yourself to adequately practice these principles can take considerable energy and commitment.

Building a retained, and possibly better paying, practice takes time. A new attorney selecting the appropriate system can generate instant business. In addition, the indigent client contacts can often lead to future retained business. Prospective attorneys should also assess the method of compensation and projected caseload size as other determining factors. Historically, both criminal defense work and prosecution employed the newer inexperienced attorneys. This no longer appears to be true. Many serving in these capacities now have more of a career orientation and considerable experience.

Attorneys for the criminally accused can offer significant services beyond trial advocacy. Since the majority of cases are resolved by agreement reached through plea bargaining, negotiation skills can provide immeasurable benefits to clients. For example, often there are subtle distinctions between closely related crimes that carry profound ramifications. In one state the legal definitions of "negligent homicide" and "involuntary manslaughter" are quite similar. Yet the former carries a two-year maximum penalty and the latter fifteen years. Rather than total exoneration, defense attorneys can actually achieve success by having their clients convicted of violations that are more appropriate than those alleged by the prosecution.

Guilty clients can further be well-served by the attorney's efforts in seeking suitable rehabilitation for various problems such as drugs, alcohol, aggression, lack of employment, etc. Certainly many criminals are as portrayed on TV—real bad guys. However, most do not comport with that image. Many are more regular human beings, having problems that can be addressed with assistance. Initially, the attorney is often their only source of help. I frequently perceived myself as part attorney and part social worker. Providing legal advice in itself is a vital service, both to the client and his or her family. The vast majority of the public are legally ignorant regarding the nuances of criminal law.

Personally, I found criminal defense fascinating. Unlike prosecution you get to know criminal defendants as real people, since they are your legal responsibility. Prosecutors rarely talk with defendants; most are represented by counsel who speak on their behalf. As a general practice, defense attorneys rarely allow clients to meet with prosecution or law enforcement.

As a prosecutor I often wondered what certain defendants "were really like"; I wanted to talk with them but rarely had the opportunity. Working with defendants as people rather than criminals changes your perspective. You'll find that you can be of assistance and, in return, often obtain great satisfaction from your efforts. It's ironic, but I believe I enjoyed criminal defense more than prosecution, just because of the individual client factor. Prosecuting Attorneys represent the public generally and often lack "real" clients.

Sometimes it is more difficult, however, for court-appointed counsel to establish positive relationships with the clients than it is for retained (privately hired) attorneys. Defendants often see publicly paid counsel as part of the "system"; overly eager to plead them guilty, disinclined to give them much time, and little concerned about their welfare. Mistrust may also be fueled by the regularity of social, racial, and economic differences between attorney and client. Attorneys believe that honesty in communication and deference to professional judgment are inherent in relations with retained clients, but not in court-appointed associations. When retained there is a certain immediate rapport since the client is paying for the experience and judgment. Attorneys who can establish relationships and "control" their clients also experience less job frustration.[5]

Research has failed to disclose any significant differences between retained and court-appointed counsel relative to "competency." It relates entirely to the clients' perception. However, an over-abundance of work can pressure attorneys to cut corners and this is more likely to occur in court-appointed situations because of the lower rates of compensation. Autonomy—that is the freedom and independence to control their work—is the goal of many attorneys. To achieve that end attorneys have to learn to control their clients.

---

[5] For further insight into these and related issues affecting the professional practice of defense lawyers' work see: Abraham Blumberg, "The Practice of Law as a Confidence Game: Organizational Cooptation of a Profession," 1 (1967) *Law and Society Review*, 15. Maureen Cain, "The General Practice Lawyer and the Client," 7 (1979) *International Journal of Society and Law*, 331. Jonathan D. Casper, *American Criminal Justice: The Defendant's Perspective*. Englewood Cliffs, New Jersey: Prentice-Hall, 1972. Roy B. Fleming, "Client Games: Defense Attorney Perspectives on Their Relations with Criminal Clients." *American Bar Foundation Research Journal* (Spring 1986).

Preparation
Essentially defense attorneys and prosecutors require similar academic training (see Chapter 10 on criminal prosecution). Trial experience is helpful, but not a prerequisite. Many begin their legal careers in these reciprocal fields. A good suggestion is to seek out attorneys practicing in your locale. Typically they are most willing to provide advice and offer insight. If you opt to solicit court appointments, talk with the appropriate local court office to determine how you can be assigned cases. They may be able to supply an estimated caseload for the year to assist you in projecting income. If you are willing to travel, you can often find additional work in nearby communities. Good luck.

Richard E. Priehs is an Assistant Professor of Criminal Justice, at Saginaw Valley State University.

CHAPTER 12:

Paralegals and Legal Assisting

by *Donna Aynessazian*

There are generally two types of positions available for persons seeking to assist in the legal profession: paralegal and legal assistant. I work as a legal assistant for an immigration attorney and have done so for approximately one year. The qualifications for the position of legal assistant are less stringent than those of a paralegal, particularly a paralegal in the litigation field. Generally a two-year degree in criminal justice, or even a business degree can qualify you for the position. It helps if you have taken some courses in law and legal research as part of your degree.

Legal Assistants
Legal assistants are utilized more than paralegals by smaller law firms and non-litigant type firms. This is because the skills necessary encompass a rudimentary, overall view of the dynamics of the legal system and concentrate more on writing, communication, and computer skills. General office organizational skills, such as filing, are also required. Legal assistants can end up doing some of the same types of jobs law clerks do, such as summarizing depositions and cases, research and fact-finding, library research, letter-writing, file organizing, court filings, and preparing of exhibits.

Most positions for legal assistants are advertised, but sometimes you can find ads for paralegals with small firms and they are often just as happy to hire a legal assistant.

As a legal assistant for an immigration attorney my duties allow me to do just about anything done by our office attorney—under her authority, of course. I have considerable autonomy and am allowed to decide whether or not to take cases based on my judgment concerning their viability or non-viability according to specific criteria that have been established for each type of visa being requested. Legal assistants each have their own caseload and sometimes their own area of expertise. I prepare and file papers relating to petitions for different types of visa status such as: non-immigrant workers visas; permanent residency petitions; investor visas; treaty trader visas; and others. We also handle political asylum cases. I am in charge of each of my clients, from the initial interview until completion and issuance of their visa status. I am responsible for expirations of adjustment of status on each of my clients. If I allow a client's visa status to expire, he or she may be required to adjust status out of the country—and to go back to some countries in order to do this can be a very unpleasant experience. I am in constant contact with our state's Employment Security Commission, the Department of Labor, and Immigration and Naturalization during each step of the process during an application.

Most non-litigation law firms prefer hiring legal assistants over paralegals primarily due to the salary disparity. Since a four-year degree is not required for the position of legal assistant, the salary can range from approximately $20,000 to $24,000 a year (average). Since a four-year degree is required for paralegals in the litigation field, their salary can range up to $30,000 or more a year. This is also why some smaller firms prefer legal assistants to paralegals.

My job is definitely not boring. I thoroughly enjoy the working atmosphere and the uniqueness of each case I am handling. I am lucky to have a wonderful boss who has been an immigration attorney for 17 years and knows it inside and out! I enjoy the interaction with different cultures and learning more about different areas of the world. I enjoy the challenge of obtaining each visa approval under the sometimes odd and complex circumstances of the client's life situation. I enjoy the chance to learn more about the immigration laws as they constantly change. I enjoy most things about my job, but there are a few things that I don't enjoy.

I find that each foreign group has a similar attitude toward the immigration process. They feel that they are disliked and are being singled out by Immigration and Naturalization to be the subject of a personal hassle. Each client feels that their case is and should be the only case that you are handling and that everything should be done yesterday. Some of the clients can be very deceptive and you have to be on your toes to determine whether fraud is being perpetrated. (After you've done this as long as my boss, you know all of the tricks!) The clients constantly badger you, no matter how much you explain the process to them. In other words, one of the primary skills necessary for this job is "people skills"—they are a must! The only other drawback is dealing with the robotic bureaucracy of Immigration and Naturalization. This can sometimes become an ongoing nightmare.

Paralegal _education beyond undergrad (Bachelor's Degree)_

A former colleague of mine works as a paralegal in a large multi-national corporation. She began her paralegal career with one of the city's largest law firms. She had not planned to become a paralegal, but began her career as a legal secretary. Circumstances, along with her education, allowed her to move into the position. Her duties include: maintenance of minute books and drafting of corporate actions for all the subsidiaries of the foreign parent company; patent and trademark liaison activities; filings with state, county and federal agencies (i.e., articles of incorporation, UCC, etc.); support of acquisitions and divestitures (including due diligence and preparation of certain closing documents); and establishment of departmental administrative procedures. Her education and degree are in the area of business administration and have been augmented with paralegal courses.

She feels that it is most important for a paralegal to cultivate attention to detail, persevere, be able to effectively follow up cases, and develop the judgment necessary to prioritize. A paralegal must become skilled at document organization, and computer literacy is becoming a necessity. It also helps to be a self-starter.

She much prefers the corporate environment to that of the "law firm" because, as she states, "It frees me from the tyranny of the billable hour." She also enjoys the opportunity to be involved with a much greater variety of projects and people. She feels that law firms tend to pigeonhole their employees into one area (probate, environmental, pension, litigation, real estate, etc.). She also believes that, in general, less respect is accorded non-attorney personnel by large law firms than by corporations.

Prospects

The current prospects for legal assistants and for paralegals in their niches (degreed paralegals primarily in litigation and legal assistants and paralegals degreed in something other than the title of "paralegal") look good. Since 70% of the world's lawyers are in the United States, the job market is open. Attorneys do not want to spend their time doing the leg work or the tedious paperwork, so they hire legal assistants and paralegals to take up the slack. Attorneys need someone to fill the void between legal secretary and themselves with someone who can work autonomously and knowledgeably. This allows them to have the time and resources to expand their clientele and it frees attorneys with sole practices to keep their heads above water without having to take on a partner! (See Chapter 11 for an expansion on this problem.) Sometimes the job offers a person insight into whether they want to continue their education and become attorneys. If this is the case, working in either position gives you the necessary contacts and connections to establish a practice when you do become a lawyer.

SECTION FOUR:
CORRECTIONS

The job of a corrections officer has changed enormously from the days of the "turnkey" or jailor. A career in corrections increasingly requires at least an associate's degree in criminal justice and several months intensive training. As with other criminal justice occupations the range of roles available in corrections is many and diverse. In addition to the correctional officer, employment possibilities include: parole officer, prison counselor, clinical psychologist, substance abuse specialist, teacher/instructor, interviewer and many others. Here we shall be concentrating on the career of corrections officer. In the next section we shall look at probation and parole officers.

Corrections officers work mainly in either federal or state prisons or county and local jails. The primary correctional setting is in state institutions which accounts for 62% of the nation's corrections expenditure and employs 342,316 employees out of a total of over half a million.[1] As a result these positions are only occasionally advertised in newspapers; more often they are announced through state civil service departments. Institutions differ with regard to their level of security, from minimum to maximum. With the 1980's prison expansion, the traditional cell-block format is slowly being replaced with dormitory-type and housing units. These have a more humanistic and open feel, and look something like college dorm rooms.

States vary in the level of qualifications required and in the extent of training offered. Those states with highest standards require at least two years of college education and provide four to six weeks training in such areas as self-defense, crisis intervention, riot control, report writing, departmental policy and health care. In the open format of the new prisons, communication and crisis intervention skills are crucial to control the incarcerated offender who is seen more as a client in need of counseling and treatment, than as a convict. Correspondingly, in these settings the corrections officer is transformed from jailor to counselor,

---

[1] Bureau of Justice Statistics, "Justice Expenditure and Employment, 1990 BJS *Bulletin*, September 1992, p. 6.

1 CORRECTIONS
Typical ads

CORRECTIONS OFFICER:
Dept. of Corrections, Lansing, MI. **Job Description:** Oversee and participate in custody, security and treatment of prisoners in correctional facilities, including major institutions, camps and corrections centers.
Qualifications: Corrections certificate or 23 college credit hours in corrections, criminal justice, psychology, sociology, educational psychology, family and/or guidance and counseling and law enforcement plus fitness requirements: 13 push-ups in 13 seconds, 10 pull-ups in 60 seconds and 5-minute step test.

CORRECTIONAL OFFICERS:
Upper Malborough, MD. **Job Description:** Entry-level position involving basic confinement services in care custody and control of inmates on an assigned shift. Assignments vary in inmate contact. **Qualifications:** 21 yrs., HS graduate/GED, vision 20/70 corrected to 20/20, weight proportionate to height. **Salary:** $23,752-$35,342.

CORRECTIONAL OFFICER TRAINEES:
NV Dept. of Prisons, Reno, NV. **Job Description:** To receive instruction and training in custody corrections. After 12 months training eligible for promotion to journey level correctional officer. **Salary:** $18,300 as trainee, $25,600 as corrections officer.

CASE MANAGEMENT STUDENT ASSISTANT: U.S. Penitentiary, Atlanta, GA. **Job Description:** Assist unit management staff in providing services to local inmate population at high security facility for male inmates. Responsibilities include evaluating progress of inmates, preparing applications release to half-way houses, and preparing inmate files for parole board hearings. **Qualifications:** Majors in sociology, psychology, criminal justice, counseling or related. **Salary:** $11,015-$25,717.

COMMUNITY CORRECTIONS STUDENT ASSISTANT:
Community corrections office, Dallas, TX. **Job Description:** Assist with drafting correspondence, half-way house placements, parole issues, problems with state "boarders", review of inmate privileges, and recommendations for furloughs and home confinement.
Qualifications: Majors in criminal justice, sociology, psychology, paralegal, law. **Salary:** $11,015-$25,717.

CORRECTIONAL OFFICERS:
El Reno, OK. **Job Description:** Supervise and perform correctional treatment of criminal offenders in federal facility. **Qualifications:** College degree can be substituted for 3 yrs. experience. **Salary:** GS6 to GS7 after 6 months probation.

98

and even confidant. Indeed, because of the relative absence of physical constraint, it is increasingly important that the corrections officer maintain control through respectful relationships rather than by reliance on force.

This is not to suggest, however, that working in a prison is comfortable or even therapeutic. These are ideals. Corrections is a semimilitary environment, with an expectation that officers will be giving and taking orders. Prisons are changing but they are also beset with some irreconcilable and recurring problems. Not the least of these can be stress stemming from fear, vulnerability, and the low morale among some prison officers who are concerned that they are not as appreciated as they might wish to be. In addition, prisoners often exist in a predatory relationship with each other and with staff, the weak being exploited for sex and favors, that is backed up by violence and homosexual rape. Prisoners manufacture their own alcohol inside prisons, they trade drugs and cigarettes, run gambling rings, exist in ethnic or other gangs and sometimes kill each other. There are also escape attempts. These are the realities of prison life. They are occasional rather than continuous but they do exist, and anyone contemplating a career as a corrections officer should appreciate this fact and put it in perspective. Indeed, consider the following statement from the job description for a corrections officer: "The work is performed in an environment that is extremely uncomfortable and...involves a considerable chance of incurring a disabling or life threatening injury."[2]

The major part of a corrections officer's job, however, does not involve incidents but is somewhat routine. It involves: watching prisoners for unusual or prohibited behavior that threatens the security of the prison, its employees, visitors or other prisoners; counting prisoners; conducting searches of persons, packages and cells for weapons, drugs and other contraband; enforcing compliance with facility rules; enforcing discipline for rule infractions; attempting behavior modification through one-on-one or group interaction; dispensing medications; transporting prisoners; assisting in classification of prisoners, parole eligibility, and counseling; controlling prisoner and personnel flow; inspecting and

---

[2] Michigan Department of Civil Service, Corrections Officer 8, E9, job description and qualifications document, 1991.

maintaining security equipment; writing reports; and training new recruits.

The U.S. Department of Justice Federal Bureau of Prisons offers internships nationwide. These are excellent opportunities to discover whether corrections is an area that you would enjoy. Typical internships include Case Management Student Assistant and Community Corrections Student Assistant. Also available are Executive Staff internships. They pay between $12,000 and $26,000 depending upon the number of college credits completed. Internships are also offered by several County Sheriffs' Departments in their jails.

The salary of corrections officers has improved in line with other criminal justice positions and in accordance with the greater demands placed on present day officers. At entry level, corrections officers can expect to earn around $23,000 which rises to $35,000 over five years. However, overtime requirements typically raise this to $45,000.

Included in this section are the accounts of one male and one female corrections officer. DJ Culkar's article describes the application process and also debunks some myths about corrections work. He compares and contrasts it to police work and indicates that, in spite of criminal justice students' reluctance to enter the profession, those who do so find it very rewarding, with many opportunities for varying work. A similar theme is presented in Lesley Jones' contribution. She describes some of the problems likely to be faced by the new recruit, and reflects on what personality types make the best corrections officers. She also identifies problems specifically related to being female in a predominantly male environment and, like DJ Culkar, demonstrates that social and intellectual skills are more important than physical abilities.

For more details on corrections officer careers:

Steinberg, Eve. *Correction Officer*. Englewood Cliffs, NJ: Prentice-Hall, 1989.

Stinchcomb, James D. *Opportunities in Law Enforcement and Criminal Justice*. Chapter on "Corrections and Rehabilitation," pp. 110-124, Lincolnwood, IL: National Textbook Co., 1990.

Whithead, John T. *Burnout in Probation and Corrections*. Westport, CT: Greenwood Press, 1989.

For more information on corrections officers contact:

American Correctional Association, 8025 Laurel Lakes Ct., Laurel, MD 20707 or call (301) 206-5100.

The American Jail Association, 1000 Day Road, Suite 100, Hagerstown, MD 21740.

National Institute of Corrections, 1960 Industrial Circle, Suite A, Longmont, CO 80501 or call (303) 682-0213.

For the latest information on developments in corrections:

Corrections Digest
Washington Crime News Service, 3918 Prosperity Ave., Suite 318, Fairfax, VA 22031 or call (703) 573-1600.
Biweekly, $249.50 annual subscription.

For position announcements:

American Jails (address above)
The bimonthly journal of the American Jails Association.

Corrections Digest (address above)

National Employment Listing Service (NELS)
Criminal Justice Center, Sam Houston State University, Huntsville, TX 77341 or phone (409) 294-1692.
Monthly—$17.50/six-month subscription.

Job Advisory Service
Available to members of the American Correctional Association which also has a non-member computer modem access service called *ACAnet* available for $60 plus a user charge. Contact the ACA at (301) 206-5050.

CHAPTER 13:

The Reluctant Profession:
Being and Becoming a Corrections Officer

by *DJ Culkar*

Why would anyone want to work in a prison? This is what I thought to myself when I received a "Notice of Examination" in the mail from the Michigan Department of Civil Service. I had originally submitted an application hoping to take the State Police Trooper exam, not the Corrections Officer examination. I had never considered working in a prison in Michigan or any other state! The job I had at the time paid just as well as the Michigan Department of Corrections (MDOC) and was much more appealing than working inside a state prison. I did not return the notice and did not take the examination. Little did I know that eventually I would actively pursue a position in the prison system and ultimately find corrections a rewarding career.

For some time, I had been working as a stock clerk with one of the larger national grocery store chains. I felt secure that this job would continue and that my financial condition was stable enough to allow me to get married and to purchase a new car. This turned out to be incorrect. Shortly after I refused the examination for the prison system, the grocery store, along with 54 other branch stores in Michigan, closed permanently. I was left jobless with rent and car payments, and a marriage that soon failed during my unemployment. Faced with the sagging economy of the early 1980s and a lack of marketable job skills, I sought out the civil service exam I had so blindly turned down earlier in the year. Eventually this examination was offered again and I took it very willingly. Unemployment had a very humbling effect on me. I no longer saw working in a prison as undignified.

My individual circumstances may seem exceptional, but this is not so. Talking with newly hired officers I have come to realize that the majority of correctional officers hired in Michigan over the last 10 years came from other career tracks outside of corrections. Several of our staff have been automobile workers who have been laid off or former police officers who are looking for promotion prospects or better pay and hours. These people, like me, typically seem to fall into employment

*Few people grow up wanting to be in corrections.

with the Department of Corrections, not having intended to ever work inside a prison. This reluctance may be due to the relative obscurity of corrections or the unappealing nature of the job. This career may be so repugnant and distasteful to the average person that they do not even consider this type of employment as a possibility. However, many of those who do find their way into corrections, and who may have initially believed that they'd move on when something better turned up, decide to stay.

Many students currently finishing high school or college may not have considered the thought of a career inside a prison. Most find the idea of working in a prison not only distasteful, but done by a different class of people from themselves. The stereotype of the corrections officer is of a low class authoritarian male who enjoys tormenting others and inflicting pain on people. But this perception, like so many public images of corrections and police careers, is very far removed from the reality.

Some people may have fleetingly considered corrections as a career, only to change their mind to go into police work, believing this to be a more noble and respected career choice. I have repeatedly heard how criminal justice students plan to work for a police department upon graduation. They have an illusion that policing, with its many rewards, is a preferred career over corrections. They mistakenly believe that careers in prisons and jails are low paying and unrewarding, reserved for those who "could not make it" as police officers. This is not true. Many of the officers with whom I work and have trained over the years hold degrees in criminology, criminal justice, sociology, etc.; and they all could have held a position in any police department. In fact several have tried law enforcement as an auxiliary or regular police officer, but realized, after some exposure, that the MDOC offered better working conditions—especially in terms of pay, hours, and promotions.

Others might be put off by the examination process. I found this to be a very simple, but lengthy affair. Approximately two months after I mailed my application I received the examination notice from the Department of Civil Service. Taking no chances the second time, I sent this one back immediately via certified mail! I was eager to take the exam and to return to earning a decent living. About a month later I received an admission letter for the exam at a local test site. On the date of the test I arrived with my admission letter, pencils, and driver's license, as required. I was pleased to find that the examination was simply based on aptitude. I always seem to score well on standardized tests such as this. About six weeks after I took this test I received my results. I scored 98%. I felt great. Shortly after that I had an interview at a prison in Ypsilanti, Michigan. I was hired and began a training program for my new career. The whole process had taken about six months.

The training program I experienced ten years ago as a new corrections officer has since changed dramatically. The current program has evolved into a residential academy, centrally located in Lansing, Michigan. The entire program is sixteen weeks and involves both classroom and field training. Included in the field training is an "On the Job" (OJT) phase that allows new recruits to work alongside certified corrections officers during their daily duties inside any one of more than 40 prisons and work camps.

During this training phase the new recruit experiences a rigorous program that provides the future officer with: a detailed history of Michigan's prison system; familiarization with the dangers and rewards of corrections as a career; education in race relations, discrimination, affirmative action, sexual harassment, and racial and cultural minorities; prison operations; restraint equipment; firearms; chemical disabling agents; riot control techniques; and self-defense skills. Also provided are situational lessons, such as report writing skill enhancements and what to do when taken hostage or how to defuse a violent confrontation with an angry prisoner. These lessons, and numerous others, provide the foundation for the duties that recruits will eventually be expected to perform. However, it is not the academy that will teach them how to work inside a prison. This will just prepare them for what to expect. The academy training, and the college degree are only tools for the new corrections officer to use in their career. The prisoners, the staff, and the actual concrete and steel of the prison will be the real teacher and trainer of the new corrections officer. This is not to downplay the importance of the academy and formal academic knowledge but to emphasize that the majority of learning how to work in a prison is learned *inside* the prison.

Why didn't I find a different job when the economy improved or why didn't I educate myself for a new trade or career? The reason is that, to my surprise, I found corrections to be an interesting profession. Also, the longer I remained in the profession, the more my pay and benefits increased.

Corrections, a profession? It is a career that is unlike any other job. Corrections has its own set of ethics, duties, responsibilities and, in the end, is the ultimate enforcer of society's sanctions. Without corrections there is no deterrent and no ultimate enforcement capability to our legal system. Of all the available responses a society can make to crime, prison as a concept offers the widest range of possibilities, depending how it is used. It can satisfy the numerous goals of protecting the public, punishing the offender, and rehabilitating, treating, or training the offender for a life without crime. It can do some or all of these things at the same time.

So what is it like to be a corrections officer and why do people stay? I cannot fully explain it. Working inside a prison as a corrections officer can be very dangerous but, statistically, many more police officers are killed than corrections officers. The corrections officer plays many different roles, everything from big brother to the cop on the beat; he or she may assume the role of prosecutor, defense attorney, judge and jury when disciplining a prisoner. The corrections officer operates computerized cell locking systems, prevents escapes, and transports injured or ill prisoners to hospitals. Perhaps the best way to illustrate the corrections officer's duties is to describe a typical day.

Your day will normally begin with a very short chat with the officers you are relieving. They will tell you who has certain restrictions or who may become a problem throughout the day. They will also inform you of any changes in your normal operations, which are frequent in corrections. You will then probably start your shift by taking a count to see who is inside your cell block, and to determine where those who are not there have gone. This is a safeguard, not only for you and the prisoners assigned under your control and care, but for the people who pay your salary; the general public who are always threatened and often harmed when a prisoner escapes. You begin to fill out some daily reports and call in your count to an officer who is responsible for the daily control of all activities within the prison. Daily activities begin.

After meals are completed prisoners are normally locked in their cells and another count is taken. Once all prisoners are accounted for, they are released a second time for work and school assignments or for recreational activities. Prisoner work assignments are normally those associated with the service industries (janitorial and food preparation); although·there are some factory assignments inside prisons, these are often very scarce jobs for which prisoners compete.

Various counts and checks are made throughout the day to ensure that the prison operates normally, i.e. without disruptions and incidents. It is the norm that the daily duties are well-organized. However, there are those infrequent instances where any amount of planning could not have averted an incident. Escapes, stabbings, assaults on staff, fights between prisoners, and rapes do occur within a prison. These incidents, even though much more infrequent than their presentation in the media would indicate, are part of the reality of prison life. It is your duty to recognize these in the early stages and react as quickly as you possibly can to avoid any harm to yourself, your fellow staff members, and any prisoner who may fall victim to one of these violent acts.

Your work day will normally be filled with much less severe confrontation than those I have mentioned. It will be common for you to run into a prisoner who does not want to be locked into his cell or the prisoner who does not want to be transferred to a new prison. It is here that your academy skills will come into play. You will defuse situations more easily as your time inside the prison increases. The more situations you are involved in, the greater your knowledge of what works to calm a prisoner.

You will also have to account for tools, chemicals, solvents, and firearms during your daily duty. You will search prisoners and prisoners' rooms in attempts to find prison made weapons or other contraband. You will write reports and make log entries, describing your routine and unusual duties throughout the day.

The material rewards for your professional activity as a corrections officer will vary depending upon your state and what position you eventually obtain. The Michigan Department of Corrections, for example, hires new officers at an initial pay scale of $21,715 per year. At the end of their first year of service a corrections officer will be paid $26,079 a year, plus overtime. At the end of five years a corrections officer's base salary will be $34,535, which is supplemented by the availability of overtime. It is not uncommon to have corrections officers routinely earning a salary of over $45,000. The career comes with other benefits: vacation starting at almost 3 weeks per year; almost 3 weeks of sick time per year; his or her birthday off and one personal day each year; full medical, dental, and retirement benefits which begin the first day of employment. This is not to mention the possibility of promotion, which is almost nonexistent in most local police departments.

Promotions within the MDOC can come very quickly; and shift transfers are plentiful enough to allow almost every employee the chance to occupy any work schedule that they desire. The prisons are so diverse in their function and security level that transfer to a security level or prison type best suited to an officer's personality and career goals is always a possibility. Prisons, minimum security work camps, parole supervision units, tethering units, probation services and community placements are all fields and services that employ corrections officers. Presently the MDOC employs over 8000 corrections officers and numerous other sergeants, lieutenants, captains, inspectors, wardens, parole agents, probation agents, counselors, and others. These varied positions allow corrections officers to advance their career in almost any direction with ease. Career choice is further facilitated for those who go on to complete their bachelor's degrees in fields such as criminology, criminal justice, sociology, and psychology.

Ultimately only you know why you want to go in a certain direction, but if you do want to pursue a career in corrections, or any other in criminal justice, you must begin with an informed assessment of the job and some insight about yourself and about your long-term objectives. You also need to keep an open mind and be willing to defer some job satisfaction for a few years. The first year will be the most frustrating. You will be placed in an alien environment with people, unlike your family and friends, who resent you and generally are very uncooperative.

To be a corrections officer you must be flexible and be able to shake off your work duties at the end of the shift. If not, you will find that the job will eat you alive. Prisoners will get away with rule infractions, just as criminals in the street get away with some crimes. All you can hope for is that you catch the major ones and do not allow a majority of minor rule infractions to get past your authority.

You must also be willing to learn new cultures, some of them foreign. You will come into contact with people who do not read or write, people who do not know their fathers, people who have killed their fathers, and people who have committed crimes and acts that may seem so heinous that they do not deserve to live. This is where you use the tools from your education and corrections academy. You have a job to do and that job is not to be the punisher for society, but the keeper of the punished for society. It is your job to carry out the laws of the people of your state, not your own personal agenda or beliefs.

To get started on a career in corrections you will go through the following process. In several states you will have certain requirements to meet before you can become a corrections officer. These may include taking a civil service exam, meeting certain formal education requirements, along with having some level of physical fitness. To begin with you will have to be a high school graduate or hold a GED. In addition, in Michigan for example, you will have to complete 15 semester (23 term) hours of college credits in one or a combination of human service classes. Your physical abilities must be on a level that will not impede your duties. Once these conditions are met you can then submit a "Civil Service Application" to take the corrections officer exam. This is not an application for a position. It is only an application to take the appropriate standardized test. Once you have taken and passed this examination your name is placed on a roster for interview. This roster is used by prisons and other work sites to interview and hire new corrections officers.

Once selected, the newly hired officer is still not solidly established in a position. The new recruit must now pass a medical examination, complete background investigation, drug use screening, and physical agility test. With these conditions met the new recruit must satisfactorily complete a 16-week training program that consists of academy-type training along with on-the-job training. Once these are completed the newly hired officer actually begins work. But permanent employment is still not fully established. The new recruit must now undergo a 12-month probationary period. Once this is satisfactorily completed the officer *now* has a permanent full-time position in corrections. Even though I have described the application and training process in Michigan, you will find that in your own state or jurisdiction, many of the same elements of the process will be present.

Should you decide to embark on this career path, I can assure you that you will find corrections to be a very rewarding career filled with opportunity.

CHAPTER 14:

Being a Female Corrections Officer

by *Lesley Jones*

I joined the Michigan Department of Corrections (MDOC) strictly for the paycheck, job security, promotion opportunities and the benefits. This might sound like a rather unfulfilling and unrewarding attitude, but it has worked exceptionally well for me. I'm afraid that being a corrections officer, or prison guard, as it is more popularly known, is not something that small children dream of becoming when they grow up.

For 13 years I had a job that I really enjoyed, working as an assistant instructor of horticulture, and it was immensely gratifying. However, over time, as my children grew and I matured, I experienced "burnout." There was no opportunity for promotion, nor even to change areas, and the pay became less and less acceptable. To top it all off, I worked in a rather isolated area, at least as far as other staff were concerned. When a new co-worker and I started having severe problems getting along, I knew it was time to move on.

Having foreseen this dilemma coming, I had returned to college to earn my bachelor's degree. Earlier I had a small start on a degree, but this time I was determined to finish, no matter what. I knew that a degree was the only way I was ever going to gain more control of my work situation. I looked for employment for about a year and was always "runner up" for the position. These jobs had wonderful status names, but didn't fit my definition of a career nor did they have adequate pay. During this time, I heard that the small community I lived in was being considered as the site for two state prisons. When the local newspaper started running employment ads for corrections officers, I immediately applied. However, as I soon learned (and it has been reinforced on numerous occasions since), the state does not move quickly. I knew certain college classes were required, so I included them in my already active college schedule and was ready when they told me to take the civil service exam.

Upon passing the exam, I was interviewed and given little quizzes about short "inmate dramas" that we were required to watch. I passed numerous tests like physical fitness, a doctor's exam, and a urine screening test. Then, and only then, was I put on a waiting list to attend the corrections officer academy. I was very fortunate in that I received the call to report in only a few weeks. For many it takes a year or more.

The actual academy is located in Lansing, but many satellite academies are set up when the state needs new employees or when the state needs officers faster than one academy can turn them out. Although the criteria and agendas vary from time to time, generally the academy is run along military lines, in three phases. There are four weeks of classroom learning and physical training (phase 1), followed by four weeks of on-the-job training at an actual prison (phase 2). If you are fortunate this training will be at the one you are assigned to for future employment. The third, or last phase of the academy covers four more weeks of classes and physical fitness training. The exposure of having had four weeks "inside" changes everyone's perspective during this final phase.

When an officer is on the second phase of on-the-job training, she is known as an OJT or a "red tag," because her name plate is red. This makes the officer readily identifiable to other staff who must always keep this trainee in their sight. Regretfully, the inmates also know that the red tag indicates a beginner, and during this time, the trainee will get some of the best and toughest training. A person who can make it through this phase can generally make it through anything.

Upon completion of all three academy phases, the officer is issued a "green tag," which means that they will be on probationary status for nine more months. The officer can now hold most of the positions within the department, except those considered "one person" positions. These are areas where an officer works for long periods of time with little staff contact. One person positions generally have little or no inmate contact, except in emergency situations. Some examples are the Alert Response Vehicle (ARV) officer, who patrols the outer perimeter roads; the entrance area whose officer controls all foot traffic through the institution, including inmates, staff and visitors; and the officer controlling the Sallyport, through which all vehicle traffic must enter.

Green tags cannot work on third shift or work overtime hours except in an emergency. The state can waive these restrictions if a true need arises, and all were waived for me during my period as a green tag. In my first summer I worked twelve hour days as we were desperately understaffed. The two new prisons were opening just as huge budget cuts and spending restrictions were being enforced by the new governor. The big prison building era was over, so the funds went dry. The inmates still kept coming though, and continued to fill an already overfilled system.

I trained at one prison then, as a green tag, was involved in opening a new "pole barn" prison called a temporary, and after about a year, I was transferred to another new prison when it opened. This one was made of brick, had multi-million dollar landscaping, and is called a regional facility.

Once an officer has completed one year of service, she becomes known as a black tag, or a status officer. The title remains as corrections officer unless she chooses to work housing; then it becomes a Resident Unit Officer (RUO). This is a small promotion in status as well as pay, although many prefer not to take it. An RUO usually has two years of service with the department. I am presently an RUO. I had the wonderful learning experience of being one of the first staff involved in opening the unit in which I work, which allowed me a lot of leeway in how things were set up.

I have worked the same unit for about a year and a half, which is a long time to stay on one assignment. Many institutions feel it is better to regularly rotate staff. I like staying in one place right now, so I have been very fortunate. Two hundred forty inmates reside in the housing unit that was built for 120. Double-bunking was planned before the institution ever opened. Although this creates more problems, it is unlikely that the situation will change during my career with the department.

Inmates are classified by security levels, with "Level 1" being minimum security and "Level 6" being maximum security. Our housing unit is designated for level 3s, who have a lot of free movement. We also have some 1s, 2s and 4s. The state will sometimes waive restrictions for both inmates and staff when it is convenient or worthwhile.

I work the first shift which is from 0600 to 1400 hours. (Notice the use of the 24 hour clock which seems to be standard for all military-type organizations). During this shift there is basically unlimited free prisoner movement for the entire time, except at formal prisoner count which runs 11:15 until around 11:45. At this time all inmates must be in their rooms and on their bunks. The rest of the time they are free to enter and exit their cells whenever they choose. Inmates even have keys to their cells.

As an RUO, I am in charge of the condition of the unit, and the actions of these inmates. Three RUOs work a unit each shift, so it's 240 prisoners to 3 officers. Needless to say, communication skills are extremely important for successful day-to-day management. This is essential to remember, but easily forgotten by many staff and much of the public. Even though I am a slightly built female, I manage my job well. If I were male, and weighed 250 pounds, I still wouldn't be able to fend off 240 inmates, so size doesn't matter here as much as other skills such as demeanor and attitude. These make the difference between compliance and having a safe day, or of going home stressed out, or hurt. An officer has to be in charge, and if they are unable to tell an inmate "no!" this is definitely not their field. Inmates are generally renown for their need of immediate gratification, and this need seems to intensify as the inmate population gets younger. They are used to taking what they want, and doing what they want, when they want. One of their hardest adjustments to prison life is doing things on **our** schedule. When problems arise they want instant solutions. For example, when problems with health or money matters occur, they always ask the officers to make phone calls instead of writing a kite (note/memo) themselves. They want the officer to do the work for them, and they want it done now.

It is very important for an RUO to be consistent and fair in teaching the inmates how to handle their own crisis and stay out of it themselves. An RUO must respond to emergencies within the unit, such as a fire, a fight, a missing inmate, or a plugged up toilet (which happens more often than you would imagine and not always because of faulty plumbing!). Although there is usually very little physical contact between staff and inmates, an officer must always be on the alert and stay aware of her surroundings. Officers do get hurt, but more often than not, it is from running to a duress (call to assist) when one is out of shape. We lose more staff from bad knees and backs than from assaults.

Females definitely have a harder time working in a male prison than their fellow male officers. The inmates test them constantly, calling out names and trying every way they can think of to become special to that female officer. They can become possessive of a female corrections officer which is very dangerous. Also, male staff do not always like female officers working in the department. Many male officers and sergeants have told me they feel that they always have to watch out for the females, making working with them much more work. I feel this is definitely a wasted concern on their part, and reflects inherent chivalrous attitudes if not sexism. However, females at least need to be prepared for this job knowing that the situation exists, even if they don't want to fully accept it.

So far, while degrees are increasingly becoming the minimum standard for entry level corrections officers, my degree has not helped me to get promoted. Because of state cutbacks, there have been no civil service exams for those of us ready for promotion. Hopefully this will soon change, for I am ready to learn more of the legal aspects of incarceration. The knowledge I have obtained about human beings since I joined the department is unmeasurable. It would fill volumes and one never stops seeing something different every day.

The prospective corrections officer needs to be aware that this profession is only for people who are sure of who they are. People with weak personalities or identities, who are easily swayed by others, do not belong in a prison. Also, if you're looking for "buddies" among the prisoners or if you think that prisoners are misunderstood and in need of care and help, then I think you should look elsewhere. These are convicted felons, most of whom will use you to their benefit in a heartbeat, no matter what they're telling you to your face. If name-calling hurts your feelings, stay away. But if you're strong enough to resist these supposed insults, you may have a good career in corrections. Once employed by the state, the avenues for promotions when you have a degree, are varied and fairly plentiful. Sometimes it takes awhile, but I'm very pleased with the amount of income I am already earning. A promotion will be exciting and challenging, but is really just icing on the cake.

SECTION FIVE:
PROBATION AND PAROLE

For many criminal justice students, helping people is the primary motivation for their career choice. While law enforcement is the first career choice for most students, others prefer a career that assists those who have been in trouble with the law to stay out of trouble in the future. Consider the goals that led one former student, Susan Rich, to choose probation as a career:

> I don't want to become a paper pusher. I want a job where I feel like I make a difference in someone's life. I want a job that offers an alternative to sentencing people to jail...I want a job that shows real rehabilitation possibilities for people, not one that just shuffles them through the system. Finally, I want a job where I work with people one-on-one. I don't want files with names on them. I want to know these people for whom I make life-changing decisions.

As we shall see, while some of these goals are met by a career in probation, there is no question that the amount of report writing, form filling and telephone communications is considerable.

There are several ways to contribute to a treatment or rehabilitative approach within the criminal justice system and corrections provides just one opportunity. However, while the emphasis in corrections is security and protection of the public, with rehabilitation a secondary goal, the careers we shall examine in this section are centrally concerned with supervising, treating and counseling the offender to become a less offensive citizen, with the aim of preventing him from harming others, and helping him to lead a productive future life.

The positions covered in this section involve both counseling and supervision; they are part social work and part law enforcement. The content of counseling varies depending on the job's institutional function to the criminal justice system, on the caseload of the agency, and on the nature of the clients' problems and needs. We shall consider two types of careers: (1) parole officers and (2) probation officers. In Section Six we shall consider the more varied and more specialized therapeutic work of human service workers.

Approximately 57,000 probation and parole officers are employed nationwide. Probation and parole are quite similar in content. Parole is

117

1 PROBATION AND PAROLE
Typical ads

PAROLE AND PROBATION ASSISTANT: State of Michigan. **Job Description:** Parole and Probation Assistant for the State Department of Corrections. **Qualifications:** 60 college credit hours required.

VICTIM WITNESS ASSISTANT: Pittsburgh, PA. **Job Description:** In-take and counseling work. **Qualifications:** Bachelor's in criminal justice, social work, human/social services or psychology and 1-yr. experience in social service or in-take in criminal justice program. **Salary:** $18,221.

DIVERSION SERVICES OFFICER: St Paul, MN. **Job Description:** Pre-trial diversion program. **Qualifications:** Experience with probation, investigations, treatment plans, and community resources. Bachelor's degree required. **Salary:** Low 30s to start.

HISPANIC/LATINO OUTREACH SATELLITE COORDINATOR: Toledo, OH. **Job Description:** Toledo-Lucas County Victim Witness Assistance Program, implement services to Hispanic/Latino victims of violent crime. **Qualifications:** Must speak, read, and write Spanish. Bachelor's degree preferred.

Salary: $15,000-17,000/yr. with benefits.

PROBATION OFFICER: Hartford, CT. **Job Description:** Court probation officer. **Qualifications:** Bachelor's in sociology or related field. MA preferred or comparable experience. **Salary:** $25,000.

PROBATION COUNSELOR: Detroit, MI. **Job Description:** Work with adjudicated youths. **Qualifications:** BS/BSW required and 2 yrs. experience.

PROBATION AND PAROLE OFFICER: Cheyenne, WY. **Job Description:** Supervision of adults and juveniles on probation-parole, writing pre-sentencing and pre-dispositional reports, counseling of offenders and families, coordination of community resources, confer and cooperate with law enforcement agencies. **Qualifications:** B.A. and two yrs. related experience. **Salary:** $21,564.

ADULT PROBATION OFFICER: Bowling Green, OH. **Qualifications:** Degree in criminal justice, psychology or related field and one yr. experience. **Salary:** $18,000 plus benefits.

118

used to test a convicted offender's readiness for release into the community. Parole Officers supervise and assist juvenile or adult offenders who have served part of their sentence in a correctional institution. They take each parolee on a case-by-case basis, familiarizing themselves with the client's social history prior to incarceration. Work with the parolee involves interviewing them, evaluating their progress, and advising them on a plan of action towards obtaining education, employment, housing and other help that they may need, perhaps for a substance abuse problem. Another aspect of the job is communicating with other agencies about such issues as: corrections in relation to a release plan; families in obtaining background information and counseling them to adjust to the parolee's impending release; and lawyers in regard to pre-hearing and pre-sentencing investigations for subsequent offences. Also important is the remedial action necessary should a parolee breach the conditions of parole. This requires taking action to initiate the return of a client to court. In spite of the appearance of a people-oriented position, parole, like probation and other positions in criminal justice, requires a considerable amount of record keeping, evaluation and report writing.

The work of probation officers is very similar except that it involves pre-hearing and pre-sentencing of clients and supervision of them as an alternative to prison when the person convicted has had their sentence suspended. Probation officers are used as an alternative to incarceration when it is believed that the client will benefit from the experience and when the offender is believed not to be a further danger to the public. Probation officers conduct interviews, do case research, write reports, counsel probationers and cooperate with community agencies.

The basic qualification for either probation or parole officer is a bachelor's degree in criminal justice, sociology, psychology or a related discipline. Since competition is high for these positions, the successful student will usually have completed some form of voluntary work in a related field. This might include volunteering in hospitals, or direct care work, helping at youth camps or assisting at various criminal justice agencies. However, the most important activity that can enhance the prospective student's employability in these areas is an internship. This enables the agency to look at you in action as a prospective employee, to train you according to their needs, and to let you know if this is really the kind of work you desire. For others the success route may involve initial employment as a direct care or case worker in one of the many low-paying residential homes or detention centers. Pre-employment in corrections or a court often makes hiring easier since one is already employed by the agency, which is a particularly valuable status during hiring freezes when agencies are generally restricted to internal hires.

The application process varies depending upon the employer. In most states probation and parole officers are hired by the department of corrections. However, they are also hired by the federal government which requires going through the office of personnel management. Probation officers are also directly hired by district courts.

Salaries in these occupations vary widely and depend upon the region. Nationally, federal probation and parole officers' salaries ranged from $26,798 to $50,516 in 1992. Entry-level salaries ranged from $21,564 to $31,860. In addition to the material rewards the satisfaction comes when clients change their lives for the better. The complete credit for this is not the probation or parole officer's, any more than it is their complete responsibility when things go wrong. Clients are responsible for the choices they make. However, widening the choices available, facilitating their implementation and enabling personal change, and seeing the outcome can be immensely satisfying.

In this section we have three contributions to illustrate the finer details of the various areas that we have described. The first, by Jim Robertson, describes the working life of a parole officer. Jim began his career in parole by starting as a federal corrections officer which gave him good insight into the experiences of those who would be his future clients. After explaining the purpose of parole he goes on to describe the dual role of the parole officer as both law enforcement officer and social worker, and details the daily work activities. He discusses the parole officer's use of interviews, of visits to the parolee's home and with local area employers, as well as what happens when parolees abscond and how he deals with this. Jim points out the challenges of the job, not least of which are the large case loads, political and organizational obstacles to effective parole supervision, and the clients' substance abuse problems. He highlights some of the more satisfying aspects of the work, such as getting clients through substance abuse programs and fixing them up with a job.

The next article is by Keith Jones, a former student who went on to work in probation with young offenders. Keith's paper is a diary of his experience as an intern with the Intensive Probation section of a County Juvenile Court. Here we are introduced to the kind of work and clients that might be typically encountered by a student pursuing a career in probation. Keith's article illustrates the mix of client contact, supervision, court appearances, record keeping and research, as well as describing both the routine and exceptional events that comprise the work of a juvenile probation officer.

The final article is by Linda Peck, a probation supervisor working for a misdemeanor court. Linda describes what it is like to be in probation and gives insight about the kinds of clients to expect. She began her career with many idealistic notions about what probation was about and what, as a probation officer, she would be able to do. Her experience in probate court as an intern was an invaluable "eye-opener" that also focused her career goals. She recommends that anyone going into the field today obtain some substance abuse training and that they do an internship. Linda's article raises questions about the limits placed upon the probation officer's work by the caseload; by the social and environmental conditions in which the client lives, expecially their substance abuse history; and by the politics of the criminal justice system and the manipulation of it by some clients.

There are few resources on careers in probation and parole. Most are short pamplets:

"Probation and Parole Officers" (Career brief) Moravia, NY: Chronicle Guidance Publications, 1987.

"Probation Officer" (Pamphlet) Sauk Centre, MN: Vocational Biographies, Inc., 1986.

For further information about probation and parole contact:

American Probation and Parole Association
c/o Counsel of State Governments, P.O. Box 11910, Lexington, KY 40578.

Federal Probation Officers Association
c/o U.S. Probation Office, 3rd & Constitution N.W., Rm 2800, Washington DC 20001.

For position announcements in probation and parole:

National Employment Listing Service (NELS)
Criminal Justice Center, Sam Houston State University, Huntsville,
TX 77341 or call (409) 294-1692.
Monthly—$17.50 per six-month subscription.

CHAPTER 15:

Being a Parole Agent

by *James B. Robertson*

I became interested in a career in corrections while studying for my bachelor's in criminal justice at Wayne State University. Shortly after graduation I applied for a position as a corrections officer with the Federal Bureau of Prisons. Although entry level educational requirements are still comparatively low in some places, bachelor's and master's degrees are becoming more important as selection criteria and/or practical requirements for promotion and professional advancement. After passing a background investigation and interview, I was hired as a corrections officer at the Federal Correctional Institution at Milan, Michigan.

As a corrections officer I provided custody and ensured the safety and security of the institution. Although the job description of corrections officer involves a high degree of responsibility for people, genuine threats to personal safety, rotating shifts and unpleasant surroundings, I feel corrections officers have the most important job in the prison. Today the role of the corrections officer is much more than merely providing custody to inmates. There are many tasks required and the officers must understand the philosophy and function of the entire correctional institution. A good officer must know the limits of their responsibility, the extent of their authority, and their relationship to other employees, the courts and the legislative process. I worked at Milan for three years. This period provided me with invaluable experience to prepare for a parole agent position. I decided to pursue this and applied to take the standard civil service examination.[1]

After passing a civil service exam for the parole/probation officer, I was hired as a parole agent for the State of Michigan, and placed at a parole office in the inner city of Detroit. The educational qualification

---

[1] This is the avenue of entry for all state positions, including circuit court, state police, corrections, and probation/parole.

for the position is a bachelor's degree in criminal justice, sociology or related field.

Parole is a release from prison while continuing to serve a sentence. Being "on parole" means being returned to the free community under the legal control and custody of the Department of Corrections and the Parole Board. Parole is considered an opportunity for the prisoner to show restraint from further criminal activity. It is a test of their readiness to return to the community. Supervision is provided by the agent, both to assist the parolee in making an acceptable adjustment, and to protect the public in the event that his or her behavior deteriorates.

As an agent you have to handle each person's problems or situation on an individual basis. Supervision of parolees includes all activities and techniques of investigation, counseling, casework and surveillance, that are consistent with the major mission of the Department: the protection of the public. Experienced parole agents will work to acquire and develop all of these abilities during their career. The goal of supervision is to minimize risk to the public while assisting the offender in identifying problem areas and controlling and/or correcting his or her behavior. The parole agent's role is to motivate the offender to change their behavior by directing efforts and community resources (through the appropriate use of rewards, punishments and social pressures) toward the problem behavior to encourage conformity with the law. If this is not achieved, the parolee can be returned to prison.

As a parole agent working in the city of Detroit for six years I have come to realize that I have dual roles. I am part law enforcement officer and part social worker. In the role of enforcement officer my goal is to ensure that offenders do not violate the conditions of their release, do not abscond, and that they attend any special functions, such as drug programs, assigned as conditions of their release. Parole agents are asked almost daily to decide if violators should be returned to prison for failing in any one of these areas. However, I not only observe the offender's behavior for conformity or violation, but I also engage in counseling, assist clients regarding employment issues, and broker community services such as drug programs. This is the social worker part of my job.

In order to give you a better understanding of what we do I thought it might be helpful to describe various aspects of the work, concentrating especially on: pre-parole investigations, interviewing, supervision, field contacts, home calls, employment contacts, and our relationships with other agencies.

The process of parole begins prior to the prisoner's release. At this time we must investigate the proposed home placement of the potential parolee. Our report is used by the Board of Parole in deciding advisability in granting paroles and to assure the best possible adjustment of offenders who are about to be released on parole.

The initial interview with a parolee, which takes place at the parole office, is the beginning phase of the intake and supervisory process. It establishes the foundation of the relationship between the parolee and the agent and provides an opportunity for the agent to assess the strengths and weaknesses of the client. Parolees approach this initial phase with a great deal of apprehension and the initial impressions they give can impact on the rest of the supervision. Through the initial interview I aim to establish a time-frame for the remaining period of supervision. The content of discussion in the process includes: 1) the parole rules, including Michigan rules for out-of-state cases; 2) the client's home and employment plans and addresses; 3) the client grievance procedure; 4) the parole loan repayment and supervision fees; 5) classification of the parolee to establish initial level of supervision; 6) implementation of a supervision plan; and 7) the client's reporting schedule.

The office interview is one of the main techniques through which I am able to implement supervision. The frequency of such reports by the client are established by the supervision standards and case needs. The office interview provides me with an opportunity to review client progress toward their supervision goals. Beyond this, I have an obligation to verify what they say and to seek out any other relevant information available that can help me determine their behavior. This is done through contact made in the field.

Field contacts may be made with anyone, including the client, who can provide me with information about what they are doing and how they are adjusting to the community. Sometimes these contacts are made at the client's home, at their job or elsewhere, and they may include family members, friends, or representatives of community agencies. I have enjoyed making field contacts and found it to be a valuable tool in assessing how the parolee is really doing.

Home calls are another part of my job that serve several purposes. At a basic level they enable me to verify the client's residence subsequent to an initial field interview. Another important purpose of home calls is to keep me informed of interpersonal relationships from a vantage point different from that of the client. I have found it especially important to communicate with family members about supervision planning and to enlist their help in the process.

As an agent in the field I have the responsibility of assisting and monitoring the unemployed client's work-seeking efforts and of verifying employment when the client is employed. Job verification is an important supervision technique and can be accomplished either by my contacting the employer directly or through the examination of client pay stubs. Frequent field contacts with local employers also give me the opportunity to be aware of job possibilities for other presently unemployed clients.

Part of my responsibility is to become fully knowledgeable of available community resources. Many agencies are partially or fully publicly funded and have a responsibility to serve our clients. Active liaison with agency personnel is essential. Obviously, my assessment of the particular individual's needs will dictate the type and frequency of community contacts, but I must be aware of a broad range of community resources in order to be an effective agent.

Another key element of the job is what to do when things go wrong, such as when a parolee absconds. In these cases I must conduct an investigation and write several reports. The parole is violated when a parolee stops making his regularly scheduled reports. My first report includes the parole violation charges, parole adjustment, my efforts to locate the parolee and a recommendation to issue a warrant for the parolee's arrest. Another report is needed when the parolee is arrested for absconding. This must include the details of the arrest, the parolee's statement, and a recommendation as to whether the parolee should be reinstated or returned to prison. In addition, I must investigate any new criminal charges with local police agencies and recommend that an administrative warrant be issued to maintain jurisdiction over the parolee where local charges are pending.

In practice, report writing and investigations are the two most important aspects of the parole agent's job. Reports are used throughout the system as sources of information for making rational decisions about the treatment and correction of the offender. Investigations assure the best possible adjustment of offenders about to be released on parole and document an act or failure to act by a parolee that does not conform to the conditions of his or her parole.

When there is new felony-behavior, parole is usually revoked regardless of the sentence. Parole revocation may result from technical violations as well as law violations, especially for violent and assaultive offenders. If an agent discovers criminal action or rule violations through surveillance and investigative techniques, the agent's role is to incapacitate the offender before serious new crimes are committed.

As you can see there is much more that goes into parole than people imagine, but the use of parole is subject to much controversy. Detractors assert that despite its lofty intentions, parole has failed to release people at the right time. They also claim that desirable post-release services have not been delivered in a manner which would adequately meet the needs of the client. Part of the explanation for these criticisms stem from the working conditions of parole agents, especially the caseload.

While the recommended caseload for an individual agent is fifty or fewer, average caseloads in Detroit, for example, are 110—the number determined as the maximum possible to do an effective job of supervision. It is very difficult for us to maintain frequent personal contact with parolees when caseloads approach this size. When caseloads are too high we are reduced to "cops", interested more in the timeliness, if not honesty, of monthly reports made by the clients, than in their actual problems or progress. Based on the high caseloads, parole supervision has been radically relaxed. Since 1987, parole agents in Michigan are operating under an emergency waiver system that supersedes the Department's more stringent supervision policy. Under the waiver system, the most dangerous parolees (those under "intensive" supervision) see an agent only twice a month instead of weekly. Parolees under average supervision see an agent once every 60 days. Minimum cases report once every 90 days. Since 1982, the Corrections Department has increased its parole staff by only 11 percent while the number of felons under supervision jumped 70 percent. Some of my colleagues complain that "they've turned this job from a field job to a desk job," and that juggling paperwork and telephones reduces their ability to supervise what many believe are more sophisticated criminals being released into communities to make room at overcrowded prisons. Parole agents are struggling to do a frustrating and difficult job during a period of overwhelming workload increase and simultaneous budgetary cutbacks.

Although there are many criticisms of the parole system, on the positive side, there are a number of reasons to become a parole agent, even in these difficult times. These have to do with satisfaction from the work we do. My two favorite duties, for example, are helping clients and protecting the public. These seem to be contradictory. I feel very useful when I am identifying and utilizing community referral resources for parolees in need. I also get much satisfaction knowing that I am protecting the public from a dangerous offender.

The services needed by offenders are varied and depend, in part, on the client's environmental and socioeconomic conditions. Meeting their needs often requires that I use specific resources in the community such as: education, housing, vocational training, employment services, psychological and psychiatric counseling and treatment, medical services, religious guidance and training, welfare, family counseling, substance abuse programs, and a host of others! It is imperative in using community resources that I select these as part of a specific program tailored to the client to enable them to return to the community and remain there in a noncriminal role. However, before I am able to refer a client to a program, I must first assess their needs and link these to the range of available community services.

Many factors affect the client's needs. This varies by region, as well as by the nature of the locality, their past education and employment, and their emotional maturity. Two of the biggest problems for parole agents in Detroit are unemployment and substance abuse problems. Employment programs are contracted by the Department of Corrections to develop and implement activities that are designed to combat, for example, the causes and effects of poverty through the provision of services and opportunities for residents of poor neighborhoods. Often included in this type of agency are programs such as the Peter Claver Career Training, which provides work, job experience, and training opportunities for underemployed and disadvantaged parolees. This program often serves as a job bank for offenders who need on-the-job experience, or who need basic and remedial education. I believe in the old saying: "idle time is the devil's workshop." From my experience as a parole agent, employment is a necessary ingredient for the parolee to successfully complete his or her parole. Clients need to be involved in a job, or in a training or educational program to give them the motivation to become productive members of society. If parolees are working, there appears to be less chance they will support themselves through illegal means.

The biggest problem parole agents face in Detroit is the substance abuse by our clients. At least 50 percent of parolees violate their parole because of a drug-related issue. They either are arrested for selling or possessing drugs, or for committing new crimes to pay for their drug habits. Alternatively, violation occurs as a result of testing positive for urine drug tests, or for leaving drug treatment programs after incurring three positive urine tests for illegal substances (mostly cocaine or heroin). As a parole agent I've encountered parolees who would strip their own mother's car and sell the parts to pay for their "crack" habit. As parole agents we can refer parolees with substance abuse problems to NA/AA meetings, out-patient programs or in-patient programs such as Share House or Salvation Army's Harbor Light.

When you are able to help motivate a client to obtain a job or complete a substance abuse program, it can be very rewarding. When the offender shakes your hand after completing parole, and thanks you for your assistance, you can be assured you have provided them with the maximum opportunity for growth and development, and hopefully, have reset them on a course to live a crime-free life. Equally satisfying to me is placing a dangerous offender in custody to protect the public. Crime causes poverty in Detroit. It instills fear in its citizens. It forces many businesses to close and takes away our freedom to move safely in our homes and on our streets. The costs and consequences of crime affect all of society and it has changed the city of Detroit. As a parole agent I am concerned that the overcrowded correction system is becoming the domain of serious, violent, repeat offenders thus raising considerable supervision problems for agents. Offenders are being released from prison early—regardless of their conduct while in prison—because of crowded prison conditions. These violent repeat offenders are very difficult to supervise in the community. It's important to get "tough on crime" and hold offenders accountable for their criminal behavior.

Prospects for employment in corrections have improved. In the state of Michigan, parole services are currently expanding, and they are hiring parole and probation agents. The 1990s present a difficult dilemma for corrections in that the public wants offenders punished rather than treated, but they do not want to spend the money to build new prisons. Thus arose the challenge: to identify and develop community-based intermediate sanctions which would satisfy the need for punishment at a reasonable cost while also addressing the issues of public safety and treatment. There is a critical need to establish a greater array of options strong enough to ensure public safety.

One promising approach the Department is now using is parole boot camp programs to ensure more reasonable control through the use of intensive supervision programs. Boot camps invoke strict curfews and require offenders to maintain employment, report weekly, and remain drug and alcohol free. Their long-term effectiveness is still being researched.

Another new approach that our department is utilizing is electronic monitoring for parolees using the electronic ankle bracelet or "tether." Our ability to enforce house arrest, curfews, and intensive surveillance programs may be revolutionized by electronic monitoring devices. Generally the tether is placed on a parolee after a parole violation has taken place, as an alternative to incarceration. If the wearer is not where he or she should be, the violation shows up on a central monitoring screen at a local correction center. Hopefully, this tool will help reduce repeat crimes by those already entrusted to the parole system. It appears to be cost-effective and a viable alternative to incarceration for non-violent offenders.

I would like to conclude on a personal note about the problems and prospects for someone becoming a parole agent. As you may have deduced from the description of the work I do, parole agents experience a great amount of role conflict. They serve as police officers, caseworkers, and prosecutors (in parole revocation proceedings). As an agent I spent less than 50 percent of my time in actual contact with parolees and more than 50 percent of my time on paperwork and other chores associated with the various roles. Based on my experience as a correction officer, parole agent and parole supervisor, I believe the supervision provided by the parole agent affords the public some measure of protection and safety, and provides at least one person to whom the offender can turn for guidance and assistance.

Continuing education and training are critical to the maintenance and advancement of professional skills, and to the professional development of parole agents. With these skills will arise new ideas and action for the improvement of parole. For example, based on scoring well on a civil service promotional exam, completion of a master's degree from Eastern Michigan University in criminology and criminal justice, and my experience, I have recently been promoted to parole supervisor. As a first-line supervisor, I coordinate and direct parole agents and the operation of a parole office in the city of Detroit. The opportunities are out there for those who want to balance the care and control that is required to be a successful and effective parole agent.

CHAPTER 16:

Diary of a Juvenile Court Probation Intern

by *Keith Darnell Jones*

I was surprised how easy it was to get my internship in the county juvenile court. I just talked to the intern organizer on the phone and it was set up. I've heard that at other courts there is a waiting list so I guess I was lucky. They gave me a choice of whether I wanted to work with the regular caseworkers or to intern in the Intensive Probation Program. I spent a day with both and decided on Intensive Probation (IP). This was because the regular caseworkers spent a lot of time in the office whereas the Intensive caseworkers spent much more time in the field dealing directly with the clients and their families. I worked with four male probation officers who were committed to helping their mainly high school-age clients. These professionals did not get too emotionally involved, as they knew that to do so would result in early burn out. I found it interesting that all of these probation officers have their own children, which might have explained their dedication. The team worked well together. If you saw them in action it would remind you of a well-oiled machine. The following is a summary of my activities during the twelve weeks of the program.

Week One — On my first day I was assigned to a juvenile probation officer with whom I would spend the majority of my time. I was shown the office and familiarized with the clients' files. Then we went to a city high school to pick up a client who had violated his probation. It had to be decided whether this individual was to be held in detention or just disciplined for his actions by being put into a more secure phase of the program. I was also instructed that I would be a "Big Brother" to this individual. On Wednesday I reviewed the files of two persons due to appear in court and then sat in on their hearings. The individual I was supposed to "brother" was held in detention instead of being released, which was a little disappointing.

Week Two — This week I learned how to prepare a review file for a client. Some of the clients desire to be placed at a particular type of treatment facility. Before they are selected the facility has to review the client's file. The files contain police records, court orders, the results of urine screening and drug tests, psychological evaluations and victim reports.

I accompanied a caseworker on "school checks," where a caseworker checks up on the juvenile's progress in school and examines their attendance record. In addition, I went on a few "night checks." This is where a juvenile is supervised at night by finding out if they are where they are supposed to be. If probation is violated the individual would risk being put into detention.

Week Three — This week I rode with the night probation officer and we checked on all of the clients in the program to see if they were in their homes by curfew. We covered the whole county but the majority of the clients lived in one particular city. We visited about ten clients, all of whom were at home except for one. This youth had run away and had told his family not to worry because he could take care of himself. A pick-up order was issued so that when the person is caught he will be put into detention awaiting placement.

While visiting with the clients we spent a lot of time interacting with the family. The caseworker has created a special relationship with the parents. They look at him as an equal parent, which reflects the reality because the caseworker has considerable authority over the child.

Week Four — The beginning of this week started out slowly. I had little interaction with the clients. My caseworker was out of town taking a client for an interview with a special group so I was assigned a lot of paperwork. I had to total up the number of personal contacts and phone contacts that staff had had with the clients over the last four months in order that the appropriate data could be entered into the budgeting process.

As the week progressed client interaction picked up. I did some more high school checks for attendance and attitude in the classroom. When we arrived at one client's class, he was dead asleep right there in the classroom. He was sitting right in front of the door. He sure heard it from the probation officer! Later in the week we did more night checks.

Week Five — This week we had more court hearings than usual. One of the clients sabotaged an interview with a sexual therapy group for which he was being considered, so that he wouldn't be accepted. As a result the court was left to decide what to do with him. This had been his last hope before being put in placement.

We journeyed to four area high schools to check on the progress of all our clients. I was introduced to the newest client and it is more than likely that I will be his "Big Brother." This individual has a lot of anger and no positive male role models in his life. Hopefully, if I can become his Big Brother, the situation will be rewarding for both of us.

Week Six — This week the caseworker and I did many high school checks. The majority of the clients were doing well in school and there were no complaints from any of the teachers. On Thursday I went on my regular night check with one of the probation officers. We went to one client's house and he was baby-sitting. It seemed that everything was okay. His mom had just been released from jail and we wanted to see how their interaction was going. We left the client at about 8:00 P.M. At 9:00 P.M., his mom called the juvenile court and said he had "gone wild!" She said that he had a temper tantrum, stormed out of the house and didn't tell anyone where he was going.

Week Seven — I started a project this week that will probably take two weeks to complete. The Intensive Probation Supervisor gave me this research project that is aimed at helping him support a new program he wants implemented in the juvenile court. I have been asked to make a list of the inmates that are in the County Sheriffs' Jail, cross reference the names with all of the closed files here at the Juvenile Court and list all the inmates that are involved in both. From this list I create a file for each person, listing all the charges against them in both courts. The aim is to discover if there is a trend in the types of crimes committed. The Probation Supervisor believes that the majority of clients have committed more serious crimes **after** Juvenile Court, and if that is shown to be the case, then our methods of therapy must change.

Week Eight — On Monday I went with two probation officers to pick up a young male who was going to be locked up in detention for violating his probation. While we were waiting for him to get dressed we noticed that he seemed to be taking a long time. We went up to his room. He had cut the screen and jumped out the top window of a two-story house. It was incredible that he jumped without injuring himself.

The rest of the week was mainly routine. I worked the night shift on Thursday and it was normal. I also continued work on the research project that had been assigned to me.

Week Nine — This week was mainly the same routine as the previous weeks. I had a chance to review the case files of all the clients. Since the clients in Intensive Probation change periodically, it is necessary to keep up with all the new ones. The caseworker and I took a client down to an area boys' home for placement. This individual had been sexually abused by his father and some of his father's friends and his mother wasn't able to care for him. The only alternative was for him to learn independent living skills at the home.

This week the police picked up the client who last week had jumped out of the window to escape detention. I talked with him and asked how he managed not to injure himself and he explained that when he landed, he rolled.

Week Ten — A young man we had placed in a foster home really messed up this week. His foster parents are farmers. He took his foster father's pick-up truck without asking permission. Don't ever take a farmer's pick-up truck! He was furious and threw the young man out of his house and told him not to come back. Since we had no place to put him until the next day he had to spend the night in detention. After getting to detention he told us that he had taken some LSD a few hours ago and his "trip" was bad. We spent the next three hours in the emergency room of the hospital while he was under observation. The doctor said he was fine and released him.

Week Eleven — This week was pretty routine. We did more school checks and many referrals. Quite a few of the kids got in trouble at their high schools so we had to get them placed in other facilities where they could be taught. This week I was offered a position as a part-time Probation Officer. I'll be working on Sundays and covering any days off that the regular Probation Officers have scheduled. The organization did a background check on me to see if I was qualified and I passed with no problems. This week my "little brother" here at the court started to open up to me more.

Week Twelve — In my last week I had to refer a client to a foster care agency. I had to sit with the client's mother and fill out a twelve-page history report for the agency which took about an hour and a half. My "little brother" got expelled from school for a week because he was horsing around with one of his friends and the teacher thought he was fighting. We closed a case on one of our clients who was charged with carrying a concealed weapon. The case was closed because he is 17 years old and has charges pending in the adult court.

I start working as a part-time probation officer on Sunday.

Final thoughts — Overall, the approach of the Intensive Probation team was very positive and, in part, this stemmed from the Juvenile Court judge who has a very positive attitude toward probation for youths. She has given our court a positive reputation. One negative aspect of this court is that, because of limited resources, each caseworker has too large a caseload. Another is the division of responsibility between the different agencies who do their own evaluations of clients. Those done by the probation court caseworker sometimes don't agree with the agency evaluation and the agency relies on their own interviewer's assessments. This means that the manipulative kid can put on an act and get themselves rejected by an agency. The result is that those youths who need treatment for their problem often go without it.

This internship was well organized and well implemented. It also had a major impact on my career goals. Before the internship I really didn't even consider working in a human service capacity where children were involved. My main goal had always been to join the FBI. But the internship exposed me to an atmosphere that I found most pleasant and rewarding. I experienced immense joy working with these children. I think that they've been given the short end of the stick by society. The majority of the youths just crave the stability and attention that adolescents need when growing up. It's hard to learn responsibility if your father is not around and your mother is a "crack head."

CHAPTER 17:

An Officer of the Court:
Working in Probation for a District Court

by *Linda Peck*

I decided to go back to college when I found that I couldn't support myself and my three sons on the kind of jobs available to someone with no more than a high school diploma. When I went through the colleges' choice of degree programs, I came across criminal justice. I looked over the required classes, many of which were sociology, psychology and law courses and decided I was interested in studying these areas. The more courses I took, the more they excited me.

I thought that in the criminal justice field I would be part of upholding the laws of the land. I believed there would be clear-cut rules of right and wrong. I saw the job as black and white; the good guys against the bad. Of course the law breakers were bad and the criminal justice system was good. It had to be. It was upholding the laws of the American people.

I had never been involved with the justice system personally. I relied only on outside images: book learning, media news and the movies. While in college I interned for six months at the Probate-Juvenile Court as a juvenile intake worker and for six months at the 15th District Court as a probation officer with adults and misdemeanor offenders. I also worked as an auxiliary police officer for 10 months. Each of these positions gave me a different insider perspective on the criminal justice system. Fortunately I met and worked with some very good and dedicated people. They shared their knowledge and experiences with me. I also saw those who were burned out and discouraged with the system. My intern experiences helped me the most in deciding on my career choice as a probation officer. I liked the idea of working as a probation officer better than anything else I had tried or the other careers I had read about. I decided to work towards that goal when I finished college.

Besides a bachelor's degree in one of the social science fields, I found job experience and substance abuse training were required by most courts and probation departments. Maturity also ranked high as a requirement. I graduated in 1983 with a B.S. degree in criminal justice and with a minor in sociology. I then obtained Michigan's apprentice Substance Abuse Counselor Certification credentials. I worked retail while watching for criminal justice openings in my area and then moved to the west coast.

While in California I worked as a counselor in juvenile residential homes for two years. The children in these homes and/or their parents had all been involved with the criminal justice system in some way. Most of them were wards of the court and state. Counseling them was often a difficult task. Some had lived through more bad experiences than most adults. The counseling experience, however, was valuable in preparing me for a successful interview for the position as a probation officer which I obtained when I moved back to Michigan.

I really felt I was going to make a difference. I believed our justice system was fair and that, as an officer of the court, I would help and counsel those in need and help to turn their lives around. I would assist the judge in obtaining background information and in preparing fair and equal sentencing recommendations. I was so excited. Here was a position in which I'd be respected and serve my fellow human beings. It was a position where I could do some good while upholding the laws of my state, where criminals would see the errors of their ways and change their ways or go to jail! I was naive.

I was not prepared for the numbers of clients. The number of clients each probation officer has on their case load far exceeds real manageability; it ranges from 250 to 350 clients per probation officer. The officer will do 6 to 10 new assessments and/or interviews per week and write full reports on each of them. She will get background information and verify information when needed for the written reports. She will see up to 25 clients a day who are reporting to her monthly or bi-monthly. While seeing these clients she will keep a written report of their visits and monitor all things that they are ordered to do by the court. She will also take daily telephone calls from clients, attorneys, family members, police officers and counselors. In some courts the probation officer spends from half to one and a half days per week in court. She will read mail daily and monitor clients who are reporting by mail. She will notify other courts when she has a client who is on probation in another jurisdiction but now has a new case with her court. She checks her court's records and the state and federal criminal information system's records (Law Enforcement Information Network—LEIN) when seeing new clients. One to three days per week she may see the new clients out of court after their sentencing. She will go over their probation orders with them and set them up with their first appointments or put them on mail-in probation. She will interview defendants brought to her office from lock-up by a court officer when the judge needs their background information and a recommendation in a shorter period of time. On some occasions she will interview a defendant while they are locked up. This may be because the court officers are busy or because the defendant is a security risk and may be violent and endanger the lives of others if released. These "quick interviews," as we refer to them, are hand-written and delivered to the judge in court so that the defendant may be sentenced that same day. Two or three times per month we have "violations of probation" and "show cause" hearings. These may take a half or a whole day each. Each probation officer will see their clients prior to the client going before the judge in the court room. At that time the probation officer will try and work out with the client what is going to be done about the client's violations. It could be they have failed to pay court costs or it could be multiple other problems with their probation. If the defendant pleads guilty to the Violation of Probation, they will be sentenced that day. They may go to jail for one day or up to one year, whichever is the maximum penalty for the offense. Alternatively the client may incur more costs and/or more provisions for probation and that probation may continue or be extended but will not exceed a two year period (misdemeanor courts). If the defendant pleads not guilty, the Violation of Probation is set for a full hearing at a future date.

At the hearings the defendant can be represented by an attorney. At the second hearing the probation officer will again talk with the defendant before they go before the judge. They will then go into court. If the defendant pleads guilty, sentence is passed by the judge. If the plea is not guilty the client must prove that the charges brought by the probation officer are not true. I have never seen any defendants prove that they were innocent. The probation officer is there in court because she has documented the behavior of the defendant. The defendant is sentenced by the judge. If the clients/defendants fail to show, the probation officer asks the judge for a bench warrant to be issued for the defendant's arrest.

The probation officer works closely with other probation officers, the judges, court recorders, the court administrator, court clerks, police and counselors. She also works closely with the department's secretary who is a very important part of any probation department. Courts vary in size, this being determined by the population served. Our city has a population of 72,000, so we have two judges and one magistrate/court administrator and two court officers. We are fortunate to have a new facility which houses the courts, clerks and probation department all in one building. We are also located beside the police department which is convenient. Many courts are in separate buildings from their probation departments which makes court operations much more difficult.

Probation officers put in a minimum of 40 hours per week. In some departments, one day a week they stay until 8:00 pm so they can see clients who work daytime hours. Probation officers' salaries are often lower than they should be for the job qualifications required and the duties of that job.

I am now the supervisor of the probation department. We have a full-time secretary and two full-time probation officers. The department takes interns from local colleges. We have them, usually two at the same time, for a period of 6 to 8 months for 16 hours per week. We also have 10 volunteer probation officers who give 3 to 12 hours per month of their time. They are assigned a case load and I supervise them. Some of our present volunteers have been with us for up to 8 years.

I look forward to going into work in the mornings and I feel the other probation officers I work with feel the same way. We are fortunate to have a good working relationship in our office. It is a job that can bring a lot of frustration and stress. We try to use humor to lighten up situations and not take client behaviors personally. In this field, burnout is a reality that we discuss in order to get things off our chest. We also ask each other for ideas, opinions, and advice.

The defendants are as diverse as the areas they come from and quite representative of this area's population. They are more often on the lower end of the income scale, with many making only minimum wage. They frequently have not completed high school and often have no real job skills or training. A small percent cannot read or write. In this jurisdiction they are mostly caucasians, with blue-collar and service jobs. A large percentage have moved here from the south, searching for work, either by themselves or with their parents or grandparents. Many come from families where education was not important. Most are trying to do the best they can with what they have. Over 50% have a substance abuse problem with the majority having a problem with alcohol. Many of them do not see their problem or understand it. The majority do not have any health insurance. Around 50% made a bad choice and that's why they're in court. Most of them will not return. The one-time encounter will be enough to steer them clear of the courts. Some need counseling and assistance in other ways and, for the most part, it is given and they too will not return. The other approximately 40% will return. Some see nothing wrong with their behavior and actually like what they do until they get caught. Many are drug users and alcoholics who refuse to see their problem. Others come from backgrounds in which this behavior is the norm.

There are some very bad people on the streets who should not be anywhere but behind bars for the rest of their lives. They are habitual criminals that will never change their behavior and, in the course of their lifetime, they hurt and injure many people. Unfortunately, these people know the system as well as I do. They play it, use it and manipulate it. They make a probation officer's job frustrating and cost the taxpayers thousands of dollars. The ideals of justice being served increasingly go out the door with our overcrowded prisons. Probation officers and judges compromise because there's nowhere to put these criminals. Usually the judge and probation officer both want them in jail or prison but can't get them placed there for lack of space. If they go at all it is just for a short time and they're back on the streets again. Most of the time, a person on probation or parole for a felony can commit a new misdemeanor offense and not expect to be returned to prison. They know it. Occasionally we are able to put them in jail through the district courts. This is where the legislature and governor—politics—enter the picture. It is an enormous problem that will not be corrected overnight.

Most courts and probation departments are understaffed. Some probation departments are so overloaded that they aren't able to do much monitoring of clients at all. Taxpayers think more probation officers will cost them more money but the truth is that the court with its probation department pays for itself with revenue in excess of its expenditures.

After stating these frustrations of the criminal justice system it might seem that I am cynical about probation, but I still enjoy my job. There are always those clients who improve because you have been there for them. And on a few occasions you get a "Thank you." Like most of life you just know you are doing what one person can do and doing it well. I plan to finish my master's degree and move up administratively in the field. I also am working on making people aware of the prison system and campaigning to get new prisons opened and for more alternative sentencing programs. Things are more gray than they are black and white!

SECTION SIX:
HUMAN SERVICES

The role of human service workers is generally tangential to the criminal justice system. However, several areas of human services overlap with criminal justice. Clients often have a mix of problems including poverty, criminal histories and mental health problems. Although their often violent background might suggest criminal confinement, many are placed in psychiatric and community-based settings where they receive various treatments and therapies from psychologists, counselors, social workers and therapists. Therapeutic human service work can vary enormously and include: direct care in group homes, casework, youth counseling, victim support or advocacy, domestic violence counseling, social work with clients having substance abuse problems, and art therapy with schizophrenics. These are the kinds of jobs that we shall focus on in this section.

Human service workers are hired by federal, state and local social work agencies and by private agencies, hospitals and mental health programs. Workers who deal with deviant, disturbed or legal offenders perform a similar kind of counseling and rehabilitative function to that of probation officers but it is more therapeutically focused. It attempts to satisfy educational, health, occupational and other needs. These employees may rely on their specialized therapeutic skills in handling clients with self-esteem problems arising in relation to substance abuse, child abuse, spouse abuse or mental illness. These workers, therefore, are often required to be more qualified in a particular therapy and may deal with populations of clients all suffering from certain types of problems. Consequently, while for social work the typical requirement is a master's, for the more specialized therapeutic services a master's degree in clinical psychology, guidance and counseling, or such things as occupational therapy, recreational therapy, substance abuse therapy or art therapy, may be required.

While social worker's salaries are comparable to those in probation and parole, other employees' income can range from as low as $5.00 per hour for some direct care workers to $40.00 per hour for therapists, with around $20.00 per hour being typical for those with more specialized therapeutic training.

1 HUMAN SERVICES
Typical ads

144

CHEMICAL DEPENDENCY COUNSELOR: Sandusky, OH. **Job Description:** Provide counseling in both inpatient and outpatient settings to adults and adolescents. **Qualifications:** BA/BS with 2 yrs. experience in chemical dependency counseling. Licensed or eligible CDC or CAC.

CHEMICAL DEPENDENCY COUNSELOR: Bridgeport, CT. **Job Description:** Individual and group counseling, educational presentations and case management. **Qualifications:** BA and substance abuse therapy certification.

SUBSTANCE ABUSE COUNSELOR: Athens, GA. **Job Description:** Provide sub-acute 14-day program with didactic group, individual & family therapy services. **Qualifications:** C.D. knowledge base with one yr. experience preferred. MSW/MA/BA and current licensure.

SUBSTANCE ABUSE THERAPIST: Coldwater, MI. **Job Description:** Working with women inmates. **Qualifications:** BA, MA preferred. Substance abuse therapy and relapse experience.

DRUG/ALCOHOL COUNSELOR: Mansfield, OH. **Job Description:** Crisis intervention, counseling, aftercare. **Qualifications:** Skilled chemical dependency counselor, experience with children, CAC or CCDC required, and MSW/MA.

SUBSTANCE ABUSE COUNSELORS: Chicago, IL. **Job Description:** Counselor for adolescents involved in substance abuse program. **Qualifications:** BA/BS.

SUBSTANCE ABUSE CLINICIAN: Macon, GA. **Job Description:** Community coordinator for jail-based program. **Qualifications:** Master's degree preferred. Prior training and experience with ASI, SASSI or McAndrews. Knowledge of available community resources.

PROGRAM DIRECTOR: Toledo, OH. **Job Description:** Treatment Alternatives To Street Crime (TASC). **Qualifications:** 5 yrs. experience in criminal justice or substance abuse field, 2 yrs. managerial experience, BA, MA and CCDC Certification. **Salary:** Mid-$30,000.

In this section we have three contributions that illustrate the diversity of work confronting the human service employee working with legal offenders in a therapeutic setting. In order to obtain a position in a clinical setting it is necessary to gain experience. Typically this comes through one of several minimum-wage, entry-level jobs such as "psych-techs" (technical assistants in psychiatric settings) or direct care workers. Such employees do the most basic routine tasks with patients or clients. These can range from regular checks on patients to establish that they are where they are supposed to be, to food preparation, and/or helping with personal hygiene. The first article provides one example of this kind of entry-level position. Linda Nelson was employed in "community care" as a case worker for a group home caring for brain trauma injury patients. Linda's account describes her first experiences with these clients, who exhibit a number of similarities to offenders in the criminal justice system. A common reason for brain trauma injury is auto-collision and a typical contributing factor in their collision is alcohol and drug related behavior. Linda illustrates how this behavior can continue while they are in care, and can result in severe security problems for which the entry-level human service workers are inadequately prepared. A related difficulty is the self-centered behavior and violence stemming from the condition itself that might lead to problems with the law if not adequately supervised.

Carolyn McGillis is a psychiatric social worker responsible for discharge planning of mentally ill patients, many of whom are on parole, have past criminal records or substance abuse problems. Her article describes the legal limitations on her work and the pressures stemming from heavy caseloads and the unpredictability of her clients.

Our final contribution by Lee Doric-Henry, who is an art and recreational therapist, explains the extreme difficulties of working with schizophrenic and chronically depressed clients, whose severe illnesses prevent them from functioning normally within a family or community setting. She runs groups aimed at improving these patients' socialization skills, cognitive abilities, coping skills, self-esteem, and leisure planning. She encourages them to participate in art and music projects, recreational activities and therapeutic exercises. Lee also identifies the stressors stemming from the nature of the patients' illnesses which can cause suffering by therapists, psychiatric nurses, psych techs, and social workers. Through her work she comes in contact with rapists, murderers, child molesters, drug abusers, and suicidal and self-mutilating patients. Working with these persons can be both highly fulfilling and emotionally draining.

For more information about human service careers and the role of human service work with legal offenders:

Neale Baxter, *Opportunities in Counseling and Development Careers*, Lincolnwood, IL: National Textbook Company, 1990.

National Association of Social Workers, *Careers in Social Work*, Silver Spring, MD: NASW, 1987.

National Therapeutic Recreation Society, *About Therapeutic Recreation*, Alexandria, VA: NTRS, 1987.

Albert R. Roberts, *Social Work in Juvenile and Criminal Justice Settings*, Springfield, IL: Charles C. Thomas, 1983.

Paul Schmolling, *Careers in Mental Health: A Guide to Helping Professions*, Garrett Park, MD: Garrett Park Press.

"Prison Social Worker" (Pamphlet) Sauk Center, MN: Vocational Biographies, 1988.

For further information about related human services:

National Association of Social Workers
750 First St., NE, Washington, DC 20002.

National Association of Alcoholism and Drug Abuse Counselors
3717 Columbia Pike, Arlington, VA 22204.

National Rehabilitation Counseling Association
633 S. Washington Street, Alexandria, VA 22314.

American Art Therapy Association
1202 Allanson Road, Mundelein, IL 60060.

For position announcements and news or features in various human services, contact state departments of mental health and:

The Family Therapy Networker
>Subscription Services, 8528 Bradford Road, Silver Spring, MD 20901 or call (301) 589-6536.
>Bi-monthly, $20 per year subscription.

NASW News
>National Association of Social Workers (address above) or call (800) 638-8799.
>Monthly, available to non-members for $25 per year.

Social Service Jobs
>Employment Listings for Social Services, 10 Angelica Drive, Framingham, MA 01701 or call (508) 626-8644.
>Bi-weekly, $39 per year subscription.

National Council News
>National Council of Community Mental Health Centers, Suite 320, 12300 Twinbrook Parkway, Rockville, MD 20852 or call (301) 984-6200.
>Monthly available to non-members for $21 annual subscription.

CHAPTER 18:

Casework in a Group Home

by *Linda Nelson**

To get a professional position in a psychiatric or human services setting you not only need required educational qualifications but also experience. Obviously, an internship helps but, one of the main ways to gain experience is through jobs as direct care caseworkers. Because they are low-paying and routine, such jobs are relatively easy to come by. If you pick up the classified section of any newspaper, most likely one or more will be advertised at any time. These jobs can be with any type of problem population such as substance abusers, sex offenders, juvenile delinquents, mentally ill or the elderly. They seem to be the most frequent entry-level jobs for people who later go on to mental health care or institutional care. From my personal experience and that of my past and current co-workers, these jobs vary vastly from generalized care to more specialized therapies. Caseworker positions can also occur in independent living situations where the client lives alone in an apartment or house.

The job advertisement I answered said, "case worker, brain trauma." No specific requirements were listed. I filled out an application and was called for an interview. The supervisor who interviewed me said the company was looking for people who were "caring and client-oriented," but admitted that sometimes he was snowed by applicants who were only looking for a paycheck (the job paid basically minimum wage!). The company hired college students—psychology, social work, and nursing majors mostly. I had just graduated from a New Jersey college and entered a master's program in psychology but had no experience in the mental health field and this seemed as good a place to start as any.

The interview was pretty ordinary except for the unusual environment in which it was conducted. The office was in the basement of a house that had packaged food, cleaning equipment, and disorganized piles of paper everywhere. Being used to such chaos, I hoped the mess was a sign of creativity. I also noticed several animals roaming through the

*This is a fictional name used at the request of the author.

149

house and inquired about them. I was told that the clients were allowed to bring their pets with them and that other animals were part of the environment. This was especially encouraging, as I had read several articles about the benefits of pet therapy.

In order to get to the office—"the inner sanctum of the operation"—one entered the side of a house through a kitchen, passed by a couple of friendly inquisitive dogs and went through a child-gate down steps, through a furnace room, past piles of accumulated "heaven knows what" stuff, into a large room piled everywhere with papers. The interview itself was pleasant and positive, though full of distractions and interruptions from ringing phones, and staff discussions and queries. I did not seem to be the main event of my interview.

After many phone calls I was called in for a final interview. The person doing this interview was beginning her first day in a supervisory capacity. She needed much instruction and didn't actually interview me. I **concluded** that I had been hired when I was asked to fill out the necessary paperwork and sent for a physical and TB test. Only being prepared for an interview rather than my first day of work, I was a little surprised. After my physical, the company wanted me to come back and begin work. I was given several articles to study regarding closed head injury. There was never any formal job training.

Caseworkers in group homes can be required to do a wide variety of things from feeding, bathing, dressing and catheterizing clients, to transportation, shopping, laundering, cooking, housecleaning, dispensing medications and providing physical therapy. The list is endless.

My first assignment was not in a group home but an apartment setting where I was to watch a male client, document occurrences, dispense medication, and act as his chauffeur—basically baby-sitting an adult. But this was not just any adult. At the time I was hired, I assumed the client would be high-functioning and near recovery. This case seemed, at first, to fit that category. After all, he lived in his own apartment rather than in a group home. I later discovered that some clients are placed in independent living situations **primarily** because insurance funding is available and/or the client is unable to cope with group home life. In the event that a client is so lacking in self-control that they are continually involved in conflict with other group home members, separating them can solve the problem or create new ones; not the least of which is endangering the life of the caseworker. The particular client to whom I was assigned, I later discovered, was gay, extremely manipulative, unpredictable, uncooperative, and demanding, had drug and alcohol problems, and was violent as well. He had physically assaulted nearly all of his previous caseworkers. At another of my assignments a client who was closed head injured, as well as schizophrenic, had repeatedly beaten his mother and sister who refused to let him live with them afterward. The client was furious with them and, because of his lack of insight, was incapable of associating the beatings with their refusals, and repeatedly demanded that they let him come live with them.

Rather than these being exceptional cases that I was unlucky enough to encounter in my first psych job, it turned out that many of these clients were similar multiple problem sufferers. Part of the reason for this has to do with the nature of the injury itself. Persons with brain trauma injuries have low tolerance for frustration and their physical, as well as mental abilities, are often impaired. Part of the tragedy of closed head injury has to do with the profile of the type of person who suffers brain trauma. I was told by an administrator of a hospital closed head trauma unit, that the "typical profile" of a client was "male, 20s-30s and reckless." Risk-taking is often what precipitates the accident itself and most victims are the result of car accidents. The next time you're on the road and a young male passes your car, narrowly missing the vehicle oncoming in the opposite lane, you are probably looking at a future victim of closed head injury. I made the, perhaps biased, observation that the clients seem to retain their original personalities in spite of their injuries and that the easygoing likable characters were always that way, much like we read that older adults retain much of their earlier outlook on life after senility sets in. Others are devious, uncaring, unlikable and violent.

After a short time I discovered, from reading the case histories of the clients at my particular group home, that they all had physical or mental disabilities **prior** to becoming closed head injured; schizophrenia, mental retardation, personality disorder, post-traumatic stress, alcoholism, drug addiction etc. Many were also violent and seemed prone to outbursts of temper and rage. After being at the group home a while longer I discovered that nearly every worker had, at one time or another, been physically assaulted by one of the group home's clients. One worker told me that she had been beaten for 45 minutes by a client while outdoors and unable to get help. She suffered a fractured arm and massive bruises all over her body. She admitted that she knew she could have sued but chose not to. Instead she kept the job and faced the ever-present possibility of it happening again. This was encouraged by the employer's attitude that violence only occurred because the employee didn't handle the situation adequately, filling the employee with self-doubt and a sense of guilt. I'm sure violence is not a common factor in all group homes but unless the clients are properly screened and suitable for group home living, what you may be facing is the same situation. I have a friend who worked for another company who cared for closed head injured clients whose experience was much more positive than mine. The best advice I can give is to be aware of these difficulties and be ready to change jobs if the situation looks too dangerous.

What I enjoyed most about this job was the one-on-one interaction. When there was spare time, I was able to work with clients on different therapeutic activities. Some clients are able to complete only the simplest of tasks with much help from the caseworker, but the energy expended was worthwhile. For instance, a client in her 50s, with mental retardation and physical disabilities, made an angel food cake with me. After lots of direction and physical assistance, the cake went into the oven. The client got enormous pleasure and sense of achievement from the experience and talked about it for days afterward. Another time, several members of the group home and myself all planted seeds indoors for the backyard garden. The clients couldn't wait to see them sprout and patiently watched and watered them. A male client who was severely affected by his closed head injury had such a poor memory span that he didn't know if he had or hadn't eaten a meal nor could he remember anyone's name or the date. All day long he would repeatedly ask my name and repeat the same phrases over and over. He was partially paralyzed and was able to use only one hand and leg. I assisted him with a "tissue collage," showing him how to apply the paper and use the paint brush. Giving him an assortment of colors, I asked him to choose which ones he wanted to use. He chose only three. We proceeded to work. Each time I asked where he wanted the tissue, he decided, then I helped him glue it in place. The client gave the collage to his sister when she came to visit. The next week she came again and was talking about the collage her brother had made when he walked into the room, heard us talking, and said "I made that." We were both stunned.

One topic that became a major issue for me in the group home setting was drug use by both employees and clients, and sometimes together. Many group homes randomly screen their employees for drugs. Two of my co-workers showed positive on their tests and were asked to leave.

One worker actually acted as a go-between for clients and drug suppliers. This was highly irresponsible, not to mention illegal, since these clients were already prone to unpredictable violence. Depending upon what drugs were taken in conjunction with their prescribed medications, death could have easily resulted. While I was at the apartment assignment, my client's roommate slashed his wrists in an alcohol-related suicide attempt. We were left to clear the blood-soaked sheets.

Most of these group-home jobs pay just above minimum wage. Some more reputable places pay about $7 per hour. Because the pay is so low (mine was about $5.50 an hour) and the work so stressful, employee absenteeism is high. Lots of caseworkers pull double shifts to make extra money and to fill in for absent co-workers. When you're the only caseworker in a group home and responsible for 3-6 clients, and your relief worker calls in sick, there isn't really anyone to cover. When this happens the pressure may be high to work a 16 hour shift.

I stayed in this job for 6 months. Toward the end of my first assignment I asked for a transfer to another location where I worked for about a month. When I quit I gave only a weeks notice, which I considered short. However, some employees actually quit after their first day at work. The longest anyone ever worked there that I know of was two years. Usually the reason the caseworkers stayed on the job that long was because they were students and trying to get experience for future employment after graduation. Also, the company didn't discourage studying on the job. While I was employed there I was able to do homework, study for tests and write papers. Quiet time starts between 6 and 9 pm and you could get a lot done. Food is free for lots of group home workers. They either help the clients prepare meals or cook it themselves and are expected to eat with the clients. Although the pay is possibly lower than McDonald's, the perks of free food, studying while at work and getting job experience, make casework attractive employment for nursing and psych students.

On the negative side, as I have said, violence among certain populations is common. Anyone entertaining the idea of working with them should carefully investigate the safety measures employed by the employer! Room searches often reveal concealed weapons. At the group home a schizophrenic client concealed steak knives, bottles and rocks. When confronted with a hidden fork and questioned about what he planned to do with it, he said he planned to use it to poke out the eyes of another client.

As I previously mentioned, the casework experiences of many of my current co-workers have been far more positive than my own. In fact, some now employed in professional positions have related that they miss their old caseworker jobs and actually would return to them if their salary were not an issue.

CHAPTER 19:

Psychiatric Social Work

by *Carolyn R. McGillis*

Had I known when I started college it was going to take me 12 years to complete undergraduate and graduate school I probably would have not accepted the challenge. Moreover, when I decided to pursue a master's of social work (MSW), being employed as a psychiatric social worker was not in my repertoire of professional expectations.

Getting there
I decided to start college in my early thirties. I was a full-time mom with three children in elementary school. I felt there had to be more. However, I wasn't quite sure what "more" was suppose to be. I had been out of school for fifteen years so I applied to a junior college and began with easy classes. Four years passed before I completed junior college with an associate's degree in liberal arts, and this was followed by several interruptions before I attained my bachelor's in social work (BSW) and eventually my MSW.

A BSW and MSW are two degrees that can be applied in many areas. A BSW has career limitations which include a ceiling on pay, and job restrictions due to a need for continued education. However, with a BSW, an MSW can be obtained in ten months of full-time study through an Advanced Standing Program at an accredited college; otherwise it will take two years to complete the program. Currently, in my state there are three colleges with this accreditation. I applied for and was accepted by an Advanced Standing Program in one of these.

At the master's level the employment field is wide open. The main career directions include: social work with legal offenders, psychiatric social workers, therapists, counselors, school social workers, working with an EAP (Employee Assistant Program), medical social work, social work community mental health, and several more.

By the time I graduated with an MSW in 1989, I had obtained my ACC. I had also acquired credentials to qualify as a school social worker, and had numerous experiences through my internships at the BSW and MSW level. By this time money was the name of the game. I

155

was now single and my livelihood was at stake. One month after I graduated I had three job offers. Unfortunately, the pay was poor; tops $21,000. I was angry and insulted. With a master's, $21,000? Forget it! Fortunately, within a week I was offered a position as a psychiatric social worker in a hospital setting with a reasonable rate of pay and good benefits. I grabbed it, knowing it would be on-the-job training and a new learning experience. I stayed in that position for one and a half years, then moved to another hospital with an increase in pay. I am in that position currently.

My clients/patients

Many of the mentally ill are indigent—without housing, money or clothes. Others are linked to community mental health agencies and many live on the streets. I work with those who have been in prison, others may be on parole or probation and yet others are substance abusers. I work with people who are diagnosed as having chronic schizophrenia, manic-depression, major depression, substance abuse, personality disorders and several others. Their symptoms may include being delusional, hyper-verbal, agitated, physically aggressive, extremely depressed, sexually preoccupied, religiously preoccupied, and nothing if not unpredictable. I have been trained in physical management to protect myself should the need arise, however, it is a rule of thumb not to let your guard down because you do not know when a patient could strike out. Fortunately, I have never found myself in this situation. However, when I sense there is the potential I will initiate skills I have learned in physical management.

The legal framework governing my job

The expectations for my position are governed by law that is spelled out in the state Mental Health Code. These guidelines have been written to protect the mentally ill. Years ago a patient could be "committed" for lengthy periods of time with no legislation to protect them. The Mental Health Code specifies that I have to meet with a patient within 24 hours of hospitalization and have to complete a Comprehensive Social History within 72 hours of admission. This time-frame may sound insignificant but an eight hour day is never long enough to complete my work. Due to budget cuts in our state, the length of hospitalization has decreased, and demands and expectations of my role have increased, resulting in my days being frantic.

Ninety percent of the patients at my facility have been screened at a crisis center or an emergency room of another hospital before admission to our facility. They arrive at our facility with a "petition" and physician certificate (PC I) which makes them involuntary admissions. A petition is a legal document requesting hospitalization. It describes observed inappropriate behavior of the patient that justifies the need for hospitalization. A petition may be completed by a family member, police officer or a social worker from a community mental health agency (anyone can complete a petition). A PC I is a legal document which is completed by a psychiatrist, after the petition is completed, which substantiates the need for hospitalization. These two legal documents accompany the patient to the hospital. The petition and PC I are further examples of specific procedures defined in the Mental Health Code. If the psychiatrist does not feel a person needs to be hospitalized, the petition becomes invalid and the person is sent home.

When persons are admitted they may sign in voluntarily. This means they have acknowledged their need for treatment or, if they feel that they do not need to be hospitalized but the psychiatrist does, the psychiatrist then completes a PC II and these three legal documents (petition, PC I and PC II) are taken to court. The person has a court appointed attorney and a hearing is scheduled within the next seven days. In most cases, during this period, the patient is not on medication. The petitioner is subpoenaed to testify at the hearing. Ninety-nine percent of the time the judge will issue an order for 30 days of hospitalization for the patient.

I have been a petitioner and have been subpoenaed to court. When a voluntary patient has not stabilized in 30 days they are transferred to a state facility for long term treatment. Numerous times I have been the petitioner in these cases, resulting in me being subpoenaed to testify. With these particular cases (state transfers) there is a Petition Log on our unit and we rotate disciplines (Nursing, Social Work and Rehab), with each unit taking responsibility for the petition.

When you are subpoenaed you can plan on spending at least three hours in court, time which is not there to spare. I have also been subpoenaed to court in child custody cases involving my patients or when I have had to notify Child Protective Services when neglect and abuse was suspect.

My job
My main objective as a psychiatric social worker is discharge planning.
As a discharge planner I spend my day planning and preparing for the
impending discharge of a patient into the community. I have numerous
resources to assist me in this preparation which include Adult Foster
Care Homes (AFC Homes) and Residential Care Alternatives Homes
(RCA Homes). They provide a more structured living environment.
There are also Community Mental Health (CMH) agencies for those who
are returning home and Assertive Community Treatment (ACT
Program), which is part of a CMH designed for those who are able to
live independently. ACT staff will go to a person's home several times
a week, if necessary, to make sure they are doing well and taking their
medication. Their goal is to keep their clients out of the hospital. There
is also a Fairweather Program, which is a home for the mentally ill that
is managed by the residents. Partial Day Programs are similar to
hospitalization except the patient resides at home or an AFC Home and
returns daily to the day program. There are several other resources for
substance abusers and battered women; and support groups for
schizophrenics, manic-depressives and many more, all of which I utilize
for discharge planning.

Every morning I plan my day. However, within an hour everything
changes. I roll with the punches and start to prioritize my day. I have a
caseload of 11 or 12 patients at all times. A typical day may begin with
three new patients being assigned along with two discharges. I have had
as many as five new patients in one day, all with needs. Some may be
manic and demanding while others are completely confused. Suddenly,
the long-term application that was filed five days ago at the Mental
Health Board has been approved for a patient to be transferred to a state
facility and the wheels begin to turn. I now change my priorities. My
new patients are on hold and I begin to facilitate the transfer. A "packet"
(admission   summary,   history   and   physical,   lab   reports   and
comprehensive social history) needs to be copied for the state facility. A
petition and PC I need to be completed, transportation needs to be
arranged, and the family needs to be informed of the transfer. Now, one
of my discharges decides he is not going to return to the AFC Home
today. One week ago I called in the referral, copied a packet and he was
interviewed by an agency who has a contract with the Mental Health
Board to locate an AFC home with a room available. As a result of his
refusal all my work may be going down the tubes. I have two options

here: try to talk him into returning to the home or he can be discharged to a shelter. You have to remember, the patients have rights. If he is not harmful to himself or others, he has the right to change his mind and go to shelter if he wishes. Unfortunately, this does happen. Meanwhile, one of my new admissions is a substance abuser and the doctor feels he does not warrant hospitalization. He is to be discharged immediately. I have to put together a discharge plan and will refer this person to a substance abuse program. A patient cannot leave the hospital without a plan. Most of the patients are discharged with a month's supply of medication and I make an appointment at a community mental health agency in their area.

By this time (my new patients are still on hold) I have received phone calls regarding other patients and family members of my new patients are beginning to call. However, I cannot talk to them due to the laws of confidentially. A patient has to sign a Release of Information form that grants me permission to contact those who have called. In some cases, the patient will not sign a Release, resulting in irate family members. But, once again, the patient has rights.

If my day settles down, I can now begin to interview my new patients and dictate their comprehensive social history. I begin making contact, depending on the case, with family members, probation officers, parole officers, therapists, community mental health agencies, and AFC providers, in an attempt to get a complete picture of the patient in order that I can begin discharge planning. In many cases families will not allow the patient to return home and some patients have legal guardians who need to send me a copy of guardianship papers along with signing all legal documents in the chart. There are also patients who need legal guardians, so I make the recommendations to the family to begin that process. I also meet with family members, CMH liaisons, parole officers, members of the ACT team, and many more.

Weekly, for one and a half hours, I meet with the other specialized disciplines who are on my team. We complete treatment plans and discuss each patient. Four times a week I do group therapy. This is the only part of my position that I dislike. Not because I do not like doing group therapy but because I do not have the time either to do it or to adequately prepare a group session. To me it is an added burden because I have so many other priorities. However, group therapy is good for the patients. The focus for group may change daily depending on the severity of illness for each patient.

The unwritten qualifications

Being a psychiatric social worker is definitely a high stress job but I have learned to keep my job where it belongs, at the hospital. Anyone who would consider this position needs to be able to work independently and be well-organized with the ability to change plans at any given moment. If you have any bias against the mentally ill, former prisoners, or substance abusers, this position is not for you. You need patience, the innate ability not to personalize being called every name in the book, and understanding for those who are confused, delusional, paranoid and afraid. In addition you need the capability of acknowledging when you are burned out, and the determination to do something about it. With all the upheavals in the work force and the restructuring of employment that has occurred in recent years, I do not believe this is the time to be changing positions, unless there is a lot of security in your next position. However, to be aware of your own limitations and the emerging possibilities for the future is a necessary survival tactic for the present.

CHAPTER 20:

Recreational/Art Therapy with Mentally Ill Offenders in a Psychiatric Setting

by *Lee Doric-Henry*

I work at a psychiatric hospital in the Detroit area as a recreation/art therapist. My educational background is a bachelor's in art with a teaching certificate, K-12. At the time I obtained the job, I had completed half of a three year master's degree in art therapy, and had 17 years retail experience! At college I had taken many psychology courses and had always been interested in the area. Art therapy was the ideal career in which to combine my interests. Unfortunately, I didn't discover it until 1990 and by then I had been considerably side-tracked. After college I owned a retail store for ten years and worked in retail sales for seven years following that.

With this background, obtaining my current position was difficult. I had applied for several jobs in the mental health/juvenile delinquency area, but was not successful. The application for this particular job started out as just another "possibility" in the newspaper's Help Wanted section. When I read the ad for a Recreation Therapist, I thought it was worth an application so I sent a resume from my resume kit.[1] Since I had not yet even completed an internship, had never worked in the field, and had no contacts, networking wasn't a possibility for me.[2]

I was invited to an interview and didn't really know what to expect. I went prepared to tell them about my teaching and art therapy background, art and crafts experience, and willingness to do physical

---

[1] This is a portable case where I keep copies of my resume, letters of reference, envelopes, stamps and copies of each application letter I have sent to potential employers, together with their replies. Having all these things in one place really helps.

[2] Now that I am in mental health care, I've actually seen a full-time position advertised for our department and filled by the sole applicant (also from our department). No one except an employee or their network contact could have possibly gotten this job. So knowing someone "in the business" certainly can't hurt!

recreation with patients. I brought samples of art work I thought relevant to the hospital's population, notes I had compiled from my student observation at another psychiatric hospital, and photographs of a project that I had developed for older adults as part of my master's program. The interview, with a three person panel, went extremely well. A few weeks later I received a phone call in which I was told that they were offering me the job. I still didn't really know what I would be doing and what exactly was expected of me. Sometime later I found out that there had been many applicants for the job who were better qualified regarding their degrees but the judgement was made that I would be best suited to the work in spite of my lack of experience. I later also discovered that the job offer had been turned down by several applicants, most likely due to the population, pay, or personal reasons. The population was largely schizophrenic, the pay about $13 an hour, and the time schedule evenings and weekends.

The work I do is group therapy, mostly with mood disorder and schizophrenic patients, although I also work with substance abusers. Our hospital doesn't allow its therapists to specialize in their own discipline but has them conduct the same kinds of groups on each unit. I run groups on initial orientation, occupational therapy (O.T.) workshops, leisure education, group games, cooking, art and crafts, exercise, and recreation. Our department places lots of emphasis on the positive use of leisure time. So far, I've been at the job for eight months; working part time while going to school. I'd estimate that the average stay for therapists in my department is about three years.

Our patients/clients

Most of the clients we see at our hospital are involuntarily committed. The police are called to a scene where a person is displaying violent or bizarre, uncontrollable behavior. Often the relatives or friends have to make the call and later are blamed by the patient as responsible for their hospitalization. Sometimes the patients threaten these same people by phone or in person when they come to visit. We see many "repeaters" (patients with a history of multiple hospitalizations). The primary reason they return is that they stop taking their medications because they don't like its side-effects.

When they come to us, they're often hallucinating and need physical restraints and medication. For days they lay in their rooms or pace the halls in an agitated frenzy, responding to internal stimuli until their medications begin to take affect. When the patient is in this state, they're often a threat to themselves, the other patients and the staff.

Many of the patients I see have a past prison record, are currently on parole, or face future incarceration due to features of their illness such as poor impulse control, lack of insight and a tendency toward violent behavior. Of the general prison population, a staggering 25% are reported to suffer mental illness of one kind or another. Schizophrenia is high on the list. It's not surprising then that a portion of our clients are from this population. One of my patients was admitted directly from jail where he had attempted to hang himself in his cell. Currently I have a patient who is in his early thirties and has been released after serving a sentence for murder and another who was formerly convicted of rape. Some patients boast about "doing time" while others have expressed fear that their lack of control may result in them going to jail someday.

We deal with a variety of psychiatric illnesses that afflict a wide range of people of varying education, income, and socialization skills. Some are middle class, college educated and employed, while others are lower class, illiterate, unemployed and homeless. Those with jobs often suffer added anxiety about whether their jobs will be held open for them while they are hospitalized. Some of the patients, especially "first timers," are worried that co-workers, friends and family will think they're "crazy". Often coupled with the mental illness are drug and alcohol dependency. Then, of course, we have developmentally disabled and physically impaired patients. And let's not omit the aged.

I've also worked with patients who were extremely high-functioning. One was a male in his early twenties. The staff all agreed that he did not exhibit overt signs of mental illness. It appeared that, because he was from another culture and seen by his family as acting deviant, the family sought to have him committed to a psychiatric hospital, using this as a control measure. The psychiatrist may have been convinced by the family as well. Dealing with all these different types of patients on a daily basis takes a lot out of all of the staff members.

Working with patients
Hospitals operate 24 hours a day. The morning shift is the most hectic. Patients receive their medications, doctor consultations, breakfast and lunch, and the majority of their therapy sessions during this time. The afternoon shift is a little more laid back and the evening shift is the

quietest. Nurses and "psych techs"[3] attend to the patient's needs and are perpetually pelted with requests, demands, condemnation and harassment by them. Therapists, in contrast, have limited contact with the patients. Therapy in a psychiatric hospital entails about 75% paperwork and meetings versus about 25% actual patient contact. Out of a normal 40-hour week, therapists conduct an average of twelve, 50-minute therapy sessions, i.e. 10 hours therapy compared with 30 hours of meetings and documentation. Therapists, nurses, psychiatrists and social workers all interact in ITP's (Interdisciplinary Treatment Plans) where the patient's treatment progress and discharge plans are discussed. These meetings can be meaningful, useful, and of great benefit to the patient, or they can be mere rubber stamping, paper shoving sessions. I see both things happen at my hospital.

The therapy I do consists of running groups of clients/patients who are encouraged to focus on certain pre-designed activities that reaffirm their connection to the real world and also increase their self-esteem. These projects may range from simple recreational games such as Pictionary or indoor croquet to therapeutic art projects. We've made calendar collages, paper mache piggy banks and handmade Easter cards. I've run percussion music groups and put together activities like "Mystery Motown Music," a name-that-tune program. I run one therapy session about leisure education in which the clients are asked to describe a trip or vacation that was a positive experience and to trace their travel route on a map for the rest of the group to see. The group interacts with questions and comments and, in the process, the presenter's status is transformed from "mental patient" to "traveller," in their own and others' eyes. Patients have fascinated their groups with accounts of travels to such places as Alaska, Egypt, the Bahamas, as well as to local theme parks. On one occasion we were aghast by a patient's account of a drug run to Florida!

In an art therapy exercise the patients were asked to write a word that had special significance to them on the top of a piece of blank paper. The papers were then shuffled and a different patient was asked to draw a picture of the word on the paper. The papers were shuffled again and a

---

[3] These are usually undergraduate psychology or social work students who are employed to check on patients regularly and to provide "technical" i.e. physical restraint in cases where patients become out of control.

third patient was asked to write a story about the picture and word, which could either be true, or a complete fabrication. After everyone had written their stories they were each asked to read them to the group, who had to decide whether the story was true or not. Some of the patients were revealed to be fabulous fakers and fooled us all. Others wrote soulful poetic stories that left the group in awe. After the discussion of each story, the writer of the word and the drawer of the picture describe what they originally had in mind. For schizophrenic and chronically depressed patients this exercise gave them a focus outside of themselves and an opportunity to display original and creative thoughts.

I personally have a great deal of difficulty with the extent to which there can be carry-over from our hospital-run groups to the patient's life after discharge. Trying to put together activities in which a client will realistically engage after he or she leaves the hospital is tough. With art projects, I try to stick to ordinary, easily obtainable materials so the patient can replicate a project at home. At the same time, the activities themselves have to be considered "adult." Last weekend I was thoroughly chewed out by a man who was going to be sent to an AFC (Adult Foster Care) home because I ran a weekend activity of Pictionary. He said it was childish and angrily refused to attend the group. He demanded that he be allowed to go to the O.T. workshop to make a leather bracelet instead. The patients who attended the Pictionary group enjoyed it and didn't think it was childish at all. One thing I've learned in this business is that it's nearly impossible to please all of the patients all of the time.

Then there is the daily struggle of discharge plans. The patients need somewhere to go. Lots of families refuse to have the patient come back home to live with them. Often the best that can be done is a homeless shelter or an AFC group home. Patients have discussed AFC (Adult Foster Care) homes with me. Some like them and others do not. The chief complaint is that the homes receive the resident's support checks and dole the money out to them rather than the resident receiving it in one lump sum. Patients with poor insight and substance abuse problems don't seem to like this and try to stay out of this housing which presents the hospital team with a dilemma of where to place them.

Depending on the particular program in which you are employed, the hours of patient contact can vary drastically. One of my patients recently told me about a drug rehab clinic he had attended in Florida where the clients were involved in therapy sessions all day long, 7 days a week.

Also, a nursing home where I interviewed recently described a rigorous schedule of sessions for their clients. When the interviewer told me the residents went to bed early, I wasn't surprised. Their elderly clients must be pooped after all those activities and therapy sessions. Our hospital recently changed over to seven-day programming, meaning that therapists will be conducting sessions on weekends. Many mental health facilities offer programs only five days a week which allows the patients to vegetate for two days. A large facility which keeps patients on a long-term basis nearby, offers their patients practically nothing in the way of therapy.

Tension, stress and coping
The nature of our population does not readily lend itself to a peaceful work setting. These people are here because they have mental illnesses that disrupt their own lives and the lives of others. Those that also have tendencies to violence and intimidation do not simply stop behaving that way just because they are committed. This necessarily affects the way we work. Whenever especially violent or disturbed patients are in close proximity, the staff member has to switch to hyper-vigilance. Anything said or done could be interpreted negatively by the patient. At times, the mere appearance of staff could trigger an aggressive response. A nurse told me about a client who saw her from the other side of a room and rushed toward her and pulled a patch of hair out of her head. The patient had hallucinated that the nurse was the woman who had stolen her husband. Sometimes the patient will be responding to internal stimuli which tells them to harm someone. When working with patients who are this unpredictable, we have to constantly check our surroundings and be aware of any possible danger.

People cope with these stressors in different ways. The therapist has to decide whether he or she wants to expend maximum or minimum energy. I've seen employees range from sleeping on the job to going far beyond the call of duty, putting in considerable preparation, research and their own money for one hour sessions that may or may not be a success.

Another frustration is that there is little or no time available for the therapists to develop many new activities for the clients. Being part-time, and having started a new job area, I've found that I had to drop school courses in order to keep up with the job demands. Each new activity takes somewhere between one evening to days of hunting down materials, testing methods, making samples, and timing projects. Safety and success are key issues in all the projects I develop for clients.

When working with schizophrenic, paranoid, and depressed patients, the therapist must constantly be on guard lest they manage to harm themselves or each other with the implements and material you've provided. Our hospital is under severe safety measures. Even blunt children's scissors must be monitored carefully. Last week a client came to me saying he knew where something was hidden that could be used as a weapon. It turned out to be a heavy steel curved door handle that a patient had managed to remove from a shower door.

Another important source of stress for therapists is race and ethnicity. Most of the therapists are white middle class females age 24-45. The patients, in our hospital, tend to be disproportionately young African-American males; roughly 1/3 of our census is African-American. At first I found myself extremely sensitive to this issue. Often, a patient I didn't know would pass by and hurl racial and sexual insults and intimidations. Race and class were often used as a manipulative device by the clients. When I started the job, I was extremely intimidated. As time went by, and I worked with the clients, they became more open to me and vice versa, especially those undergoing their second or third hospitalization. It took about three months to adjust to the setting and its patients. I have found that after eight months of working with this population, although the tension hasn't lessened, I'm able to cope with it better.

An additional fear for those working in the mental health field is exposure to HIV positive individuals. A few weeks ago, a fellow therapist was bitten by a patient with a history of drug abuse, and had to go through the anxiety and terror of HIV infection. Other patients who have tested HIV positive and are schizophrenic are especially worrisome given that their behavior is sometimes uncontrolled. A patient recently spit in a nurse's face and while we know that HIV is not transmitted from saliva, to experience this behavior still produces stress.

Very soon after they start, many co-workers make comments about wanting to get out of our in-patient psychiatric setting and into something less stressful. Absenteeism may be one way that some staff cope. Unfortunately, this makes it rough for the remaining staff who are expected to cover for the missing employees. Staff who regularly and systematically call in sick wear everyone out, forcing people to work overtime, which in turn makes people physically ill, emotionally exhausted and more likely to call in sick and keep the cycle going. It's hard to say no sometimes but you must keep things in focus and décide just how much you're willing to give. Then you must stick to your decision or you will be the next one calling in sick.

Some employees get by with as little as possible; sleeping, eating, reading, or gossiping the time away while others go out of their way to help patients and do excellent jobs. Unless you really screw up, you can choose your own method of survival.

Satisfaction and dissatisfactions
I enjoy the challenge of my current job but always feel that I need more time and budget allowance to give the clients what they really need. Clients often go out the door when no one but the insurance companies feel they're ready to go. Some days I come home exhausted and totally drained but feeling good about the work I've done and about the noticeable advances the patients have made. Other times, when the patients are extremely violent, uncooperative, angry, or completely unreachable, I leave feeling very unsettled.

Nothing about my work in mental health has been boring. It's been interesting, dangerous, exciting, exasperating, sad, creative, rewarding, and sometimes even fun, but never boring.

An ongoing frustration is that we spend more time on administration and staff meetings than with the clients. Every time I hear about the shrinking health care dollar I think of where our funds are going....into big boxes of paper. We've got rooms full of the stuff—sometimes it spills over into the hallways.

The most discouraging part of my job is what's called "decompensation." Sometimes, within a period of a few days, a patient who has been making progress takes a drastic turn for the worse. The change is so remarkable and devastating the patient seems to be someone else.

My greatest dislike is the violence. Nothing can prepare you adequately for the intimidation and terror. Eventually you begin to identify similarities in the clients' patterns of intimidation and manipulation. After the first few terrifying clients you begin to say to yourself "he or she's doing.....just like Fred/Wanda." You step outside yourself and analyze the situation. You get to a point where the whole bizarre sideshow is manageable but never enjoyable.

Prospects

Since I am only two-thirds finished with my master's program, my current job prospects are not fabulous. The best prospect of getting a better job would be to apply for another position within the same or another health care network and this time aim for a different population in order to get more experience. Within our system there are jobs dealing with outpatient drug dependency, schizophrenia, and older adult care. Right now in the Detroit area, judging from job ads, there seems to be a big demand for Occupational Therapists, especially ones with master's degrees. They even offer $4000 sign-on bonuses. However, this is now. Four years from now OTs might be in the over-supply dilemma teachers have faced.

When I finish my master's degree I need additional experience in order to qualify for my ATR (Registered Art Therapist). Although a board exam is not required after completing their master's, art therapists must complete an additional 1000 hours paid, and 500 hours unpaid experience to receive their ATR certification. With this completed several possibilities are open. The Veterans' Administration has civil service jobs for ATRs, and hospitals, nursing homes, schools, prisons, and clinics, etc., have occasional openings. Art therapists employed in schools often deal with child abuse issues. Right now jobs for art therapists are scarce and many art therapists are forced into taking other positions usually held by OTs or RTs. Others may create their own jobs by joining an organization where several therapies are offered within the same network.

Recently I was asked to substitute for a full-time therapist on the staff and I found the experience enlightening. Working full-time, the therapist has much more contact with the patients and sees them on a regular basis. I found it was much easier to establish a rapport, to elicit cooperation, and to make therapeutic progress than when working in a part-time, primarily weekend position. In fact the experience was so rewarding that I changed my mind about working with this population after I graduate from my master's program.

SECTION SEVEN:
GRADUATE SCHOOL, ACADEMICS,
AND RESEARCH

What can you do with a graduate degree in criminal justice? The short answer to this question is anything that you can do with an undergraduate degree in criminal justice, and usually for more money. There are several basic reasons students pursue a graduate school education in criminal justice. One reason is that, as current practitioners they desire promotion or salary increases or, very occasionally they may develop a need to more deeply explore and analyze the nature of their work. Another reason is that they want to go on to do research or to teach at a college or university. Here we are concerned with the latter group.

It is virtually impossible to teach full-time in college without first obtaining a higher degree; a master's or a doctorate. The exception is the practitioner who is hired part-time to teach one or two classes based upon his or her life experience in a specialized field e.g. a public defender or a police officer. Likewise, without the specialized knowledge afforded by a higher degree, it is unlikely that you will be hired as a research worker. You can obtain positions such as a data entry clerk, transcriber, data processor or interviewer with no more than an undergraduate degree, but these are often "gofer" positions for the researcher. To be a college professor or full-time researcher requires an MA, MS and/or a Ph.D. Those who successfully graduate from higher education in criminal justice either apply to colleges' Departments of Criminal Justice, Criminology, Sociology or Political Science, or else they obtain work on a private or government research grant or contract. These two areas of work involve some similar tasks.

The college professor and the academic research business
Most undergraduate students have a restricted view of what a college professor of criminal justice does. They see the in-class teaching and student advising and can imagine the out-of-class grading and teaching preparation (roughly three hours for every one spent in the classroom). What they do not see is the hidden aspects of the job. For many university professors, especially at major research schools, two

171

1 ACADEMICS AND RESEARCH
Typical Ads

ASSISTANT PROFESSOR OF CRIMINOLOGY: Eastern State University. **Job Description:** Tenure-track asst. professor to teach police and society, criminology, criminal law or corrections. **Qualifications:** Ph.D. in sociology, criminology or criminal justice. Candidates should be generalists with the potential for scholarly research. **Inquiries:** Send vita and three letters of reference.

ASSISTANT PROFESSOR OF CRIMINAL JUSTICE: Southern International University. **Job Description:** Tenure-track asst. professor to teach justice system and criminal justice policy. **Qualifications:** Ph.D. or ABD acceptable. **Inquiries:** Send statement of how you would teach these classes with application, curriculum vita, college transcripts and three letters of reference.

ASSISTANT/ASSOCIATE PROFESSOR: Central College. **Job Description:** To teach police and private security in our administration of justice program. **Qualifications:** MA or doctorate. Some previous teaching experience. **Salary:** $27,000-$36,000 for 9-month contract, depending upon

experience. Send three letters of reference and vita.

RESEARCH COORDINATOR: Minneapolis, MN. **Job Description:** Train, supervise, and direct research assistants. **Qualifications:** BA in social science, allied health, or nursing; knowledge of basic statistics and computers. **Inquiries:** Send resume.

RESEARCH ASSISTANT: Cincinnati, OH. **Job Description:** Collection of sociomedical research data. **Inquiries:** Send resume.

EVALUATION ASSISTANT: Detroit, MI. **Job Description:** Statistical research and analysis for substance abuse agency. **Qualifications:** BA, Lotus, Wordstar, statistical ability and writing skills.

DIVISION CHAIR FOR CRIMINAL JUSTICE: Central City Community College. **Job Description:** Teaching, administration and curriculum development. **Qualifications:** MA in criminal justice or social sciences. Community college teaching experience. **Salary:** $43,754-$50,853 depending upon experience.

172

dimensions of the job are paramount in consuming their time and polar opposite in terms of job satisfaction. These are administration and research.

It is the rare academic who likes administration—those who do typically go on to become department chairs or heads. They may eventually make the "dirty switch" to become deans, provosts, vice presidents, and occasionally, college presidents. For the typical criminal justice academic, however, administration means committee assignments, meetings that lead to more meetings, memo-writing, reports and evaluations, politics, arguments and, generally, wasted time and energy in battling with other people's egos. If given the choice, most criminal justice faculty would gladly drop all administration. Some do anyway.

The real substantive meat of the criminal justice professor's business is conducting research and publishing the results. The research may be on some crime problem, such as serial murder, or why corporations defraud their consumers, or on how aspects of the criminal justice system operate, e.g. how effective is community policing at reducing the fear of crime in urban areas? Either type of research involves various kinds of data gathering ranging from participating in situations where the action is occurring, to interviewing subjects through surveying populations and examining varieties of documentary data and government reports. With a problem narrowly formulated, and relevant data gathered, it is the task of the criminology or criminal justice professor to analyze the findings and interpret and report the results. If you do not like writing papers this could prove to be a problem, since much of the criminal justice professor's work involves some kind of writing for publication and, at the very least, writing papers for presentation at professional conferences of criminologists.

Usually you are writing for a professional criminal justice journal such as *Criminology* or *Justice Quarterly*. These journals are read by professional criminologists and criminal justice practitioners nationally and internationally. They have high standards and a "peer review" system in which all articles are sent out anonymously to three or more experts in the field who evaluate them. The result is that papers are often critically assessed, and revised one or more times before they are acceptable for publication. The other outlet for publication is books. These may be whole books written by the researcher or chapters individually written by different contributors, devoted to a particular theme.

Another dimension of academic writing is necessary in order to even begin the research and this is what is known as "grantsmanship." It involves writing research grant applications to private foundations or government agencies for the money to be able to temporarily buy yourself out of teaching and administration, and to pay for staff, materials and equipment to conduct the study.

As well as administration, teaching, and research, the faculty member is often asked to serve on certain professional bodies outside the university, and/or to serve as a consultant, lending their expertise to society's institutions.

Finally, related to the service function (though inconsistently valued by faculty, students and administrators) is what is known as community service. In addition to the administration inside the university such as serving on various committees, university faculty are expected to appear in public, on radio and television; be interviewed by the news media; and to talk to community groups and others about their research, their teaching, or both.

It is worth briefly mentioning that all colleges are not alike. There are three types depending upon their source of funding: public, private-independent and private-church related. Then there are at least four levels or rankings depending upon the nature of the degree programs offered. These range from highest to lowest in terms of prestige and, generally speaking, this corresponds to teaching load and research expectations. Class I are doctoral granting institutions such as the University of Pennsylvania (private) or the University of Wisconsin, Madison (public). These top-ranked universities usually have both undergraduate and graduate programs. Class IIA are comprehensive institutions (master's, bachelor's and professional programs) such as the University of Richmond (private) and Eastern Kentucky University (public). Class IIB are primarily undergraduate institutions (providing general baccalaureate degrees) such as Madonna University (private-church), and Ohio State University at Marian (public). Class III (ranked two-year college doing only associates degrees and professional qualifications and colleges without rank) include area community colleges and some branch campuses of larger schools. Generally, research expectation is highest in class I and IIA institutions while teaching and service is more valued in class IIB and below. Teaching loads can vary between one and two courses taught per semester at doctoral schools to

5 and 6 courses per semester at community colleges. The typical load at a comprehensive university is 3-4 courses per semester.

The initial appointment of a college professor is either at the Instructor level (usually while awaiting to defend their Ph.D. under the strange category of ABD—which stands for all-but-dissertation) or at the Assistant Professor (tenure-track) level, which means you are eligible for tenure within a specified number of years of teaching. Entry-level salaries for a new assistant professor vary depending upon the region or city or type of university or college. According to the 1993 annual survey of colleges and universities, the average starting salary at a four-year college or university for social sciences (under which criminal justice faculty are classified) is $34,678, rising to $43,184 on promotion to a tenured associate professor and to $62,000 as a full professor.[1] Generally, private universities pay more than public ones, with church-related universities paying the highest, especially for their senior faculty. The reverse is true at junior colleges where public community colleges pay more than private ones.

Although academic salaries may seem low relative to other areas it must be remembered that these are for 8-9 month contracts. Faculty are free for 3-4 months a year, during which time they can earn extra money, dig their garden or take trips around the world. Many do extra teaching for which they get extra pay; others get research grants. Pro-rated then, the typical average salary of $43,790 of a college professor at a comprehensive university comes out to $58,387.

As a word of caution, it is also worth noting that while students call all faculty "professors," some are "instructors" and others "lecturers" (senior or junior). These faculty are fundamentally the teaching slaves of the academy, being on short-term or even one-semester appointments. They get no job security, reduced benefits, and while not expected to do anything but teach, they typically get paid only one-fourth the rate of regular tenure-track faculty ($2000 per course). Temporary appointments may be a useful way to obtain teaching experience, but the teaching demands are so great that they often conflict and undermine the attempt to develop professionally, to complete a doctorate and to accumulate the all important first few publications.

---

[1] AAUP "Treading Water: The Annual Report on the Economic Status of the Profession, 1992-98" *ACADEME*, March-April, 1993, p. 14.

Importantly, the issue of tenure (which means a protected level of job security—not, as is often misunderstood, a job for life!) and the positions designated "tenure-track" used to depend upon publishing and research abilities, as captured in the famous "publish or perish" quotation. This is slowly being replaced with a triumvirate of demands: teaching, research and service. Newly hired faculty are expected to be equally proficient at all three, and not least the aspect of research involving grantsmanship, since this brings additional external funds to universities and pays for their salaries as well as helping to defray university administrative costs.[2]

One way that frustrated college professors can focus more of their time and energy on criminological research is to become full-time researchers, employed either by a university, an independent research institute such as The Addictions Research Foundation (Toronto) or a government agency, such as the Department of Energy or the Department of Justice. Some post-graduates go into this area from the outset as post-doctoral research workers. The typical appointment here is as a Research Fellow, Research Associate or Research Assistant. Their salaries are comparable to those in higher education, but in many cases they pay much more than entry-level college positions. This can be an attractive proposition for the hungry, indebted and impoverished post-doctoral student but it also carries a price. The job lasts only as long as the grant contract, typically from one to three years (though occasionally five-year and revolving appointments are possible). There are also considerable demands upon your time and difficulties in converting from research to teaching if you stay in research too long. How long is too long? One or two such contracts at a stretch is enough before moving into, or back into, teaching. The alternative is to become a perpetual grant writer, to move up in the institution to ultimately become a Director of Research.

In this section of the book we have four papers, each addressing different aspects of joining academia. The first two papers are by Mark Lanier. Mark is a recent graduate of Michigan State University's doctoral program in social science and has twice successfully been through the process of being hired as an Assistant Professor of criminal justice. His

---

[2] Universities take what is referred to as "overhead costs" of between 31% and 60% of the actual grant, which goes into the university's general fund.

first paper describes the key elements of the prospective undergraduate student's preparation for and transition to graduate school and what to do there, beyond taking classes, to improve your development as a novice academic. His second contribution is a personal reflective account of his own progress in going through graduate school and of his job as an Assistant Professor. The third article is by Anthony Adams who teaches sociology and research methods to criminal justice students at a comprehensive state university. He describes the struggle for a first generation college kid to make it in the academic world, the sacrifice in material and social life necessary to succeed at graduate school and the never ending hidden demands of academic life. He also reveals some of the conflicts within academia and highlights some that confront him as a black male in a white college. Finally, our last article is from Shalane Sheley, a research associate at the University of Michigan, who provides a good insight into the content of one aspect of criminal justice research work dealing with archiving large data sources.

For more information about academia and how to become a college professor:

Altbach, Philip G. and Lambert, Richard D. (eds). *Academic Profession, Annals of the American Academy of Political and Social Science* (No. 448). Philadelphia, PA: American Academy of Political and Social Science, 1980.

Heiberger, Mary M. and Vick, Julia M. *Academic Job Search Handbook.* Philadelphia, PA: University of Pennsylvania Press, 1992.

A classic, if you can get a copy:

van den Berghe, Pierre. *Academic Gamesmanship: How to Make a Ph.D. Pay.* New York, NY: Abelard-Schuman, 1970.

Some good detailed discussion of what it takes to obtain a Ph.D. in Europe, much of which also applies to the U.S. is contained in:

Phillips, Estelle M. and Pugh, D.S. *How to Get a Ph.D.* Philadelphia, PA: Open University Press, 1987.

For criminal justice in particular, read the following:

Flanagan, Timothy J. "Criminal Justice Doctoral Programs in the United States and Canada" in *The Journal of Criminal Justice Education*. Vol. 1 (No. 2, Fall 1990), pp. 1195-1213.

McElrath, Karen. "Standing in the Shadows: Academic Mentoring in Criminology" in *The Journal of Criminal Justice Education*. Vol. 1 (No. 2), pp. 135-52.

Teaching Sociology, "Special Issue of Graduate Education". Vol. 19 (No. 3), July 1991.

For other information on academic criminology:

The American Society of Criminology
1314 Kinnear Road, Suite 212, Columbus, OH 43212.

The Academy of Criminal Justice Sciences
402 Nunn Hall, Northern Kentucky University, Nunn Drive, Highland Heights, KY 41099.

The American Sociological Association
1722 N Street NW, Washington, DC 20036.

Also consult the following:

ASA Guide to Graduate Departments of Sociology
ACJS Guide to Graduate Programs in Criminal Justice and Criminology

For position announcements and what's happening in colleges and universities:

The Chronicle of Higher Education
P.O. Box 1955, Marion, OH 43306, or call (800) 347-6969.
Weekly—$37.50 for 6-month subscription.

Also:

Employment Bulletin (from ASA)
Employment Bulletin (from ACJS)
The Criminologist (newsletter of the American Society of Criminology)
CJ Update: Anderson's Newsletter for Criminal Justice Educators
Available at no charge from Anderson Publishing Co., P.O. Box 1576, Cincinnati, OH 45201.

CHAPTER 21:

Preparing for Jobs in Academia and Research

by *Mark M. Lanier*

Virtually all jobs in academia require advanced degrees. The purpose of this article is to outline some of the preparation necessary to enter graduate school and then to obtain a position in an academic setting—as a researcher, professor or practitioner. Since advanced degrees and/or attending graduate school are prerequisites for these jobs, the main focus of this discussion is on that aspect.

Deciding to go to graduate school

Given students' perpetual self-doubts, the decision to pursue graduate education in criminal justice and/or criminology (or any other academic discipline) produces varying levels of tension in most students. This tension can be reduced by obtaining information about the process with the result that it will be easier to make the appropriate choice. My purpose here, then, is to define, clarify and debate the various stages involved in pursuing graduate education. I begin by taking a look at the steps prior to graduate school admission, and go on to consider alternative methods of overcoming various academic hurdles placed before the prospective academic.

Admission

One of the first questions that will confront the prospective graduate student is whether to take the GRE or MAT. In many cases this is not a choice. In spite of their low prediction of graduate success,[1] doctoral

---

[1] Robert Jacobson, "Critics say Graduate Record Exams Do Not Measure Qualities Needed for Success and are Often Misused," *The Chronicle of Higher Education*, March 24, 1993, pp. B1-2; James Wood and Amy Wong, "GRE Scores and Graduate School Success," *Footnotes*, American Sociological Association, November 1992, who in a letter to the editor of *The Chronicle of Higher Education*, April 28, 1993, p. B3, say "Any policy basing much of a decision about graduate admissions, and graduate assistantships or fellowships, on GRE scores is seriously misguided and

programs and competitive master's programs require applicants to take the Graduate Record Exam (GRE). The extent to which the results are valued by graduate schools varies enormously. For most students this is little consolation since not knowing what to expect will make for an unpleasant experience. One strategy, especially if you are going on to a doctoral program after master's, is to take the GRE as early as possible (after enough courses have been taken to provide you sufficient exposure to content areas—particularly quantitative). This will permit you the opportunity to take the GRE again if you should not do well the first time. To do well it is crucial to **study and prepare**.

There are several good study guides. Arco and Barron's are good, but the Princeton Review's *Cracking the System: The GRE* is the best. Spend several hours a day for at least three weeks preceding the exam date, taking practice exams and studying. Alternatively, you can take a specially designed course to help you prepare. These courses usually cost around $500 and are really no more effective than **dedicated** self-study programs.

The Miller's Analogy Test (MAT) is accepted by some master's programs. It may be in your best interest to take this 45 minute word association test for admission to the master's program. When nearing completion of master's course work (especially after your quantitative course work) take the GRE.

Finally, some schools allow admission without taking either test. Look at your career ambitions closely (practitioner, professor or researcher) and decide if the reputation of the school will help you with your career decision. Don't hesitate to ask other graduates of the program and faculty advisors.

Selecting a college or university

Of all the decisions made, this is the one decision that will **always** follow the student. While the common saying among academicians that, "pedigree is everything" is perhaps overstated, the university affiliation attached to your degree is of considerable importance. However, many factors must be considered in addition to the particular program or university reputation. For example, can you afford the tuition? Can you afford to move to another location? Do you have current work or family

---

should be abandoned."

obligations that restrict your choice of location? Would you be happy spending several years in another geographic region? Is faculty contact important to you? Small schools may facilitate this more easily than large ones.

Another consideration is the availability of funding. All doctoral programs and many master's programs provide financial incentives to students to attend their school. Remember that as a well-prepared, hard-working student you are a valuable commodity. If you ultimately make a name for yourself in the field you will enhance your school's reputation. Lacking that, you will always (at least from the funding institution's viewpoint) be an advocate of your school and send future students (funded and non-funded) in their direction.

If all other factors are equal, apply to as many reputable schools as possible and go to the one that makes the most attractive financial offer. If you are not funded do not despair. Quite often funded positions become available throughout the academic year (through drop outs, grants, etc.). If you do well your first semester you will be in a much better position to receive funding during the next cycle.

Finally, do not attend a school only because you desire to work with specific faculty members. Faculty often leave universities before students have completed their studies, take sabbaticals, and may be inaccessible either time- or personality-wise.

Preparing your vitae
Your academic resume, what we call a vitae (which is short for curriculum vitae and is often abbreviated to cv or vita) is extremely important. This is a summary documenting your accomplishments. The particular style is a matter of preference. Ask all the professors whom you respect for a copy of their vitaes (I still keep a file of faculty vitaes). Then combine the best elements of each individual vitae to create your own—or copy the style you prefer. While style is variable, content is critical. As a student there are several things that you can do to begin working on your vitae as well as to improve your chances of becoming acceptable.

Join professional associations
The two major organizations in our field are the Academy of Criminal Justice Sciences (ACJS) and the American Society of Criminology (ASC). As a student you should join each (students are eligible to join

at a reduced rate of around $20 per year). As a member you will receive academic journals (*Justice Quarterly*, *Journal of Criminal Justice Education* and *Criminology*) as well as job notices, graduate school announcements and information about student paper competitions. Perhaps more importantly, membership will demonstrate that you are a serious, concerned and active student and it will keep you in touch with the latest debates and controversies within the profession.

Attend conferences

Professional organizations, and regional ACJS organizations, hold yearly conferences in which students can participate by presenting papers on student panels, or accompanying a faculty advisor on regular panels. Four students from Florida International University presented one of the best papers I have heard during the March 1993 meetings of ACJS in Kansas City. If you do not feel comfortable presenting a paper, attend the conference, attend sessions to broaden your exposure to topical issues, and most important, socialize (network). Rely on your faculty advisor or mentor to introduce you to professors at other universities. When faculty are making admission and funding decisions, it helps if they remember you as an individual as opposed to a name on paper.

Volunteer for community service

Take advantage of volunteer and/or community service opportunities. One of my students, for example, volunteered for several months at a shelter for homeless families. This type of community service is a large part of what higher education is really about. Involvement in such work shows that you are concerned with "real world" issues, take an active role in helping to resolve them, and are not afraid to "get your hands dirty." If you can couple this activism with a research project on the same subject you will enhance your competitive edge.

Volunteer to help faculty

If the opportunity presents itself, or if you can convince one of your instructors to allow you, teach a class for at least one period. The experience of preparing lecture or discussion notes and then getting up in front of your peers and presenting the material will be very revealing. In some teacher training programs trainee instructors are encouraged to video-tape their presentation and then review all their faults with the object of correcting them in subsequent performances. Whether or not you view the trial teaching as a training exercise, you can say that you "guest lectured" at such-and-such university on your vitae. I did this at universities where I was not a student to further enhance my credibility.

Finally, seek opportunities to assist faculty with their research. Code data, run analyses, conduct literature reviews, ask if you can do some interviews or accompany the faculty member when subjects are being interviewed. Not only will your help be appreciated but you will learn what Ph.D.'s really do (and gain an excellent letter of recommendation!). If lucky, you may even gain a publication or two in the process. You can also put this activity on your vitae. You may need to educate faculty on your usefulness. Many faculty do not think about joint publication possibilities with graduate students until it is suggested to them. A colleague of mine once had a student from another university turn up at his advising session saying that he'd done an undergraduate thesis based on the professor's previous work and would be interested in doing an independent study with him. They ended up co-authoring a book chapter together as the independent study, and this was before the student had even graduated with his bachelor's degree!

Biting the bullet
Having selected a school and gained acceptance (and hopefully funding), the next stage begins. How you spend the few years (and believe it or not the time passes very quickly) completing your master's and/or doctorate will have ramifications for the rest of your career. A particularly important dimension of graduate education is to get involved very early on in what will come later. In short "don't put off till tomorrow what you can do today." The key to future success is research and writing.

Some universities provide master's level students with an option of writing a thesis or taking a few additional classes and perhaps writing a paper. If you ever plan to continue your education by pursuing a Ph.D. you **must** take the thesis option. The training and experience you will gain cannot be obtained inside the classroom. Plus, this research task will provide a strong indication about whether this is what you want to do with a large portion of your time. Finally, most reputable doctoral programs demand the successful completion of a thesis for admission. However, if you desire to attend law school or want to work in the field, writing a master's thesis is probably not your best option.

Doing well in classes is extremely important, though not for the reasons most people think. For example, when applying for a job as a professor, some schools never ask about your GPA or to see your transcripts. Despite this, your reputation can be made in the classroom. The Criminal Justice/Criminology academic community is relatively small. Most competent professors know many other professors, and most of your classmates will become professors one day. If you are lazy, indifferent or unprepared in your classes you will develop a certain reputation. Regardless of how well your vitae looks, informal conversations will taint you. More importantly, you can learn something from every instructor and each class. You may not know what the relevance or application of the knowledge is, but at some point it will prove useful (if only to be conversant at social events). Beyond this, there are also pragmatic and theoretical issues that need discussion.

Although some schools insist on a particular sequence of courses, it sometimes works best if you have the choice, to tackle the toughest first. Bite the bullet. Take the theory, statistics and methods classes. You will be rewarded later when others are struggling. Some faculty even suggest graduate students take as many statistics and methods classes as possible. Unlike some other topics, these courses are difficult to self-teach. For example, you can read a book on delinquency and get a good understanding of the problem and its analysis. Reading a book on rank ordered probit analyses will not be as useful to most students. Advanced techniques require a good instructor to complement the text. This should not be construed as favoring quantitative methods over qualitative, although many criminal justice programs have that bias. However, as a student you should understand and appreciate each approach. Then you can make an informed decision as to which to use in your own work (or like me, combine the two).

At early stages in your career as a student be circumspect about arguing your theoretical views with those of your professor. This is not to say you shouldn't discuss your ideas but do not become overly committed too early on. My strategy was to accept each professor's theoretical orientation as my own (at least for that class). I learned more that way and developed a better rapport with the instructor. While this may sound Machiavellian, it is a good learning technique. More importantly, as a young student you cannot know which theoretical beliefs will ultimately become your own. For example, as a first-year student do you know of Critical Semiotics? Phenomenology? Field

Theory? Popper? The many versions of radical criminology thought? Realism, conservative and radical? The utility of the dialectic? The theoretical basis for varieties of Feminism? The measurable support for Control Theory? Integrated Theory? Hold your tongue and open your mind until you have had time to develop an appreciation for each. For example, don't reject Marxist thought simply because the Soviet Union failed. You will learn that Soviets never practiced/developed communism as Marx envisioned it and that many Marxists are not arguing from Marx's viewpoint, but that of Lenin. If you reject the genius of Marx because of his conception of human nature you may make a valid argument. But you must first open-mindedly learn Marx, then Marxists and then the detractors.

Finally, always think critically. This does not mean accepting ideas as truths. Seek to understand them in a comparative context, suspending your judgement until analysis and debate has taken its course. By your last year of classes you will have established a reputation as a competent student and can then argue theory with your professors. (Incidentally, the most useful and rewarding debates that we enjoyed at MSU occurred in local taverns—perhaps the alcohol loosened reluctant tongues. We would debate various topics for hours at an intensity level that is inappropriate for the classroom.) Perhaps the lesson here is not to isolate yourself and to buy faculty beer.

The importance of mentorship
If I had to rank the importance of the varied aspects of graduate school, I would have to call the mentor-student relationship the most important. I was very fortunate to have several faculty at each graduate program I attended who functioned as mentors. Mentors provide the technical skills, important connections, and motivation. Unfortunately, some students do not develop mentors. It is not an automatic or required activity. The student must work to cultivate the relationship. Mentorships should be actively sought by the student. By seeking this relationship you must be prepared to do whatever it takes as far as work, study, and time are concerned. However, the benefits will last the rest of your career.

Like your GPA, the value of a mentor may not be what you expect. The benefits are much more important than simply learning the mechanics. For example, ethics and integrity are more important lessons. In my opinion, researchers and professors are obligated to reveal "truth" through theory and/or research. Therefore, we have an obligation to present findings as they are and to use ethical techniques. If we deviate from this obligation we will ultimately become little more than politicians, advocates or cheerleaders for our favorite social causes. The damage to society in its effort to find objective truth will be immense. Most Ph.D.'s recognize this obligation. One of my mentors withdrew from a major, large-budget, federal research program because they did not adhere to the previously agreed upon research protocol. Years later, in part because of my exposure to that situation, I refused to put my name on a one-sided research publication. Each of us lost several additions to our vitaes but retained something much more valuable. Once academic integrity is lost it can never be completely regained. The dedication of my master's thesis read, in part, "... Dr. Belinda McCarthy has not only helped me to acquire the technical skills necessary to become a social scientist, but has, by example, shown me the importance of personal integrity in social scientific training and research." To me, this is the real value of a mentor.

Finally, a word of warning is necessary on the issue of personal integrity in relations with faculty. As in any situation where two people are in an intimate working relationship, and one is in a relative power position over the other, problems can arise. With the growth in awareness of sexual harassment and university policies to that effect, this problem may begin to decline. Recently the University of Virginia became the first to ban all sexual relations between faculty and students and others are likely to follow. Having provided this warning I must also acknowledge that several lasting and rewarding marriages have been the outcome of similar relationships.

A related issue is the exploitation of graduate students either as teaching assistants or researchers. Tales are rife in the halls of academe about faculty who get graduate students to teach all their classes, and grade all their students' papers. Others may be developing a line of thought that is very original which may prove so intimidating to faculty that they incorporate it into their own papers with no mention of the graduate student who originated it, or worse a cursory acknowledgement. Like sexual harassment, this tradition may also be in decline with the recent award to a University of Michigan junior female faculty member of 1.1 million dollars as a result of being removed for blowing the whistle on her senior colleague for using her ideas to obtain a government research grant. The key point is to be involved but also alert to the possibility of unhealthy power plays and try to pre-empt these before they develop enough force to destroy your possibilities of graduating.

Dr. Mark M. Lanier is Assistant Professor of Criminal Justice at the University of Central Florida in Orlando, Florida.

CHAPTER 22:

Experiences of Graduate School

by *Mark M. Lanier*

Writing this paper required that I be somewhat reflective. Looking back, my decision to attend graduate school was probably the best career choice I could have made. My career ambitions were determined and developed by the experiences of being a graduate student. For me, this was no small accomplishment. Having worked in a variety of occupations (pipe welder, fire-medic, machinist, to name a few), and having never really enjoyed working for someone else, the freedom afforded by academia was exhilarating. When I began graduate school, I had little ambition to be a professor. However, the experience of being a student and working closely with faculty led me to conclude that this profession was perhaps one of the few that permitted me the freedom and diversity that I desired. Despite the many positive benefits there are drawbacks to being a graduate student. In the following pages I outline the sacrifices required, the changes I experienced and the rewards I obtained from being a graduate student.

Sacrifice
After the birth of my first child I made a decision to try and better myself. Higher education seemed the logical route. Never having been a serious student (I had a "C" average to show for my first three years of undergraduate study) serious reservations existed about my ability (motivational more than intellectual) as a student. Nonetheless, after finishing my bachelor's degree I decided to apply, and was accepted, to a graduate program at the University of Alabama at Birmingham.

Because of my unsuccessful undergraduate work, throughout my career as a graduate student I always thought that the next hurdle would be the one to "weed me out." The first hurdle faced was entrance exams. Successfully completing the Graduate Record Exam and Miller's Analogy gave me a sense of accomplishment and more importantly—relief.

The next hurdle was classes. I attacked each course as if it was all that stood between me and the successful completion of my master's degree. The transition from unconcerned undergraduate to overly concerned

191

graduate student was essential. For one thing, the graduate workload was large compared to that of an undergraduate student. For many classes, a book per week was the required reading. Therefore, it was probably a good thing that I was so apprehensive about my abilities. In graduate school I would usually have read much of the text(s) before the quarter started and always had the required readings outlined prior to each class session. Using this method I learned a lot and could participate in class discussions.

During my first semester a strange thing happened. I learned that the sense of accomplishment was greatest with the more demanding classes. In a masochistic sense, I came to enjoy the difficult courses. The more effort required the more I learned. This sensation was extremely surprising for me.

During these first few semesters in graduate school I also discovered that my professors were real people! They became my friends, mentors and therefore, much more effective teachers (or, more likely, I became a better student). I would have been conscience-stricken attending their classes unprepared. Despite these positive changes, my lack of confidence remained. Many of my acquaintances in academia have also told me that they shared similar feelings as graduate students. In fact, one of my closest friends (an associate professor who has published 3 books and numerous articles) has termed the sensation "the imposter syndrome," implying that we will somehow be found out.

My next challenge was a doctoral program. I decided to attend Michigan State University. I maintained the same attitude that I had at the University of Alabama at Birmingham. While my confidence was building, I still thought that each stage would be my last. This feeling persisted through the doctoral comprehensive exams and dissertation defense. When I successfully defended my dissertation several people asked "Aren't you thrilled?" In reality, I experienced an enormous sense of relief with little "thrill." Again, having talked with others in similar positions, they also revealed feeling relief. I must add that feelings of accomplishment and pride were also strong.

Changes
Attending graduate school will have ramifications in ways the student never envisioned. Certain sacrifices are expected (e.g. financial and time) while others are completely unanticipated. I was exposed to a whole new way of thinking. Exposure to empiricism, (ir)rationality, and critical

thought can question many long-held, perhaps invalid beliefs. For example, I remember being surprised at how few of my professors were religious. As exposure to higher education increased, their position became more understandable. As a scholar you almost feel like part of a new religious order. Religion, if nothing else, provides comfort in the "knowledge" about how things will be—if only in the hereafter. Science provides insight into how things are now.

Other more tangible sacrifices should also be considered. For example, I had a family. My partner was not satisfied living many miles away from her home and friends and this contributed to the eventual dissolution of our relationship. Some develop a commuter relationship (as one my colleagues has so far successfully managed—taking three small children three states away from their home and father). Another student was 900 miles away from her home state and she was miserable the entire 3 years. She was constantly seeking the economic means and time to visit home, which detracted crucial energy, effort and motivation from her very demanding graduate program. Personally, I found the move and new environment very stimulating.

Another change that can prove both worrying and rewarding is that of working with faculty. I have mentioned that choosing to go to graduate school because of the possibility of working with certain professors is probably a bad move (see CHAPTER 21). One of my primary reasons for attending the University of Alabama at Birmingham (UAB) as a master's student was that I wanted to work with Belinda McCarthy which I did. However, a master's program is of shorter duration than a doctoral program and I was lucky that she elected to help me and that she remained at UAB the entire time (she left for another university shortly after). Five years after the fact, I still have professors from other institutions refer to me as "Belinda's student"—which I still take as a compliment.

Looking back, it was naive of me to attend a school based on the desire to work with a specific faculty member. For example, when I left UAB to attend Michigan State University (MSU) I assumed that I would work with Tim Bynum or Merry Morash since my interests and publications concerned juvenile delinquency. Having never taken a class or developed an interest in policing, I was surprised to be assigned to community policing expert Bob Trojanowicz (which incidentally worked out extremely well). Steve Cox (a fellow student) had taken many police classes and the police were his only interest while a master's student - he was assigned to Tim Bynum and now does juvenile delinquency work. However, since Steve and I selected MSU based on the overall reputation of the school, and not specific faculty members, there were many competent faculty with whom we each developed relationships.

Graduate school is a place for you to take some initiative and to make changes as well as to be subject to them. For example, many schools suggest or require that classes be taken in a specific order. Perhaps because of my desire to succeed, or perhaps because of my fear of failure, it worked best for me to **not** follow the required sequence. I took what I had heard were the more difficult courses first. Thus, the research methods class came first, followed by statistics and then theory classes. That sequence allowed me to start working on my thesis much sooner, and have it completed simultaneously with my course work. There were other benefits to this sequence. For example, in the methods class a research proposal was required and this became the methods chapter in the thesis. This "system" worked for me and I successfully completed my master's degree.

Another of the changes from undergraduate work is to impose some order of your own on the material. This is especially important in doctoral work. While advice from one's committee chair and other members of one's committee can be invaluable, total submission to faculty ideas can lead up endless blind alleys, and to an eclectic set of data that satisfies no one, least of all yourself.

Rewards
As mentioned earlier, the freedom afforded in graduate school is very rewarding. I was able to study whatever topic interested me. I wanted to study AIDS/HIV and adolescents. If I had decided to study something else I would have had the freedom, and encouragement, to do so. In addition to the freedom permitted by working in higher education, there are many other positive aspects. Perhaps one of the most important is the feeling generated by meeting, working with, and helping other students—especially those that are different from yourself. I made close friends with graduate students from Thailand and England. My friend from Thailand (who also went on to get a Ph.D.) had never been to an American's home. I was somewhat ashamed when, in the last semester of my master's program, I learned that he had never even been invited over to anyone's home (after 12 months living in the Unites States). He came to our home and cooked ethnic food for my family and brought his

wife over, despite her inability to speak English. This was, and remains, a very rewarding relationship. This experience also reveals that the rewards and experiences of graduate education should include those that occur outside the classroom.

At another level, having research findings published and quoted provides unique and very fulfilling rewards. While a master's student I published two articles with my mentor in refereed journals. (This is where the article is sent anonymously for evaluation by independent experts in the field.) This was shocking to me. Learning the process of how to get published was like having the complicated and guarded secrets of the academy revealed.

Knowledge in all its forms (e.g. sensitivity to others, learning oneself, theory, methods) is what being a graduate student was really about to me. As social scientists, most of us are exposed to knowledge, some of us expose knowledge, and a very few of us even create knowledge. However, the acquisition of knowledge is only part of the reward. Learning to learn is as important. Learning the basic methodologies and principles of science was fascinating to me. At last I thought I could discover the "truth." I still think that, but realize now that there are many truths, of many types.

Knowledge has often been compared to power. While you won't feel powerful, you will notice that you are respected. The day after completing my Ph.D. I was the same person, knew the same things and expressed myself in the same ways. Yet, I was often surprised when new casual acquaintances would express respect (also disbelief from some of my older acquaintances!) for my academic credentials.

For me, the single most rewarding experience was being mentored by the people that I respected, and in two cases, was awed by. I was flattered that these great scholars, who had written many books, would take the time to work with me. Once they took the time I felt obligated to succeed.

In summary, the university environment is stimulating, the people are diverse and the options for study and research are broad. I strongly recommend it for those with the desire to grow intellectually.

Dr. Mark M. Lanier is Assistant Professor of Criminal Justice at the University of Central Florida in Orlando, Florida.

CHAPTER 23:

Becoming a University Professor

by *Anthony Troy Adams*

I made the decision to pursue a career in academia mid-way through my second year of a two-year master's degree program. Uncertain about future employment possibilities, having earned only a bachelor's degree in criminal justice, I spoke with several of my former professors. It was through my former professors' encouragement and my independent thinking about academe which ultimately influenced my decision to pursue a university professorship

Preparation for academe

My selection of an undergraduate degree in criminal justice and criminology was very much determined by my past academic performance and immaturity as a student. As a high school student I was not in the college-preparatory track. In fact, more likely, I was viewed as an athlete-student who took primarily general studies courses. My focus was in sports. I was voted most valuable player but lacked the physical attributes of size and speed which were most attractive to major universities. My physical limitations and my desire to continue participating in athletics influenced my decision to select a Division II school over the more robust Division I universities, and this also provided a less demanding academic curriculum. Having doubts about my ability to succeed as a college athlete, I renounced my scholarship in favor of becoming a full-time student.

The first two years of my undergraduate experience were spent learning how to become a college student. Because I lacked many of the skills necessary to perform at above-average levels in college, I spent hours studying. But my hours of labor were reduced to fifty minutes of multiple-choice (multiple guess!) and true-false items which never seemed to measure my retention, knowledge, or understanding of course materials. I studied meticulously, but did not know what to study. It was frustrating!

To compound matters I worked part-time off campus. The commute to and from work, and the hours spent at work, drained me physically, psychologically, and at times emotionally. Part-time employment affected my academic performance. I never seemed to be able to stay afloat. It was like losing two days every week. In spite of the negative impact that work had on my studies, it was a means to finance my car, engage in social and extracurricular activities, and it gave me the necessary money for books, supplies, and miscellaneous tangibles.

The fact that I was a first-generation college student contributed to my below-par academic experience. The demands placed on me by school and family frequently conflicted. I was performing poorly in school and my family did not understand my problems. None of my siblings had traveled that far in school. I began to question myself. Was I cut out for this? It was a constant psychological tug-of-war. Perseverance and a sense of pride, however, kept me going.

I was a late bloomer in college. It was not until the end of my second year that I finally began to understand what was necessary to become a serious student. I learned how to pass exams with A's and B's instead of C's and D's. It was at this juncture that I began to enjoy being a college student. I was recognized by other students as a "good" student. Students called on me for help. I had successfully learned how to piece together a university term paper. My oral communication skills were above average and I had garnered the confidence to do something! I graduated at the end of four years. What was I to do after my undergraduate years?

I had aspirations of going to law school. Poor performance on standardized examinations, a marginal overall grade point average, and swelling numbers of qualified applicants desiring a legal education deferred this dream. Discourse with friends, former college instructors, co-workers, and family friends spoke about the advantages and value of graduate school education. I matriculated into a master's program at the same university where I had taken my bachelor's of science degree.

Graduate training requires a great deal of reading and writing, statistics and methods courses, and many oral presentations. It was demanding. The challenges of graduate school gave me the faith and confidence that I could handle the rigors of doctoral study at a prestigious university.

After having completed all course work requirements for the master's I transferred to a highly prestigious mid-western research university. The first year of graduate school is a weeding process. Many students do not return for the second year; some do not even return for the second semester of the first year. The curriculum is structured so that the most difficult and rigorous courses are required during the first year and a half of study. I was thrown into the company of students who were academically prepared for the quantitative oriented program that I was about to pursue. They had come from such name-brand institutions as Harvard and Yale, Brown University, University of Chicago, and other elite schools.

As a minority and non-traditional student, I felt lonely and somewhat alienated. I was the only "minority student of color" among my classmates. The competitive nature of the course work forced me to abandon many of my childhood friends and family. I alienated myself from family and friends in order to survive the demands of doctoral training.

Fortunately, the formation of new friendships helped me to deal with the pressures associated with graduate school at a prestigious university. They served as a buffer from the realities of estrangement and servitude experienced inside the academy. For instance, my first semester was disastrous. Because I was receiving a departmental merit-based fellowship, which carried a nominal stipend when compared to the more glamorous and sexy externally funded fellowships, I taught part-time at a nearby Division II university. Teaching at the university level proved to be both rewarding and distracting. On one hand, it provided me with the additional money which put me slightly above destitution. On the other hand, the energy expended in the classroom meant time away from doing enjoyable things that may have helped me to remain balanced. I inevitably sacrificed much needed study time. It was my friends, however, who understood and supported my need to work. They provided me with unconditional support. My friends gave me a place to vent my feelings of anxiety, frustration, inadequacy, and ineptitude. I survived the first semester "wash out" and four and one-half years later **earned** the Ph.D.

Inside the academy
My primary responsibilities as a university faculty member can be summarized in the following three categories: teaching, research, and service. If we use the forty hour work week as a baseline, roughly twenty-two percent of my time is dedicated to actual classroom instruction. Factor in office hours associated with each contact hour, instructional preparation, and you get another nine hours (22.5%). About 45 percent of my time is spent on teaching related activities. Classroom

instruction requires good oral communication skills, compassion, mastery of the subject being taught, enthusiasm, and above all patience!

Teaching is a not-so-easy task. It is frequently assumed that college students are homogenous and come to the university environment with similar skills and abilities. In reality students are as diverse as the institutions they attend. Many students have only remedial skills in this area or that. Other students are extremely adept. But as college teachers we must teach all students. Unfortunately our doctoral training does not emphasize teaching, and the Ph.D. is not a teaching degree. In order to effectively teach we need practice and we must understand the clients (students) being served. Many college instructors will flounder in the academic abyss for several years before they become competent educators. Only a handful of the teacher/scholars will eventually pass muster in the classroom. Those who make it are rarely recognized or celebrated for their teaching skills or accomplishments. I have adopted the philosophy of trying to teach for my worst student.

University professors who teach well are uncompromising, steadfast, and possess an unyielding devotion and dedication to teaching. To do this means to never feel satisfied with any one method of teaching. Quality classroom instruction means the desire to change, modify, and develop innovative styles of presentation. It means changing delivery styles frequently. Effective teaching means learning about students and having the willingness to try new techniques. We do not learn this in graduate school, unfortunately.

Teaching at the university level can be very rewarding. My energetic, enthusiastic, and highly animated style of teaching may have something to do with this. It is an interactive and collaborative approach to delivery that encourages students to become "active" rather than "passive" learners. Sometimes I can see it in their eyes when they clearly understand new terms, concepts, and the interconnectedness between ideas and relationships. I can watch students come into fruition. Just as important, I learn from the learning-teaching process. Students investigate and prepare written assignments about a variety of subjects. Their papers take me to other cities, countries, and continents and to terrains untraveled by me. Students' ideas are expressed from a multitude of angles. In as much as I teach students, I learn from them.

Teaching also has a negative side, unfortunately. Students can be very demanding and complacent. Many students feel free to interrupt me and barge into my office at their any or every whim. This can be distracting to the creative process. Students frequently want consultation beyond assigned office hours at their convenience. They want letters of recommendation, support, special privileges, and suggestions about what career choices to make. Students demand extensions on assignments, term papers, and make-up examinations. Students are complacent because they study only for exams; they do not study to appreciate, grasp, or comprehend the wider applications and significance of the issues under investigation. It is not uncommon for students to ask "Will this be on the exam?" This experience often makes my fingers cringe, especially knowing the amount of time and preparation that go into fifty minutes of comprehensive lecture notes. I try to overlook this seemingly grotesque feature of education.

Teaching non-white students can sometimes present special problems. Some non-white students make certain assumptions about minority professors, particularly if they are a member of the same minority or ethnic group. These students assume that they are entitled to special privileges. They believe that we should relax the course requirements in their favor. They believe that we should make it easier for them. And to compound problems, some non-minority faculty often refer "students of color" to minority faculty. This puts an additional burden on minority faculty, many of whom are not tenured, to assist minority students just because they are minority students rather than "students." I was never trained in graduate school to deal with these complexities, and I do not feel equipped to deal with them.

I spend approximately forty-five percent (22 hours a week) of my time engaging in a variety of research and scholarly activities. As a junior faculty member one of my top priorities is working toward tenure. Research and scholarly activity play important roles in the review process. Research and scholarly activity means writing and submitting articles for publication in scholarly and professional journals, preparing proposals for internal and external funding, reviewing books, articles, monographs, and proposals as a professional courtesy for colleagues who exchange the same services. Seeking external funding and submitting scholarly papers for publication is a precarious and humorous business.

In the world of academe you must learn to accept criticism and rejection. As junior faculty we are primarily apprentices learning the educator/scholar trade. Much of our time is spent preparing papers for publication and proposals to fund our particular research interests. I have grown accustomed to being thrashed by criticisms as an academician.

This process is like being battered and abused without any means of recourse. But it is a learning process that one grows to appreciate. It sharpens our analytical and writing skills. Criticism may add to our perspective and hone our thinking. It offers us new ways to approach problems. We also face many more letters of rejection or acceptances with modification than we do out-right acceptances to receive funding for research or publication in scholarly journals. A proposal or scholarly paper can be theoretically, methodologically, and strategically sound, but it may not be funded or accepted for publication. We learn to accept both facets of the business.

Approximately ten percent (4 hours a week) is spent doing service-related activities. Service means to perform certain tasks either at the departmental, university-at-large, or the community levels. At the departmental level, we review colleagues' papers, attend committee meetings and act on decisions made at these meetings, speak at "brown bags" (informal presentations of research), and serve as student advisors by often itemizing student transcripts to determine the courses students need to take in order to graduate in a timely fashion. We also attend university-wide meetings which may affect the larger college structure and policies. These committees meet with some degree of regularity. We serve the surrounding community too. We make presentations at local middle and high schools, work as consultants in community-based programs, and review documents for local, state, and federal auspices. All of this can involve a great deal of time and energy.

I can make several recommendations to those desiring to pursue a career in academe. First, because teaching at the university level is demanding, spend some time learning how to teach. Take some teaching courses coupled with courses that emphasize effective oral and written communication skills, and higher order thinking. The more ways professors offer students to approach problems, the greater the likelihood that students will address problems analytically from a multitude of angles. Second, spend some time outside the academe developing a keen perception and understanding about possible career options for students. So many times we are called upon to assist students with making decisions that affect their lives. As academics who serve as mentors and advisors we must also have knowledge about other fields to help students make important decisions. Third, make sure you are well equipped for the business of being a scholar. Take many graduate courses in theory and methods. Read, research, and become actively involved in your research area. Know important people in the field. Above all, enjoy what you are doing because you will certainly become engulfed by it.

Dr. Anthony Troy Adams is an Assistant Professor at Eastern Michigan University where he has recently been awarded tenure.

CHAPTER 24:

Criminal Justice Research: A Data Archivist

by *Shalane J. Sheley*

When I initially obtained the position of Data Archive Specialist in 1989, I had been applying for jobs for almost two years. Employed as a secretary—my background before obtaining my master's in sociology—no one had even interviewed me, until I applied for this position. Once I got that far, it was my interviewing ability and the master's thesis that got me the job. Because I had completed research for my thesis— from questionnaire to analysis—I had experience in the field. Although at times it may seem painful, when writing a thesis you will gain training that may not be obtainable anywhere else.

As a Data Archive Specialist at the Institute for Social Research at the University of Michigan, my job was to "process" data. I worked more specifically for the Inter-University Consortium for Political and Social Research (ICPSR), in the National Archive of Criminal Justice Data section. Through a grant from the U.S. Bureau of Justice Statistics, the Archive receives government data collected in various areas, including the National Crime Survey, the Federal Bureau of Investigation's Uniform Crime Report and the National Corrections Reporting Program. Also, any researcher receiving government funding must submit their data collection to us for public distribution. Anyone wishing to make their research available can archive their data, free of charge. Members of the consortium (mostly universities)—worldwide—have complete access to all data through their official representative. Governmental units in the U.S. also receive the data *gratis*. Others must pay an access fee.

It is the responsibility of the Archive to create a code book (from the questionnaire or the column layout provided by the principal investigator [PI]) to identify the questions and variables, specify data definitions (variable names and positions), clean the data, and turn it over to the data archives member services section for distribution to the public for secondary research.

The extent of cleaning or "processing" depends upon the agreement with the PI. Some are only checked for the number of variables and records and released exactly as received from the PI. Others, including most government studies, are extensively processed by the staff before release.

With extensively processed data, the first step is to copy the data and give the original to the data archives library for storage. The logical record length (total number of bytes per case) of the data is checked and compared with documentation provided. The data must be visually scanned for confidentiality (e.g. respondent addresses, inmate names, etc.). A listing is made of a fifth or so of the identification variables and other sequential variables, and frequencies are run on the remaining variables to identify exactly what is in the data. Decisions are made on how to proceed according to what is discovered in the listing and frequencies. Wild cards (garbage) and out-of-range data are re-coded to missing data. All missing data codes are made uniform. These steps are accomplished using a statistical package which requires initially setting up data definitions (or control cards). Alphabetics may show up in numeric variables and have to be corrected or re-coded to missing. Contact is often made with the PI on how to deal with unusual problems that crop up.

Concurrent to the processing is the production of a code book for each study. Code books for studies released as received are only given a description and a citation page in the front. Extensively processed data requires a standard ICPSR code book with an introduction (with sub-headings tailored to fit the current study), the main variable description section (with instrument questions or statements and all their possible responses, and column locations and width of each variable), and an appendix (which can consist of anything related to the study that aids in understanding the code book).

The finished "product" must be an easily readable and understandable code book with data that is cleaned and contains no blanks. Each processor is ultimately responsible for any problems that were not resolved in the study.

The job is challenging because no two studies are alike, even if the present study is an update of an old one. Each set-up to provide frequencies or re-codes, brings with it "bugs" that have to be worked out before results are finally achieved.

Since coming to ICPSR, I have been promoted twice; first from Data Archive Specialist to Research Associate I, then Research Associate II. As I began to gain competence in my initial work, I was given more and more responsibility which ultimately led to the promotions. I am fortunate to have a boss who recognized my abilities and made the best use of them.

As a Research Associate II, I hire new personnel in the Criminal Justice section, being entirely responsible for who is selected. In this area, my sixth sense, or ability to tell who would make the best worker, has been a great asset. The most useful background a person can have is experience and/or training in some type of research that has exposed them to the concept of data sets, variables, etc., using some type of statistical package. A criminal justice background is helpful but not required. A resume will get you an interview but the presentation in the interview will either get you the job or lose it for you. In my interviews, I look for a positive/eager attitude, a willingness to work hard and take constructive criticism, a dedication to "getting it right," and the ability to fit in and cooperate with the current staff.

Once a person is hired, I give them the orientation tour and get them established at their post. Initial training is intense and requires much of my time which I would normally put into data processing. Although I am now responsible for less data processing, the jobs on which I work are very challenging. It takes a couple of months for a worker to start feeling comfortable, to feel really in the swing of things, and it takes close to two years before enough confidence is gained that you finally know what you are doing.

My promotion has required increased supervision over co-workers; making low-level decisions, answering questions, giving direction and guidance, and helping to ensure that things run smoothly. Experience in the problems they encounter has proved invaluable. But showing people what to do and how to do it is only part of the job. My undergraduate degree in social work has helped greatly in my role as a supervisor; my training in listening and counseling are paying off, especially when someone has a gripe. On many occasions just taking time to listen to their story is all it takes to head off a problem. Being able to size up a situation and act on it, or give recommendations to the boss, is an important skill in a supervisory position. I'm also being "pushed" into leading staff meetings and I'm sure with time, my confidence will increase in this area. Taking calls regarding criminal justice data is another task for which I am responsible. The caller, usually from academia or law enforcement, may only be looking for a particular data set on a certain subject, but sometimes they call because they have run into problems with a data set. When that occurs, I troubleshoot, ordering data from the archive library, running frequencies and trying to recreate or spot the issue in question. Of course, no two problems are ever alike.

My supervisor allows her employees to develop and grow in the direction in which they feel most comfortable. Mine has been in the administrative/organizational area. A co-worker hired at the same time as I has grown into the low-level computer programming area, one which I have no desire to pursue, but which is also vital to the smooth functioning of the organization (low-level means specialized programs that are needed for our particular problems in data processing).

One of the most enjoyable aspects of my position is its challenges; the challenge to myself to learn more and grow as an employee, as well as the challenge of getting things right. Stress is at a minimum as long as I keep my supervisor informed and am working at a steady pace. Only when someone is "sandbagging" or not pulling their weight are they prodded. My benefits are terrific; besides full medical coverage I get 24 vacations days a year. My only problem has been using all of them. Because I enjoy my work, I hesitate to take time off. There has been a very strong sense of cooperation among my co-workers, especially since the office has been in the preparation of not only switching the statistical package used for processing, but the computer system and media (from tape to disk storage) as well. In addition, my hours are flexible (as we do not have contact with the public except by phone) according to what is best suited for me. The biggest drawback or complaint I find in my job is the salary. Social science jobs tend to pay less than other more technical positions and salaries at ICPSR have been unusually low due to historical reasons that are hard to change.

SECTION EIGHT: FEDERAL CAREERS IN CRIMINAL JUSTICE: INSPECTORS, SPECIAL AGENTS & OTHERS[1]

The first question many students of criminal justice ask is: "How can I become an FBI Agent?" My answer is usually to give them some standard literature on the FBI; to point out how competitive it is for most college students to enter the service[2] and that the age of entry is restricted to between 23 and 34; and to explain that the FBI favors students with skills other than criminal justice such as accounting, computer science, business administration and/or a foreign language, particularly Spanish. Then I ask: "Do you know that there are many federal law enforcement positions for criminal justice majors, other than the FBI?" Thanks to the TV series *Gunsmoke* most have heard of The U.S. Marshals and, since the notorious 1993 Branch Davidian tragedy in Waco, Texas, many are now familiar with the work of the ATF (Bureau of Alcohol, Tobacco and Firearms). The 1980's Reagan era "War on Drugs" might also have sensitized some to the DEA (Drug Enforcement Administration) but most are unaware of the numerous other positions available. In fact, almost every position in criminal justice that exists at the state level, has a parallel at the federal level and several others exist that have no parallel. Figure 1 provides a listing of some of these positions and Figure 2 provides a basic description of what they involve.

In terms of the qualifications for federal careers the content of the degree is less important than having a superior Grade Point Average (GPA). Clearly, criminal justice majors are better prepared for some positions than are other undergraduates. However, a number of criminal justice careers require a specialized degree and these are listed in Figure

---

[1] This introductory section draws on information provided by the Office of Personnel Management's federal job information service.

[2] For example, the FBI student internship program takes only one student a year from the whole of the state of Michigan, and a similar number from other states.

3. Ideally a major in a related field, or in some cases a minor, would be appropriate. It is also possible to major in a relevant subject and minor in criminal justice, or to graduate with a double major.

The federal hiring process takes place in a number of ways. Overall there is the Federal Job Opportunity List (FJOL) through which positions are announced. Positions on this list fall under several categories and involve three basic methods of hiring. One method is to take the standard federal test and be placed on the FJOL list of eligibles. A second method is the Outstanding Scholar Program in which students with GPA's of 3.5

1 SELECTED FEDERAL CAREERS FOR CRIMINAL JUSTICE MAJORS:

Air Traffic Controller
Border Patrol Agent
Civil Rights Analyst
Correctional Officer
Criminal Investigator
Customs Inspector
Environmental Protection Specialist
Equal Opportunity Compliance Specialist
Equal Employment Opportunity
   Specialist
Game Law Enforcement Specialist
Internal Revenue Officer
Investigator
Paralegal Specialist
Security Specialist
Social Insurance Claims Examiner
Special Agent-Secret Service
Bureau of Alcohol, Tobacco
   and Firearms
Tax Auditor/Technician

and above are hired directly by an agency without having to take the federal test. Finally, there are several agencies that **only** hire directly and have their own tests (see Appendix II). Let's begin with the Federal Jobs Opportunity List.

The Federal Job Opportunity List (FJOL)—The FJOL is an excellent source of information about current federal job openings. The FJOL contains a listing of jobs for which the U.S. Office of Personnel Management (OPM) is currently accepting requests for applications. Criminal justice related positions are reproduced in several publications listed at the end of this section. The complete FJOL is available for viewing at any State Job Service Branch Office or at the Area Offices of the U.S. Personnel Management Federal Job Information Center (see Appendix I for a list of federal job addresses and phone numbers). Personal computer users can also obtain the same information from the OPM Electronic Bulletin Board via a modem. In recent years the

2 SELECTED FEDERAL POSITIONS
Basic Descriptions

ATF Special Agent—Investigates violations of explosives, firearms, illicit liquor and tobacco acts; prevents and solves bombings; detects illegal transportation of explosives and firearms; controls illegal possession of these items. Agency: ATF.

Border Patrol Agent—Prevents smuggling and illegal entry of aliens into the U.S.; patrols border areas; inspects trains, vehicles, buses, airplanes, ships, and terminals. Agency: INS.

Correctional Officer—Enforces rules governing confinement, safety, health and protection of inmates; supervises inmate work assignments. Agency: Federal Prison System.

Criminal Investigator—Investigates violations of federal laws. Agencies: INS, Dept. of Defense, OPM.

Customs Inspector—Enforces laws governing imports and exports; weighs, gauges, measures, samples, and collects duties, taxes and fees; searches violators of customs laws; seizes contraband; arrests violators. Agency: Customs Service.

Customs Special Agent—Investigates fraud affecting customs' revenue through under-evaluation and smuggling of merchandise and contraband, Neutrality Act violations involving illegal shipment of arms; violations involving customs employees. Agency: Customs Service.

Industrial Hygienist—Inspects businesses to determine compliance with safety and occupational health regulations. Agency: OSHA.

Internal Revenue Agent—Audits individual and corporate taxpayers to determine their tax liabilities. Agency: IRS.

Internal Revenue Officer—Collects taxes and secures tax returns; analyzes financial information on businesses and determines the methods to resolve tax liabilities. Agency: IRS.

IRS Special Agent—Investigates criminal violations particularly those relating to income and wagering or gaming devices; recommends criminal prosecution and the assertion of civil penalties against taxpayers; assists the U.S. Attorney in preparation of trial cases. Agency: IRS.

Park Ranger—Protects against structural forest fire and property damage; gathers and disseminates natural, historical, cultural or scientific information; demonstrates folk art and crafts; enforces laws and regulations; investigates violations, complaints, trespasses, and accidents; conducts rescue missions. Agencies: Corps of Engineers, National Park Service.

211

ACCOUNTING
Internal Revenue Agent
Special Agent-Internal Revenue Service
Tax Law Specialist

AGRICULTURE OR AGRICULTURAL SCIENCES
Food Inspector
Plant Protection and Quarantine Officer
Range Conservationist

BIOLOGY OR BIOLOGICAL SCIENCES
Consumer Safety Officer
Food Inspector
Park Ranger
Plant Protection and Quarantine Officer
Range Conservationist

BUSINESS ADMINISTRATION
Securities Compliance Examiner

CHEMISTRY
Consumer Safety Officer
Food Inspector
Industrial Hygienist
Toxicologist

ECONOMICS
Securities Compliance Specialist

PHYSICS
Consumer Safety Officer
Toxicologist

212

criminal justice positions listed in Figure 4 have been those with the greatest number of available openings.

Hiring for Administrative Careers With America (ACWA)—Contained in the FJOL is a category of college graduate entry-level positions which have their own special hiring method. These are called Administrative Careers With America (ACWA) positions. ACWA positions

Border patrol agent
Criminal investigating
Customs inspector
Environmental protection
Game law enforcement
General investigating
Immigration inspector
Internal revenue officer
Paralegal specialist
Safety management
Security administration
Treasury enforcement agent

are entry-level trainee positions in a variety of administrative and managerial areas, many of which relate to criminal justice. These positions begin at the GS-5 and GS-7 levels.[3] Most have career ladders that lead to the full performance level of GS-11 or GS-12.

Most entry-level positions (GS-5/7) in administrative fields are filled through lists of eligible candidates maintained by OPM offices. Passing a written test is required in order to have your name placed on the list of eligibles (although those with GPA's higher than 3.5 are exempted from this test, as they are from tests given by several direct hiring agencies). Periodic notices appear in the FJOL whenever applications are being accepted.

Qualifications for ACWA positions—Requirements for ACWA jobs at the GS-5 level include: a bachelor's degree regardless of GPA or three years of progressively responsible experience or a combination of education and appropriate experience totaling three years (30 semester

---

[3] GS is the General Schedule for salaries on which federal positions are paid and the current levels are indicated in Figure 7. College graduates start in the range GS 5 to GS 7, depending upon their qualifications and can earn scaled increases within any category as well as being promoted up in GS level. The salary scale is discussed further at the end of this section.

213

Group 1   Health, Safety and Environmental Occupations
Safety and Occupational Health Management
Environmental Protection Specialist

Group 5   Benefits Review, Tax and Legal Occupations
Social Insurance Administration
Social Services
Tax Technician
Paralegal Specialist
Passport and Visa Examining
Worker's Compensation Claims Examining
Social Insurance Claims Examining
Unemployment Compensation Claims Examining
Veterans Claims Examining
Civil Service Retirement
Claims Examining

Group 6   Law Enforcement and Investigation Occupations
Park Ranger
Security Administration Intelligence
Wage and Hour Compliance
Internal Revenue Officer
Civil Aviation Security Specialist
General Investigator
Criminal Investigator
Game Law Enforcement
Immigration Inspection
Securities Compliance Examining
Alcohol, Tobacco, and Firearms Inspection
Public Health Quarantine Inspection
Customs Inspector

hours substitute for nine months work experience). Requirements for ACWA jobs at the GS-7 level include: superior academic achievement demonstrated either by a bachelor's degree with a GPA of at least 2.9 (on a 4.0 scale) **or** standing in the upper third of your graduating class **or** you have been elected to a national honor society. You also may qualify for GS-7 if you have a bachelor's degree and at least one year of graduate study **or** bachelor's degree and one year of professional-level experience in an occupation directly related to the position.

ACWA positions are divided into 7 occupational groups. Positions covered by groups 1-6 require a written test. Positions in group 7 require only an evaluation of education and experience. The positions covered by these groups that are relevant to criminology and criminal justice majors are located in group 6 and a few others are in group 1. There is a separate test given for each of the groups 1-6. Tests are given periodically when there is a need for new applicants on the register. When any of the tests is to be given, it is announced in the Federal Job Opportunity List (FJOL). To take the test, you must apply by the published closing date. You will then be scheduled for the test. You may take as many of the tests as you like. You will receive a notice of the results shortly after you take the test.

ACWA positions in group 7 are announced separately on the FJOL when a vacancy occurs. They are listed by position title. Applicants are sent the appropriate application forms. Once you send in the forms, your application will be evaluated. You will receive a notice of the results from the office to which you applied.

Once a candidate has passed the test, they are placed on a register (list of eligible applicants). When an agency requests a referral list, they will receive a list of the applicants who are at the top of the register. If you are on this list, the agency may contact you. If they do so, they will probably ask you to fill out the Standard Form-171 (SF-171) and other required forms.

Direct hiring for ACWA via the Outstanding Scholar Program—Some applicants can apply directly to agencies for ACWA jobs under the Outstanding Scholar Program. To qualify for this program, you must have a GPA of 3.5 or above (on a 4.0 scale) for all undergraduate course work, or have graduated in the upper ten percent of your class.[4] Applicants who qualify under this program may apply directly to any agency at which they wish to work. The initial correspondence may be

---

[4] An applicant's GPA is rounded in the following manner: a 3.44 is rounded down to 3.4; a 3.45 is rounded up to 3.5. However, note that you also qualify for Outstanding Scholar if you are in the upper 10% of your cohort. Many students ignore this and needlessly take the test.

a resume with a cover letter indicating that you are applying under the Outstanding Scholar Program. However, at a later time, the agency may require the SF-171 and other forms to be completed. You will not receive notice of eligibility from OPM if you apply through this program.

Hiring via the competitive service— As we have seen with ACWA, when a federal agency has a vacancy, it can be filled in many different ways. Most positions are announced in the Federal Job Opportunities List (FJOL) which is sent every week to state employment service offices and college placement offices.[5]

People applying for these positions compete with other applicants and are evaluated by the Office of Personnel Management (OPM) or by agencies who have been given authority to fill certain positions. Most of these positions are in the Executive Branch of the government in such agencies as the Department of Defense, the Department of Agriculture, the Department of Health and Human Services, the Federal Aviation Administration and many others. Agencies have the option, however, of using other hiring authorities to fill open positions. For example, agencies can directly hire qualified applicants for certain entry-level professional positions under what is called "Schedule B Authority." These positions would not be advertised on the FJOL. Agencies can also hire qualified physically disabled persons without advertising the position to be filled on the FJOL.

Hiring via the excepted service—Some agencies, such as the U.S. Postal Service, the Federal Bureau of Investigation, and the Tennessee Valley Authority are "excepted" from competitive service procedures. These agencies establish their own criteria for job evaluation to meet position requirements. These jobs do not appear on the Federal Job Opportunities List. If you are interested in an excepted service job with any of the following agencies, you should contact that agency directly (at the address given in Appendix II): Central Intelligence Agency, Personnel Representative, Defense Intelligence Agency, Federal Bureau of Investigation, General Accounting Office, National Security Agency,

---

[5] These positions are generally open to college students, except at times of hiring freezes when certain positions may be restricted to "internal hires."

U.S. Nuclear Regulatory Commission, Postal Rate Commission, U.S. Postal Service, Judicial Branch of the Government (positions such as court administrators, bailiffs, computer operators, law clerks/attorneys, etc. This does not include positions with the Administrative Offices of the U.S. Courts and the U.S. Customs Courts).

Special programs for students—The federal government also trains students and offers several programs in that regard.

I. Federal Cooperative Education
The United States Government employs more students in cooperative education programs than any private sector company or corporation. Federal agencies are in search of highly motivated, flexible and creative students who aspire to dynamic and rewarding careers in public service. The emphasis of the Federal Cooperative Education Program is on quality work assignments that will provide a laboratory in which academic skills can be applied. The purpose of this partnership between education and federal agencies is to produce the leaders, managers and professionals for tomorrow's effective government.

The Federal Cooperative Education Program is a planned and progressive career-related, student employment program. It blends academic studies with paid on-the-job experience. After completion of the program, a student is eligible for a full-time permanent position (called a noncompetitive conversion). Each federal agency employing co-op students must develop a working agreement with the educational institution and the student involved. It should include work schedules, program criteria and the requirements for noncompetitive conversion into the competitive service. The work assignments must provide

6 ELIGIBILITY FOR CO-OP

To be eligible a potential co-op student must be:
- pursuing a professional, graduate, bachelor or associate degree
- maintaining good academic standing in course work
- enrolled in a university/college, trade or vocational school co-op program
- recommended for the assignment by the school
- a United States citizen

sufficient opportunities for students to gain in-depth experience in areas related to their academic program or career goals. The work schedule must also assure that the student will have the required study-related work hours to be non-competitively converted into the competitive service. Work may be scheduled on a full-time (alternating with periods of study) or part-time (parallel with periods of study) basis. On alternating schedules, at least two work experiences must be provided for baccalaureate and associate degree students. One work experience must be provided for all other participating co-op students. In most cases, summers may be used for one work experience but may not be used for both baccalaureate and associate degree students. Those who are working part-time may work a minimum of 16 hours per week. In two years, students may work up to a maximum of 2600 hours.

All co-op students enter the excepted service upon initial appointment. For students in undergraduate level programs appointments are made between the GS-1 and GS-5 salary range. Students in a master's degree program may be appointed at grades up to and including GS-9. Doctoral and professional degree candidates may be appointed at grades up to and including the GS-11 level. Superior academic achievement standards may be used to appoint baccalaureate students at the GS-7 level. The co-op appointment continues until 120 days after the student has graduated. After graduation, the student may be converted to a permanent position. Students are eligible for noncompetitive conversion within the 120 calendar-day period after graduation. Written tests are not required for conversion. However, they must meet the minimum qualifications for the position and satisfy the following minimum study-related work requirements in a pay status:

high school diploma	640 hours (16 weeks)
undergraduate certificate/diploma	640 hours (16 weeks)
graduate or professional degree	640 hours (16 weeks)
baccalaureate degree	1040 hours (26 weeks)
associate degree	1040 hours (26 weeks)

The student must also be recommended by the employing agency for conversion.

II. Student Trainee Program
The Student Trainee Program is a career-related experience that works in conjunction with an academic program. It enables the student to gain

valuable hands-on training. It also prepares the future leaders of the federal service.

The Student Trainee Program is a type of work experience that enhances classroom learning. It is a competitive service appointment. Student trainees are eligible for full benefits of the federal service. A potential student trainee must be: enrolled in an accredited university/college and qualified for a specific student trainee position (i.e. accountant student trainee).

Students must apply and compete on an open vacancy announcement for specific student trainee positions. Depending on qualifications, the appointment may be made at the GS-2 to the GS-4 level. The student trainee may either work part-time while in school or alternate periods of full-time education with periods of full-time employment. After completion of portions of the educational program and qualifying work experience, the student trainee may be promoted to a higher grade. Upon graduation, the student trainee is promoted to a GS-5 or GS-7 position. Check directly with the agencies in your area to find out if they participate in this program.

III. Summer Employment Program
The Summer Employment Program eases the impact of vacation schedules and the increase of seasonal jobs. This program offers various positions including those of professional standing. The program creates paid training and work opportunities for students during the summer months. The student may be employed from May 13th to September 30th. A potential Summer Employment Program participant must be 16 years of age and qualified for the position based on experience or education.

Each December a Summer Jobs Announcement lists summer employment opportunities available nationwide for the following summer. The announcement is sent to college career placement offices or a copy may be obtained from any area office of OPM. If a student is interested in a particular position or agency, the applicant should contact that agency directly.

A note on federal salaries—Every position in the federal service is classified according to the duties and the responsibilities required. This classification determines the annual salary for the position. Recent college graduates usually enter the federal service at grades GS-5 or

GS-7. The annual salary begins at the base pay indicated in Figure 7 for 1993.

Advancement to the next higher pay rate within a grade level (step increase) occurs if job performance has been acceptable. In each grade there are ten steps (1-10). The difference between each step is approximately 3% of the base salary for the grade. The amount of time required to advance to the next step varies. The waiting period between Steps 4-6 is 104 weeks; and for Steps 7-10 the waiting period is 156 weeks. In addition, Congress authorizes salary increases to keep federal pay competitive with the private sector. Employees may also be promoted to higher grades in their line of work.

In this final section we have contributions from federal employees in two criminal justice related positions. The first article is by Danny Gonzalez who describes how he began with the Immigration and Naturalization Service as a Border Patrol Agent and then moved into Customs Inspection. He tells us how he went through the hiring and training process, and about the daily work he does protecting the United States from illegal entry by foreigners. He explains the importance of computers to investigative work and how, with experience, inspectors develop profiles of suspects and how they interrogate them in search of the truth. Danny also provides tips on how to apply for a federal position. In her contribution Vickie Kopcak, an Alcohol, Tobacco and Firearms (ATF) Inspector also describes how she went through the hiring process, her training and the nature of her work. She presents a picture of government inspections work that warns prospective employees about the enormous amount of paperwork that is required and how such work requires a considerable degree of self-motivation if one is to survive.

The final chapter describes the work of the FBI agent. This is not an actual agent's inside view but draws largely on material taken from the FBI's own career recruitment literature.

7 SALARIES
COLLEGE ENTRY

GS-5	$18,340
GS-7	$22,717
GS-9	$27,789

For further information on federal criminal justice careers:

Warner, John W. (Jack). *Federal Jobs in Law Enforcement*. New York, NY: ARCO, Prentice Hall, 1992.
Profiles over 100 federal agencies and looks at necessary qualifications.

ASA. *How to Join the Federal Workforce and Advance Your Career*. Washington DC: American Sociological Association.

FOCIS (Federal Occupational and Career Information System). Available from: National Technical Information Service (NTIS), 5285 Port Royal Road, Springfield, VA 22161. Call (703) 487-4650.
This is a software package on federal careers from OPM. It contains data on 360 federal occupations and includes descriptions of the work, minimum qualifications, grade levels, salaries and related college majors. Additionally, it includes addresses to contact for employment information and the descriptions and addresses of 450 federal organizations.

For job announcements:

OPM's own information accessed by modem from your area Federal Job Information Center (FJIC).

Federal Jobs Digest
Federal Jobs Digest FT, 325 Pennsylvania Avenue SE, Washington DC 20003. Call (800) 824-5000.
Published every two weeks.

Federal Career Opportunities
Federal Research Services, Inc., P.O. Box 1059W, Vienna, VA 22183-1059. Call (800) 822-JOBS or (703) 281-0200.
Weekly—$7.50 per issue/$38 for 6 issues/$75 for 12 issues.

Federal Times

Federal Times, 6883 Commercial Drive, Springfield, VA 22159. Call (703) 750-8600.

Lists jobs at GS-7 and above submitted by federal agencies. $1.25 per issue or $39.00/annual subscription.

CHAPTER 25:

Working for the Immigration and Naturalization Service: From Border Patrol Agent to Immigration Inspector

by *Danny Gonzalez**

I currently work as an Immigration Inspector for the federal government. I got into federal service because of a relative's suggestion. I was attending school in Texas when my cousin, who was employed by the U.S. Border Patrol, told me they were hiring. I decided to look into taking the civil service test.

Testing and the Oral Board
I discovered that the Border Patrol has its own test. I took it. I didn't prepare for it. I thought, well I'm in school. I didn't know what to expect. It involved some reading and some comprehension, some mathematical and analytical abilities and, although my algebra and math weren't that great, I passed. This was a "big hire." They didn't actually tell me I had passed. They just sent me a letter telling me to show up for an oral interview.

For the interview there is a panel of three Border Patrol Agents who ask questions about your background and education, whether you've ever had trouble with the law. Then they give you scenarios to test your judgement. They don't want anybody who is trigger happy. The scenario may start out with, "You're a Border Patrol Agent, in uniform, and armed. Now what if you come across a situation with a known felon? You've heard the description over the radio and this is the man. You know it's him and you know he's illegally in the United States..." You're sitting there, going along with this scenario step by step. They tell you, "He's confronted you. He's got his hands behind his back. And he's walking towards **you**! What are you going to do?" You **have** to answer. "What are you going to do, Dan? He's still walking. He's walking toward you. He's still walking to you. What are you going to do, Dan?!" I said I'd talk to him, try to tell him to stop where he is. They are looking to see if you'd pull your weapon. If you'd pull it out

*This is a fictional name used at the request of the author.

and shoot the man, that's an inappropriate response. If I had said that, it would have been: "Well, Dan, you just messed up. He pulled his hands out and he had a flower behind his back and you just blew him away." So they are looking for your judgment under pressure and that's the key. They want to see how quickly you can respond in a crisis because that's what you face in many situations. And they'll grade you on your response. Then they'll give you other scenarios, maybe two or three. There are many steps and so many hoops to go through to get hired by the federal government.

The hiring process can vary in length. In a period where they are hiring a lot of agents it can take 2-3 months, otherwise, it could take 6-8 months. In my case, I was hired as a Border Patrol Agent in about three months. I passed all of the tests and was assigned to El Paso, Texas. El Paso is a desert and a very mountainous region. It is an area with which I was not familiar, even though I was born and raised in Texas.

Training
Training is done at the federal academy. The academy is located in Glynco, Georgia and it is where most of the federal agencies train. The Boarder Patrol academy is very militaristic. You learn Immigration laws, rules and regulations as well as being trained in firearms and physical fitness. They train you to recognize various documents such as authentic passports and "green cards," which are actually pink and blue now, and have a bar code incorporated. For Border Patrol the training lasts 18 weeks; but for an Inspector it's eight to ten weeks. At the academy you'll be working with many other agents, such as Park Police, Customs, ATF. In all there are more than sixty agencies there. FBI and DEA train at their main headquarters in Quantico, Virginia. People sometimes switch agencies at the academy. You might start with Border Patrol or Immigration but while you're at the academy, you may see another agency whose recruiters persuade you to transfer.

When you come out of training, what happens next depends upon the agency. I graduated from the Border Patrol academy and went to the field in El Paso where they assigned me to a "Journeyman Agent." This is someone who has been around a while and knows the ropes. They sent me out in a patrol vehicle with that agent. Then they gave me a post-academy test. After you've been in the field you are subject to these tests. You are initially on one year's probation. So after the academy you have eight months to go. During the probation you take a seven-month test and a nine-month test. And while you are working the field, you are still taking a day each week to learn more on Immigration law, Spanish and so on.

The academy teaches you Spanish and you better know it or you won't graduate. Although I am Hispanic, I was never formally educated in Spanish. I just knew it from the streets. You have to read and write it. I got it down and I passed. Immigration also requires Spanish. Although there is some question of its relevance on the northern border, on the southern border you better know it or you'll be lost. It is a process of elimination and there is a lot of attrition.

Policing the border
Border Patrol is an arm of the Immigration Service. They're uniformed officers that enforce the immigration laws by patrolling the borders of Canada and Mexico. They're looking for illegal aliens and contraband. Border Patrol is a real busy job that involves literally going out and physically patrolling the borders and catching illegal aliens trying to enter the U.S. You learn to pick out those who are illegal by experience and profile. I'll be patrolling in a vehicle in El Paso and I'll see an individual who appears to be illegally in the U.S. It's so commonplace there that much of the time I'll just drive up and ask him in Spanish, "Let me see your documents." In most cases, before I've even pulled over, I know he's illegal. Once we've acknowledged that he doesn't have any documents, that he's basically walking the streets, then we arrest him. That happens daily. Of course, you frisk him to make sure he doesn't have any weapons with him before you get him in the back of the vehicle!

Many people are under the misconception that all we deal with are Mexicans. But in that area, El Paso, Texas, or in California, there are many other nationalities. We call them OTM's, "Other Than Mexicans." There are Central Americans, Hondurans, Guatemalans, etc.

There are also many nationalities on the northern border: Polish, Sri Lankan, Indian, Pakistani and most recently an influx of Chinese illegal aliens. Mexican illegals are a minority on the northern boarder. Alien smugglers use trucks, 18-wheelers carrying 18-20 people who are trying to get in or they use taxi cabs with illegal aliens in the trunks.

Immigration Inspector

After one year with Border Patrol I transferred up to Michigan, staying with the INS but moving to Immigration Inspections. The overall authority for INS is the U.S. Department of Justice, which also includes the FBI and DEA. INS itself employs Border Patrol agents, Immigration Inspectors, Criminal Investigators and others. For example, an Immigration Examiner scrutinizes immigration applications and requests for green cards, and interviews applicants who are married to Americans about their marriage. They also swear-in immigrants.

Immigration Inspectors enforce the immigration and nationality laws, initially by checking passengers' eligibility to come to the U.S. We're at the airports and at the U.S. land borders such as the bridges, tunnels and other ports of entry throughout the U.S. border. At these locations immigration works alongside many other federal agencies such as Customs, the Department of Agriculture, and the Department of Public Health. We have such an influx of visitors that legal entry is terribly backed up. In an effort to address this problem, the U.S. Immigration Service is beginning to have inspectors in foreign cities, such as London, Moscow and Mexico City, so people can be pre-cleared. One officer was stationed on a temporary duty assignment in London at Heathrow Airport for three months. His stay was extended to six months. Inspectors have the opportunity for worldwide travel with this type of job.

Specifically we check passengers' passports and visas. We determine if they are U.S. citizens at the port of entry. If they are we are not really concerned with them. They pick up their baggage and go down to the customs/agriculture check. We're concerned mainly with foreigners and people that are permanent residents here in the States; foreigners with green cards. We are concerned with all those with a non-U.S. status. We have many bona-fide visitors, meaning legitimate visitors who come for business, pleasure, tourism or to work here. We have to determine if their documents, passports and visas are valid, authentic and if they have the proper status. At the same time we also have to check for illegals trying to come in.

There is a big trade in smuggling aliens. Some smugglers try to bring narcotics in, but others are trying to bring people in. There is a big market and a lot of money involved for the smugglers. You must be aware of the tricks of the trade, of the "profiles" of high risk foreigners.

The International Terminal has non-stop flights from Tokyo, Seoul, Amsterdam, Paris, Frankfurt and London. We inspect, examine and determine whether the passengers can legally enter the United States. We are paid to make sure criminals, drug traffickers and other undesirable persons aren't admitted to the United States. We check to see if those inbound to the U.S. have outstanding warrants or if they have a prior criminal record. It's a tough job because there are so many people who want to come to this country and they'll do everything and anything to try to get here. There are so many deceitful ways to get into the U.S. As an Immigration Inspector I have to try and figure these out.

It gets pretty intense in that there are many civil rights issues involved. You have to understand the reasons why people are so desperate to come here. You have to understand their nationality, their laws, their language and culture, and what's going on in their countries. That is what is interesting about this job. You have to keep up with global political events if you are to perform effectively. If you have an interest in international relations or the international political scene, you can't help but learn more about what is going on in Korea, Japan, Bosnia, Russia, etc. You become so much more involved with international matters. This is also why Immigration likes language majors. Immigration is seeking to hire them as translators or as Inspectors or Investigators because they can be used as interviewers or undercover in electronic surveillance.

When passengers get off the aircraft at the international terminal they approach passport control. Their name is entered into the computer system and we check for any outstanding bench warrants, and on their international travel itinerary. If everything is clear and there's no match on their name then they proceed down to customs. But if there are any problems or questions they are moved into a secondary area.

We send people into "secondaries" for further questioning and to clarify the situation that came up on the computer. In the secondary area there's more questioning, and accessing of computer data bases that give us much more information about that person. If they don't have a passport because it is not required (as, for example, with U.S. citizens visiting Canada), then we'll look at their driver's license, birth certificate or other documentation, in an attempt to clarify the situation. As we are running that check, we are also running several other data bases to check how long you were here on previous visits, if you "overstayed" the time granted by INS. If you're an "overstay," Immigration will ask why you didn't leave before the given time.

At the same time we are trying to determine if what is before us is a real document. Is it authentic or counterfeit? We have many impostors.

These are people with legitimate documents that they obtained by fraud. For example, I had one passenger from an international flight who presented a fake United States passport. It was made up with his picture in someone else's passport. Through the years you learn what to look for. I can tell just by a "profile." You learn to recognize what country people are from just by looking at them. You learn what to ask them, and to establish information about them, from how they answer your questions, from what they are wearing, and from how they talk. Anyway, through seeing passports and visas everyday, I know what is real and what is not. And this guy presented his passport and I knew it wasn't any good. There is big business in manufacturing fake passports and documents. The "vendors" can make anything from $1,500 to $30,000 each, depending on the price the market will bear. I asked about his citizenship: "Are you a U.S. citizen?" I knew he wasn't. I wanted him to give false information to a federal officer. So I asked: "Are you a U.S. citizen?" and he said "Yeah" and I said "Okay" and I ran the computer system NCIC (National Crime Information Center).[1] I put the man in a jail cell and eventually he was deported back to his country.

In cases like this we take them right to one of our cells nearby and hold them there until we interrogate them and try to figure out who they are: their nationality, why they did this, how much they paid for the fake or fraudulent passport, and from which vendor they got it. In other words we try to obtain the truth, the facts, from them. We want them to tell us the truth: "Alright, I'm not this John Doe that it says on the passport that I bought for $1,500." The person will have to sit there in the cell until the other passengers have been processed through INS. He's sitting there thinking about having committed a federal offence, a false claim. We take him from the cell to an office, sit him down and start asking him questions. The suspect must formally swear under oath that he is telling the truth. If it's a female, we get female officers to do this. The suspect is not under arrest yet. The federal authority gives us the right to detain suspects and we cannot admit someone to the U.S. until we are satisfied.

Much of the time they don't tell the truth. We deal with that. We leave and come back latter. One man from the Philippines, which is

---

[1] NCIC is a federal lookout system linked with Interpol which allows us to run different checks just from entering the name.

predominantly Catholic, had a Bible in his luggage. I saw the Bible. I came back, opened the door and said, "Are you a religious man?" I said, "You think about what you've done." I left. It was just a ploy to get him to be honest with us. And he did. He must have weighed it up, felt guilty and when I came back he broke. It takes time to break some of them. One person may tell you right off the bat. With others it may take two or three hours. If they continue stone-walling, then we'll handcuff them and, in certain cases, transport them to a local jail for an overnight stay. In the morning we take them to the next available plane for removal from the U.S.

If they plead political asylum, that's a different situation because the law states they have a right to a hearing.[2] They will be given a date to see a judge who decides on the credibility of their claim to asylum status. Right now someone from Bosnia, Cuba, China, or Romania may get approved for political asylum. But if he's from a country like France where there is no persecution for political views, then it is not credible, so they are denied and then they get deported. It depends upon what country they're from and what's going on there at the time.[3] Many coming here illegally aren't aware they have the right to plead political asylum. But, in some cases, they are going to be in jail until they see an immigration judge. For many, the jail conditions will actually be better than the political conditions from which they came. They don't have to worry about where bombs are falling or being shot by a sniper while standing in a food line. They are getting food, housing, and medical care.

As well as passport and document inspection we also do "adjudications." These are immigration applications that attempt to waive a foreigner's felonious conviction, thus allowing entry. We get applications and we adjudicate them, approve or deny them. We have a data base with an alien registration number that they have been given. We look at the file. We look at the convictions and at the record; we determine when the offense was committed and its seriousness; and we

---

[2] Even if they come in on a false passport, if they plead political asylum they are given a special status of asylum refugee.

[3] Haitians have been sent back because our government claims they are fleeing economic conditions, not political or religious persecution.

send off requests for record checks from the RCMP (Royal Canadian Mounted Police). We find out where they are working, what their employment record is like. One applicant was a famous hockey player. He'd been convicted for cocaine trafficking. He was coming across the tunnel with cocaine in his car. He had a bad attitude toward law enforcement. The officers searched him and found cocaine. As a celebrity getting paid big bucks, he thought he could get around things. Anyway, he had to go through due process. He originally had one conviction for possession. A year later he got stopped again for possession of a narcotic. The federal immigration judge in Chicago set up a hearing and he was convicted and deported but he appealed. It has been something like three years now. Ironically, he could not go back to Canada because if he did he would deport himself. He can leave, but if he goes he pays the price; he deports himself and cannot re-enter until he has a legitimate status. This is another interesting part of the job, adjudicating these cases.

You meet all kinds of famous celebrities. I've met Stevie Wonder and Madonna. The White House calls our office about certain people. I also do other things related to my Immigration career. I am a recruiter contact. I am not the person that hires but I talk to students and candidates to get them familiarized with the process. Of course, Immigration Officers also have routine work, such as writing reports and going to court.

There are some frustrations to the job too. These include erratic work schedules, usually six or seven days a week and, if you go for the overtime, you don't have much of a social life. Days off rotate. Maybe you go to church on Sunday; INS works on weekends. You may have a family, a wife, a young kid, and you want to spend time with them. It can be tough working seven-day weeks. You miss the kids growing up. Also working full-time on shifts doesn't allow me much time to complete my education, although I'd like to do so.

Another disadvantage is that you may get transferred or assigned to who knows where. It may be an area of the country that you can't stand. Here I don't like the long winters. I'm used to being out on the beach in January in Texas. It's quite a personal thing. With some positions, like Border Patrol, the work goes on outside and that is very enjoyable, as well as giving you the freedom to move about on patrol, at your own discretion. With others, like Immigration Examiner, it is an inside job. But if you like office work, computer work, paperwork, adjudicating, that could be ideal. You also have those possibilities with Border Patrol, if that is what you like.

We deal with people who sometimes are very impatient and irrational. They take your name and say "I'm going to write to my Congressman." I just treat them like I'd want to be treated. If they've got bad attitudes you deal with the situation.

The work can be enjoyable at the beginning. It is a challenge and something new. You can learn a lot. But after a while the challenge is met and then you get stuck at a certain level and it may be that you have to look elsewhere to improve your career possibilities. You might start looking for better positions, to better yourself through promotion. You should always be on the lookout for better positions, with different challenges. For example, I've been trying to transfer to Texas where my family and friends live.

Salary and other benefits

You start out at GS-5 that is currently $18,340. With an advanced degree you can get more but it also depends how you sell yourself and what you demand. We have one person with a master's who was hired on as a GS-5 and another who started as a GS-7. You can fight for more, depending upon what you have to offer. After one year on probation you go to GS-7 automatically. GS-7 pays $22,717. The next year is an automatic jump to GS-9, which is now at $27,789 after two years. Every year after that you get a "step increase" and now I'm a GS-9.3, which pays $29,641 annually. That stops after three years and the step increase goes in two-year increments. Then you get another step increase. Overtime, which is required, goes on top of that. There is a limit on overtime of $25,000. One officer I work with is a "nine" (GS-9) and he got the maximum overtime allowed, which brought his salary to $54,000. But he was working all the time.

The application process

Of the different methods of applying, one of the best is to take the Immigration Inspector's Civil Service Test. Another is the Outstanding Scholar Program which lets you bypass the test. If you're qualified as an Outstanding Scholar, call the agencies and let them know this. You want to apply as many ways as you can since this will increase your chances of being hired.

The minimum age requirement for certain positions with the INS is 21, and you must be a U.S. citizen. But there are other positions that are called "covered positions" (such as Special Agents, Investigators, Deportation Officers), which refers to that position being covered under a certain section of the retirement law. You have to get into these positions prior to your 37th birthday. There are other waivers and exceptions. For example, if you have prior federal civil law enforcement or military experience, they can waive the age restriction on certain positions. There is no maximum age requirement for the Immigration Inspector position.

Application forms
Application forms can be completed at any time. The basic form is called the SF-171 (Standard Form used for applying for Federal employment). This is the government's version of a resume. Filling out the form is quite a science. Basically you complete it but don't sign it until after you have copied it several times. You leave certain items blank, such as where it asks what job you want. Then you make copies of it and sign those in original form and date them. Each application has to have an actual signature. You then fill in what job you want. You have to completely fill the form. Don't leave anything blank or this will cause a delay in the application process.

Who gets hired
About 15 or 20 years ago the easiest way to get into the INS was through the Border Patrol. I started that way and transferred over to Inspections. But now it seems to have changed. Although neither Border Patrol nor Inspections **require** a degree, from what I've seen, people with degrees are more likely to be hired. We did, however, recently hire someone who didn't have a degree. He had previously worked with the government as a clerk in INS. He found out about this position as an Inspector and qualified with a combination of school experience and work experience. The more education you have the better. If you don't have work experience you will not get into some agencies, such as the FBI. Immigration will hire from any major. Of the three people hired recently, one was a sociology major, another a Spanish major and another was a finance major. It's not crucial but it helps if you happen to know another language or if you've minored in one. Many Inspectors are learning Spanish. Computer literacy is also very important.

Another consideration is affirmative action policies, which may be an advantage or a disadvantage depending on your status. The federal agencies are increasingly trying to hire women through an affirmative action program, because most federal agencies lack women. The government has policy goals in terms of hiring, and they may be emphasizing African-Americans, Hispanics and/or women. These hiring policies may seem harsh to a white male college student trying to start their career but it is still possible to get hired; the competition may just be a little keener. The opportunities are open to all. In the past, minorities, such as women or Asians, would not get hired even if they had the right qualifications. Moreover, few of the minorities who are employed by the U.S. government are employed in upper management or policy-making positions. The result is that the majority of those currently employed are white males and they also hold the majority of the senior positions. Now, however, minorities can get hired but they still have to meet the same qualifications as any other candidate. As a recruiter my emphasis is to make minorities, among others, aware that they are eligible candidates for these jobs. If you don't get a position, try again. Don't get discouraged. Just keep trying.

CHAPTER 26:

Alcohol, Tobacco and Firearms (ATF) Inspector

by *Vickie Kopcak*

I graduated from university in December of 1988. I had a double major in public administration and interpersonal communications. I had attended a job fair at a local community college the semester prior to graduation. Numerous federal agencies were recruiting. I was unaware that the Bureau of Alcohol, Tobacco, and Firearms (ATF) even existed prior to the job fair. Because it was so crowded I just signed my name on two different lists; one was for an Inspector position in the Compliance Operations (CO) side and one was for a Special Agent position on the Law Enforcement (LE) side. I was still not sure of the difference, even when two different packets of information arrived from ATF for me. So I filled out both the forms. I was scheduled to take a test for Treasury Enforcement Agents (TEA) and, at the same time, I submitted an application, called a Standard Form 171 and a narrative statement of my skills, knowledge and abilities to the compliance operations section. This narrative was required when I applied, but I am not sure if it is still used. Essentially I was asked to write down all of the things I had done and learned in school, past employment and volunteer work.

Surprisingly the process moved rather quickly and I was scheduled for an interview for the Inspector position in late December. Two days later I was scheduled to take the TEA. The interview was downtown and it went great. I immediately hit it off with the man who interviewed me, the Area Supervisor for Compliance Operations. I was in the interview for three hours. He painted a very rosy picture of the Inspector position. I expressed my interest in the law enforcement aspects of ATF. He told me the Inspector position is "just like an Agent position except you don't break down doors or do raids." He said the major difference was that it is not as "glamorous." He never mentioned a word about tax work or alcohol work. He only told me about the firearms and explosives aspects. I left feeling fairly confident that he was going to hire me and he did. I still took the TEA, but did not take it seriously (I just guessed at the math section!), but I passed. I never heard anything else from ATF Law

Enforcement, except that I receive periodic updates to this day telling me that I am still on a list to be called for an interview. In late February I was finally notified that I was hired, but not by the man who interviewed me, as he had been transferred.

I filled out the required paper work for a background check, got finger-printed on an FBI card, and submitted it all to Washington D.C. Four months later I still had not heard anything, so I called the personnel department in D.C. They apologized to me because they had lost (thrown out!) my paperwork and had listed in my file that I declined the position!

I had to start all over and resubmit all the paperwork. Luckily I kept copies from the first time (Lesson #1: Always keep copies of everything you submit). Had I not called to check on the status, I probably would be unemployed today (Lesson #2: If you think something is taking too long to process, call and check it out. Don't be afraid to double check on things that are important to you).

I finally came "on board" on September 25, 1989, some nine months after I submitted my original application. The first stage of my employment was eight weeks of training (two four-week sessions) at the Federal Law Enforcement Training Center in Georgia. There I discovered that you not only get formal training, but informally you meet people from many other agencies and it is here that much internal recruiting goes on, as well as some serious socializing!

Working for a governmental agency is very similar to a civilian job. You still have the office politics, the office gossip and the little cliques that form. In other ways it is a whole new ball game. There are mounds of paperwork that have to be completed in triplicate, and rules or written orders for everything. Then there are the forms. When you're new to the way a governmental agency runs it is very frustrating. You can only ask so many times before people look at you as if you're stupid. Many times they do that to new recruits anyway. There was little instruction. Every time a new question came up I was pointed in the direction of one of many phone book sized manuals and told to read the regulations. So a lot of research was involved. To the people who have been there for a while, it is routine; they can't see why you have a problem.

ATF Inspectors work on numerous aspects of regulation from inspecting high explosives plants, wineries and distilleries, (checking their production process and inventories) to checking up on individual firearms dealers. They also write regulations, and hold educational seminars and check on the legality of various changes that manufacturers and dealers want to make, such as new alcohol labels or alterations to firearms mechanisms. I conduct inspections, primarily on firearms dealers, although in this area we also inspect some explosives manufacturers and do some alcohol inspections. We audit the records, run criminal checks on purchasers and work with the ATF Law Enforcement on dealers who we think are acting illegally. We don't work with the Agents that often. We work explosives in the summer. Explosives Inspections are similar to firearms work; you check the dealer's inventory and the records. Fireworks (the aerial stuff used for large shows, not the roadside stand type) are also regulated by ATF. We work on those once a year prior to the July 4th holiday. So every year it is like doing them for the first time. Fireworks inspections are conducted with public safety as a primary goal. The alcohol industry is regulated by ATF also. It is based almost solely on collecting taxes when the alcohol, beer, wine and distilled spirits are produced. There are numerous rules and regulations for alcohol production, labeling the bottle and selling the product. It is very complex. The inspectors who have been around for a while generally do this work, but everyone is required to be able to do the research to be able to conduct the inspection. I find this type of work the most boring; it is largely accounting. The tobacco industry does not exist in my state; therefore, I do not do any tobacco work. In the Southern states tobacco inspections (for tax purposes) are regularly conducted.

The firearms inspections typically involve making a visit to a dealer who, in this and many other areas, lives in a private residence and has a dealer's license. You have to move into some threatening situations, but most of the time people are civilized. I have only been terrified once in the three and a half years I have worked here and that was by a dealer's neighbor! The other public contact I have is by telephone. The phone will ring and I will be asked to decide whether the various trigger mechanism changes the caller is about to make to his Beretta are going to violate some law. Usually I have to research the question and get back to him.

There are many good things about my job. I work independently most of the time. I have a government car to drive to the office and to assignments. I can set my own hours and I do not have a boss looking over my shoulder all the time. I like the freedom of working in the field. I've met a large variety of people and the work is diverse enough to eliminate boredom. It is a pretty good job. There is not a lot of pressure, except the pressure I put on myself.

The fact that there is not much pressure to get work done can allow you to become the stereotypical lazy government employee. I think this is one of the negative aspects of my job. I am still a civilian in the sense that I expect everything to be acted upon in a logical or common sense manner. Governmental bureaucracies do not always follow the most logical procedures when operating, but as an employee you just learn to do as you are told. This is another negative feature of the position. One of the aspects that does not make sense to me is the tons of paperwork required to take any action. I have to document each hour of my work day in a diary. There are certain codes for each type of activity. The only problem that we find is that the administration does not want too much "non-productive" time, yet at the same time the hours that are spent working on an assignment can't be too high either. In other words there is a constant "catch 22" with regard to recording work time.

There are also problems with feedback on our work. This may be unique to my office but it seems that there are very few times when you are told that your work is good or few times when you are given positive feedback on the job you are doing. You are always told when it is not good, however. Negative feedback is common. In many ways you have to be self-assured and self-sufficient.

One of the other negative aspects I see is that ATF compliance operations and law enforcement do not work together enough, if at all. At times it is almost as if we are two separate agencies. With the exception of a few of the agents, I have always understood that the majority of the agents think of the Compliance Inspectors more as clerical help than co-workers. My office also seems to encourage a somewhat passive-aggressive hostility towards the law enforcement side of the agency. Things are changing in this regard, but the change is slow. Now that the ATF Compliance Office is focusing on the regulation of firearms laws as a primary goal, we are working more closely with the ATF Law Enforcement Agents and I hope to see this trend continue.

Overall I am satisfied with my position with ATF at the present time. I do not feel that this is the type of position I would want to make into a permanent career, but many people do. I think it is a great entry-level position that gives the employee many different experiences from which to draw for future use.

CHAPTER 27:

So You Still Want to be an FBI Agent?[1]

If, after reading about all the career possibilities in this book, you still want to be an FBI Special Agent then you need to know the basic facts about the job, its requirements and where to find more information.

The FBI is the flagship of the federal government's investigative agencies. The FBI employs approximately 23,000 employees nationwide, 9,500 of whom are Special Agents. FBI Special Agents investigate organized crime, white collar crime, public corruption, financial crime, fraud, bribery, copyright violations, civil rights violations, bank robberies, extortion, kidnapping, air piracy, terrorism, foreign counterintelligence, interstate crime, and drug trafficking, and are responsible for enforcing over 260 federal statutes. The work can involve surveillance, undercover operations, interviewing witnesses and suspects, examination of records of businesses, computer investigations of financial transactions, sting operations, counter-espionage activity, apprehension and arrest of fugitives and criminals, providing court testimony, and numerous other highly sensitive, demanding and sometimes dangerous situations. Agents prepare detailed written reports which are turned over to a U.S. Attorney's office for prosecution. Agents also assist the U.S. Attorney's office in preparing cases for trial and are required to appear as witnesses during trials and grand jury hearings. The work of FBI Special Agents requires long hours, night work, shift work, weekend work, holiday work. They must be on duty at all times, even on their vacation.

Special Agents are recruited year round from 56 field offices (See Appendix III for the phone number of the one nearest you and contact that office's Applicant Coordinator). These field offices are coordinated by FBI Headquarters in Washington D.C. which has state of the art laboratories, staffed by expert analysts and other support staff skilled at investigation and information retrieval.

---

[1] The substance of this section is taken from the FBI's own recruiting literature, which is cited in the subsequent footnotes.

As former FBI Director William S. Sessions says, "You should know from the outset that the competition is tough. We select only the very best for FBI training."[2] The FBI's reputation and the almost insatiable desire for the law enforcement or criminal justice student to be drawn in by the public image and the TV glamour ensure that the pool is large enough that only the most outstanding candidates are selected.

The FBI provides a fact sheet (FD-257) which is periodically updated. This lists the basic or threshold requirements and any special qualities that the FBI needs to meet current and emerging deficiencies. As well as being a U.S. citizen between the ages 23 and 37, meeting specific eyesight and hearing requirements,[3] and being in excellent physical condition, the candidate must have a four-year degree from an accredited college and be prepared to be assigned anywhere in the Bureau's jurisdiction. There are five types of degrees that are acceptable: Law, Accounting, Engineering and Science, Language and "Diversified." The Law route requires a JD from an accredited resident law school and two years of undergraduate work. Criminology and Criminal Justice majors fall under the "Diversified" category. To qualify for this entrance route you need a bachelor's degree in any discipline, plus three years full-time work experience, which can be reduced to two years for those possessing a master's degree. In addition to these five programs the FBI also recognizes the importance of women and minorities who may get a priority rating in any of the basic five categories.

If you can meet these requirements you are eligible to move on to the next step which is a written application process. The application form can be obtained from any field office. This will be followed by a competitive program of selection for all those within one of the entrance groups, or in the case of criminal justice majors, the Diversified group.

---

[2] "Message from the Director" in *Face Unique Challenges with the FBI: A Career as a Special Agent*. U.S. Department of Justice: Federal Bureau of Investigations, brochure (n.d.).

[3] **Eyesight**: uncorrected vision must not be less than 20/200 (Snellen) corrected to 20/20 in one eye and at least 20/40 in the other; **hearing**: no one will be considered with a greater hearing loss than 25 decibels (ANSI) at 1000, 2000, and 3000 Hertz; single reading of 35 decibels at 1000, 2000, or 3000 Hertz; single reading of 35 decibels at 500 Hertz; or single reading at 4000 Hertz.

These components of this selection process include: (1) a series of written tests; (2) an oral board interview focussing on initial impact, interest/motivation, knowledge of current events, range of interests, resourcefulness, accomplishments, oral communication skills, and overall impression; (3) background investigation, including credit and arrest records, interviews with associates, employers, neighbors, and a verification of education and business references; (4) urinalysis screening test for the use of illegal substances; (5) medical exam; and (6) a demanding physical fitness test. A polygraph examination may also be required. The first three of these phases are crucial. You will only get to stage (2), the interview, if you score high enough on the written test. The total of the test and interview scores is the PRG (Percentile Ranking Grade) and forms the basis of the final ranking for the candidate. Only the highest ranked candidates in each of the programs is moved on to the subsequent stages.

Those who make it through the initial application process and are accepted for training will go to Quantico, Virginia for a 16-week training program. Newly hired agents will be paid their salary while in training which is comprised of classroom instruction, physical fitness, defensive tactics and firearms training.[4] Only upon successfully passing the academy training program does the graduate receive the title FBI Agent. The agent will remain on probationary status for one year.

Newly graduated agents are assigned to a small to medium size FBI field office, depending upon the office's needs and the agent's special skills and abilities. They are then transferred to a large metropolitan office.

The starting level for FBI Special Agents is GS-10 ($29,511) which increases after training to around $37,000 as a result of overtime. Agents rise thereafter to GS-13 ($46,210 base, $56,000+ with overtime) in field assignments before promotion to a supervisory or managerial capacity. There is a liberal benefits package and for Special Agents who have 20

---

[4] All training is evaluated by tests which require at least an 85% to pass and skill performance standards which must be reached within a certain period. The physical fitness tests are scored on a 10-point scale and comprised of five components: pull-ups (20 or more=10), push-ups (71 or more=10 points), sit-ups (100 or more in a two-minute time limit=10 points), 120 yard shuttle run (21.5 secs=10 points) and a two-mile run (12 minutes=10 points), for a maximum score of 50 points.

years law enforcement experience a reduced retirement age of 50. The mandatory retirement age is 57.

Many students do not realize that the FBI operates an, albeit highly competitive, paid Honors Internship program (HIP) for the period June through August, based at FBI headquarters in Washington DC. To qualify you must be an undergraduate having completed three years of college or a graduate student returning to college after the Internship. The Intern must have a GPA of at least 3.0. The applicant must complete form FD-646a and send this together with a current transcript, a resume, a 500 word essay describing your motivation for applying to the program and what you will expect to gain from it, a written recommendation from your dean or department head and a recent photograph. Past Interns have described the program as: outstanding among government internships, making the transition to Special Agent thoroughly enjoyable; "rewarding, enlightening, and challenging;" "fascinating and exciting" with numerous life-enriching learning experiences; and from one student: "My summer was so positive, educational and rewarding that it inspired me to pursue a full-time career with the FBI."[5] Indeed, many of the Interns go on to work for the FBI, though not necessarily as Special Agents.

For additional information contact your local field office (See Appendix III for phone number) or write to:

U.S. Department of Justice, Federal Bureau of Investigation
10th Street and Pennsylvania Avenue, N.W. Washington DC 20535.

---

[5] U.S. Department of Justice, Federal Bureau of Investigation, *FBI Honors Internship Program*, Washington D.C. brochure (n.d.).

APPENDIX I:

ADDRESSES OF FEDERAL JOB INFORMATION/ TESTING CENTERS

For information on job opportunities and for application forms, contact the Federal Job Information/Testing office which is nearest the location where you would like to work.

The first line of the address should **always** be:
Federal Job Information Center

ALABAMA
Building 600, Suite 341
3322 Memorial Pkwy South
Huntsville, AL 35801-5311
(205) 544-5802

ALASKA
222 W. 7th Ave, Box 22
Anchorage, AK 99513-7572
(907) 271-5821

ARIZONA
3225 N. Central Ave.
Rm. 1415
Phoenix, AZ 85004
(602) 640-5800

ARKANSAS
(See Oklahoma listing)

CALIFORNIA
9650 Flair Drive, Suite 100A
El Monte, CA 91731

Voice: (818) 575-6510
BBS: (818) 575-6521

1029 J Street, 2nd Floor
Sacramento, CA 95814
(916) 551-1464

880 Front Street, Rm. 4-S-9
San Diego, CA 92188
(619) 557-6165

211 Main St.
Second Floor, Room 235
San Francisco, CA 94105
(415) 744-5627

COLORADO
P.O. Box 25167
Denver, CO 80225
Physically located at 12345 W.
Alameda Pkwy. Lakewood, CO
(303) 969-7050.

For job information (24 hrs./ day) in the following states:
Montana: (303) 969-7052
Utah: (303) 969-7053
Wyoming: (303) 969-7054
For forms and local supplements: (303) 969-7055.

CONNECTICUT
450 Main St., Rm. 613
Hartford, CT 06103
(203) 240-3263

DELAWARE
(See Philadelphia, PA listing)

DISTRICT OF COLUMBIA
1900 E Street, N.W., Rm. 1416
Washington DC 20415
(202) 606-2700

FLORIDA
3444 McCrory Place, Suite 150
Orlando, FL 32803
(407) 648-6148

GEORGIA
75 Spring St., S.W., Rm. 960
Atlanta, GA 30303
(404) 331-4315

GUAM
238 O'Hara St., Rm. 902
Agana, Guam 96910
(671) 472-7451

HAWAII
(plus other Hawaiian Islands and overseas):
300 Ala Moana Blvd.-Rm. 5316
Honolulu, HI 96850
(808) 541-2791
(808) 541-2784 (overseas)

IDAHO
(See Washington listing)

ILLINOIS
175 W. Jackson Blvd., Rm. 530
Chicago, IL 60604
(312) 353-6192
Applicants wanting information about jobs in Madison and St. Clair Counties (East St. Louis area), see Missouri (St. Louis) listing and dial (314) 539-2285.

INDIANA
575 N. Pennsylvania St.
Indianapolis, IN 46204
(317) 226-7161
Applicants wanting information about jobs in Clark, Dearborn, and Floyd Counties, see Ohio listing and dial (513) 225-2720.

IOWA
(See Missouri listing)
Applicants wanting information about jobs in Scott County, see Illinois listing and dial (312) 353-6192; for jobs in

Pottawattamie County, see
Kansas listing and dial (316)
269-6794.

KANSAS
120 S. Market Street, Rm. 101
Wichita, KS 67202
(316) 269-6794

In Johnson, Leavenworth and
Wyandotte Counties dial (816)
426-5702.

KENTUCKY
(See Ohio listing)
Applicants wanting information
about jobs in Henderson County
see Indiana listing and dial (317)
226-7161.

LOUISIANA
1515 Poydras, 6th Fl., Suite 608
New Orleans, LA 70112
(504) 589-2764

MAINE
(See New Hampshire listing)

MARYLAND
101 W. Lombard St.
Baltimore, MD 21201
(301) 962-3822

MASSACHUSETTS
10 Causeway St.
Boston, MA 02222-1031
(617) 565-5900

MICHIGAN
477 Michigan Ave., Rm. 565
Detroit, MI 48226
Voice: (313) 226-6950
Electronic Bulletin Board:
(313) 226-4423
(300/1200/2400 baud modem)

MINNESOTA
Twin Cities:
Federal Building
Ft. Snelling, MN 55111
(612) 725-3430
For job information in North
and South Dakota dial (612)
725-3430.

MISSISSIPPI
(See Alabama listing)

MISSOURI
601 E. 12th St., Rm. 134
Kansas City, MO 64106
(816) 426-5702

815 Olive St., Rm. 400
St. Louis, MO 63101
(314) 539-2285

MONTANA
(See Colorado listing)

NEBRASKA
(See Kansas listing)

NEVADA
(See Sacramento, CA listing)

NEW HAMPSHIRE
80 Daniel St., Rm. 104
Portsmouth, NH 03801-3879
(603) 431-7115

NEW JERSEY
970 Broad Street
Newark, NJ 07102
(201) 645-3673
In Camden, dial (215) 597-7440.

NEW MEXICO
505 Marquette Avenue, NW
Suite 910
Albuquerque, NM 87102
(505) 766-5583
In Dona Ana, Otero and El Paso
Counties dial (505) 766-1893.

NEW YORK
Jacob K. Javits Federal Building
26 Federal Plaza
New York, NY 10278
(212) 264-0422

James N. Hanley Federal
  Building
100 South Clinton St.
Syracuse, NY 13260
(315) 423-5660

NORTH CAROLINA
P.O. Box 25069
Raleigh, NC 27611
(919) 856-4361
Physically located at:
4505 Falls of the Neuse Road,
Suite 445, Raleigh, NC 27609.

NORTH DAKOTA
(See Minnesota listing)

OHIO
200 W. 2nd St., Rm. 506
Dayton, OH 45402
(513) 225-2720
Applicants wanting information
about jobs in counties north of
and including Van Wert,
Auglaize, Hardin, Marion,
Crawford, Richland, Ashland,
Wayne, Stark, Carroll, and
Columbiana Counties, see
Michigan listing and dial (313)
226-6950.

OKLAHOMA
200 N.W. Fifth Street
2nd Floor
Oklahoma City, OK 73102
(405) 231-4948

OREGON
1220 SW Third Street, Rm. 376
Portland, OR 97204
(503) 326-3141

PENNSYLVANIA
Federal Building, Rm. 168
P.O. Box 761
Harrisburg, PA 17108
(717) 782-4494

600 Arch Street, Rm. 1416
Philadelphia, PA 19106
(215) 597-7440

1000 Liberty Ave., Rm. 119
Pittsburgh, PA 15222
(412) 644-2755

PUERTO RICO
San Juan
Carlos E. Chardon St.
Hato Rey, Puerto Rico 00918
(809) 766-5242

RHODE ISLAND
John O. Pastore Federal
Building
Room 310, Kennedy Plaza
Providence, RI 02903
(401) 528-5251

SOUTH CAROLINA
(See North Carolina listing)

SOUTH DAKOTA
(See Minnesota listing)

TENNESSEE
200 Jefferson Ave, Suite 1312
Memphis, TN 38103-2355
(901) 544-3956

TEXAS
1100 Commerce St., Rm. 6B12
Dallas, TX 75242
(214) 767-8035

Houston, TX
(Phone recording only)
(713) 226-2375

8610 Broadway, Room 305
San Antonio, TX 78217
(512) 229-6611

UTAH
(See Colorado listing)

VERMONT
(See New Hampshire listing)

VIRGINIA
Federal Building
200 Granby Mall, Rm. 220
Norfolk, VA 23510-1886
(804) 441-3355

WASHINGTON
915 Second Ave.
Seattle, WA 98174
(206) 442-4365

WEST VIRGINIA
For job information in West
Virginia dial (513) 225-2866.

WISCONSIN
Residents in Grant, Iowa,
Lafayette, Dane, Green, Rock,
Jefferson, Walworth, Waukesha,
Racine, Kenosha, and
Milwaukee Counties should dial
(312) 353-6189 for job
information. All other Wisconsin
residents should refer to the
Minnesota listing.

WYOMING
(See Colorado listing)

APPENDIX II:

ADDRESSES OF SELECTED
DIRECT-HIRE FEDERAL AGENCIES

Central Intelligence Agency
Personnel Representative
Post Office Box 2144
Chicago, IL 60690

Defense Intelligence Agency
Civilian Personnel Operations Division
Pentagon
Washington DC 20301

Federal Bureau of Investigation
10th Street and Pennsylvania Ave., NW
Washington DC 20535

Federal Reserve System, Board of Governors
20th Street and Constitution Ave., NW
Washington DC 20551

General Accounting Office
Room 4650, 441 G Street, NW
Washington DC 20548

National Security Agency
Fort Meade, MD 20775

U.S. Nuclear Regulatory Commission
Division of Organization of Personnel
Personnel Resources and Employment Programs
Washington DC 20555

Postal Rate Commission
Administrative Office, Room 500
2000 L Street, NW
Washington DC 20268

U.S. Postal Service
(Contact your local Postmaster)

Veterans Administration, Department of Medicine and
Surgery. Employment inquiries should be sent to VA medical
centers nationwide. (The VA employs social workers and
various categories of therapists.)

Judicial Branch of the Government (positions such as court
administrators, bailiffs, computer operators, law
clerks/attorneys, etc. This does not include positions in
administration with the U.S. Courts and the U.S. Customs
Courts.)

APPENDIX III:

FBI FIELD OFFICES

ALABAMA
Birmingham:
(205) 252-7705
Mobile:
(205) 438-3674
ALASKA
Anchorage:
(907) 276-4441
ARIZONA
Phoenix:
(602) 279-5511
ARKANSAS
Little Rock:
(501) 221-9100
CALIFORNIA
Los Angeles:
(213) 477-6565
Sacramento:
(916) 481-9110
San Diego:
(619) 231-1122
San Francisco:
(415) 553-7400
COLORADO
Denver:
(303) 629-7171
CONNECTICUT
New Haven:
(203) 777-6311

DELAWARE
Baltimore, MD:
(301) 265-8080
DISTRICT OF COLUMBIA
Washington, D.C.:
(202) 324-3000
FLORIDA
Jacksonville:
(904) 721-1211
Miami:
(305) 944-9101
Tampa:
(813) 228-7661
GEORGIA
Atlanta:
(404) 521-3900
Savannah
(912) 354-9911
HAWAII
Honolulu:
(808) 521-1411
IDAHO
Salt Lake City, UT:
(801) 355-7521
ILLINOIS
Chicago:
(312) 431-1333
Springfield:
(217) 522-9675

251

INDIANA
  Indianapolis:
  (317) 639-3301
IOWA
  Omaha, NE:
  (402) 348-1210
KANSAS
  Kansas City, MO:
  (816) 221-6100
KENTUCKY
  Louisville:
  (502) 583-3941
LOUISIANA
  New Orleans:
  (504) 522-4671
MAINE
  Boston, MA:
  (617) 742-5533
MARYLAND
  Baltimore:
  (301) 265-8080
MASSACHUSETTS
  Boston:
  (617) 742-5533
MICHIGAN
  Detroit:
  (313) 965-2323
MINNESOTA
  Minneapolis:
  (612) 339-7861
MISSISSIPPI
  Jackson:
  (601) 948-5000
MISSOURI
  Kansas City:
  (816) 221-6100

St. Louis:
  (314) 241-5357
MONTANA
  Salt Lake City, UT
  (801) 355-7521
NEBRASKA
  Omaha:
  (402) 348-1210
NEVADA
  Las Vegas:
  (702) 385-1281
NEW HAMPSHIRE
  Boston, MA:
  (617) 742-5533
NEW JERSEY
  Newark:
  (201) 622-5613
  Philadelphia, PA
  (215) 629-0800
NEW MEXICO
  Albuquerque:
  (505) 247-1555
NEW YORK
  Albany:
  (518) 465-7551
  Buffalo:
  (716) 856-7800
  New York City:
  (212) 553-2700
NORTH CAROLINA
  Charlotte:
  (704) 529-1030
NORTH DAKOTA
  Minneapolis, MN:
  (612) 339-7861

OHIO
Cincinnati:
(513) 421-4310
Cleveland:
(216) 522-1400
OKLAHOMA
Oklahoma City:
(405) 842-7471
OREGON
Portland:
(503) 224-4181
PENNSYLVANIA
Philadelphia:
(215) 629-0800
Pittsburgh:
(412) 471-2000
PUERTO RICO
San Juan:
(809) 754-6000
RHODE ISLAND
Boston, MA:
(617) 742-5533
SOUTH CAROLINA
Columbia
(803) 254-3011
SOUTH DAKOTA
Minneapolis, MN:
(612) 339-7861
TENNESSEE
Knoxville:
(615) 544-0751
Memphis:
(901) 525-7373
TEXAS
Dallas:
(214) 720-2200

El Paso:
(915) 533-7451
Houston:
(713) 224-1511
San Antonio:
(512) 225-6741
UTAH
Salt Lake City, UT:
(801) 355-7521
VERMONT
Albany, NY:
(518) 465-7551
VIRGINIA
Norfolk:
(804) 623-3111
Richmond:
(804) 644-2631
Washington DC area:
(202) 324-3000
WASHINGTON
Seattle:
(206) 622-0460
WEST VIRGINIA
Pittsburgh, PA:
(412) 471-2000
WISCONSIN
Milwaukee:
(414) 276-4684
WYOMING
Denver, CO:
(303) 629-7171

APPENDIX IV:

SELECTED BIBLIOGRAPHIC RESOURCES

General careers information

Bolles, Richard Nelson. *What Color is Your Parachute?* 10th ed. Berkeley: Ten Speed Press, 1993.

Carter, Carol. *Majoring in the Rest of Your Life*. New York: The Noonday Press, 1990.

Eastern Michigan University Career Search: A Guide For Success in Today's Job Market. Ypsilanti: Eastern Michigan University Careers Services, 1992.

Lauber, Daniel. *Government Job Finder*. River Forest: Planning/Communications, 1992.

Lauber, Daniel. *Non-Profits' Job Finder*. River Forest: Planning/Communications, 1992.

Michigan Occupation and Information Service. *MOIS*. Lansing, MI: 1993.

Savage, Kathleen M. and Karen Hill, eds. *Vocational Careers Sourcebook*. Detroit: Gale Research Inc., 1992.

Savage, Kathleen M. and Annette Novallo, eds. *Professional Careers Sourcebook*, Detroit: Gale Research Inc., 1992.

Turkel, Studs. *Working*. New York: Pantheon, 1972.

General criminal justice careers information:

DeLucia, Robert C. and Thomas J. Doyle. *Career Planning in Criminal Justice*. Cincinnati: Anderson Publishing Co., 1990.

Law Enforcement Career Guide. 4th ed. Eaton Park, FL: Harvest Publications, 1992.

Stinchcomb, James D. *Opportunities in Law Enforcement and Criminal Justice*. Lincolnwood: VGM/Career Horizons, 1984.

U.S. Department of Labor. *Criminal Justice Careers Guidebook*. Washington DC: Government Printing Office, 1982.

Test Guides

Contact the National Learning Corporation at 212 Michael Drive, Syosset, NY 11791 or call (212) 921-8888. Jack Rudman edits a series of test guides for every imaginable position in criminal justice.

Law enforcement and private security

Cohen, Paul and Shari Cohen. *Careers in Law Enforcement and Security*. New York: Rosen Publishing, 1990.

Coleman, Joseph. *Your Career in Law Enforcement*. New York: Arco Publishing, 1979.

Good, Stephen M. *How to Get a Job with a Police Department*. New York: Barnes and Noble, 1985.

Lunneborg, Patricia W. *Women Police Officers*. C. C. Thomas, 1989.

Mahoney, Thomas E. *Law Enforcement Career Planning: A Handbook*. Springfield, IL: C.C. Thomas, 1989.

Nowicki, Ed. *True Blue: True Stories About Real Cops*. Powers Lake, WI: Performance Dimensions Publishing, 1992.

O'Neill, Hugh. *Police Officer*. New York: Arco Publishing, 1992.

Orion Agency. *Obtaining Your Private Investigator's License*. Boulder, CO: Paladin Press, 1986.

Panzarella, Robert. *Police Officer*. Englewood Cliffs, NJ: Prentice Hall, 1989.

Pickens, Frank. *So You Want to Be a Cop*. Royal Palm Beach, FL: EES Publications, 1990.

The Police Employment Guide. Huntsville, TX: Sam Houston State University, 1982.

Rachlin, Harvey. *The Making of a Cop*. New York: Pocket Books, 1991.

Stern, Ron. *Law Enforcement Careers: A Complete Guide From Application to Employment*. Mt. Shasta, CA: Lawman Press, 1988.

Stern, Ron. *Law Enforcement Employment Guide*. 2nd ed. Mt. Shasta, CA: Lawman Press, 1990.

Stinchcomb, James D. *Opportunities in Law Enforcement and Criminal Justice Careers*. Skokie, IL: VGM Career Horizons, 1990.

Thomas, Barbara L. *Successful Private Eyes and Private Spies*. Gettysburg, PA: Thomas Publications, 1986.

Vincent, Claude L. *Police Officer*. Ottawa: Carleton University Press, 1990.

Yentes, Nancy A. and M. Steven Meagher. "Choosing a Career in Policing: A Comparison of Male and Female Perceptions." *Journal of Police Science and Administration* 14. Dec 1986, pp. 320-27.

Lawyers, law school and careers in law

Barron's *Guide to Law Schools*. 9th ed. New York: Barron's Educational Series, 1990.

Corkery, Jim. *Career in Law*. Holmes Beach, FL: W.W. Gaunt, 1989.

Fins, Alice. *Opportunities in Paralegal Careers*. Lincolnwood: National Textbook Company, 1985.

Fry, William R. and Roy Hoopes. *Paralegal Careers*. Hillside, NJ: Enslow, 1986.

Gerber, Rudolph J. *Lawyers, Courts and Professionalism: The Agenda for Reform*. New York: Greenwood Press, 1989.

Graham, Lawrence. *Your Ticket to Law School: Getting in and Staying In*. New York: Bantam Books, 1985.

Johnstone, Quinton and Martin Wenglinsky. *Paralegals: Progress and Prospects of a Satellite Occupation*. Westport, CT: Greenwood Press, 1985.

Kunen, James S. *How Can You Defend Those People?: The Making of a Criminal Lawyer*. New York: Random House, 1983.

Law School Admissions Council. *The Pre-Law Handbook*.

Munneke, Gary. *Careers in Law*. Lincolnwood, IL: VGM Career Horizons, 1991.

Rakoff, Dena. *Choosing a Career in Law*. Cambridge, MA: Harvard University Press, 1990.

Stuart, Bruce S. and Kim D. Stuart. *Top Law Schools*. New York: Arco, 1990.

Utley, Frances. *From Law Student to Lawyer: A Career Planning Manual*. Chicago: American Bar Association, 1984.

Corrections, probation and parole

Steinberg, Eve. *Corrections Officer*. Englewood Cliffs, NJ: Prentice-Hall, 1989.

Stinchcomb, James D. *Opportunities in Law Enforcement and Criminal Justice*. Chapter on "Corrections and Rehabilitation," Lincolnwood, IL: VGM Career Horizons, 1990, pp. 110-124.

Whithead, John T. *Burnout in Probation and Corrections*. Westport, CT: Greenwood Press, 1989.

Human services

Baxter, Neale. *Opportunities in Counseling and Development Careers*. Lincolnwood, IL: National Textbook Company, 1990.

National Association of Social Workers. *Careers in Social Work*. Silver Spring, MD: NASW, 1987.

National Therapeutic Recreation Society. *About Therapeutic Recreation*. Alexandria, VA: NTRS, 1987.

Roberts, Albert R. *Social Work in Juvenile and Criminal Justice Settings*. Springfield, IL: Charles C. Thomas, 1983.

Schmolling, Paul. *Careers in Mental Health: A Guide to Helping Professions*. Garrett Park, MD: Garrett Park Press, 1986.

"Prison Social Worker." (Pamphlet) Sauk Center, MN: Vocational Biographies, 1988.

Graduate school, academia and research

Altbach, Philip G. and Richard D. Lambert, eds. *Academic Profession*. Annals of the American Academy of Political and Social Science (No. 448) Philadelphia: American Academy of Political and Social Science, 1980.

Heiberger, Mary M. and Julia M. Vick. *Academic Job Search Handbook*. Philadelphia: University of Pennsylvania Press, 1992.

Phillips, Estelle M. and D.S. Pugh. *How to Get a Ph.D.* Philadelphia: Open University Press, 1987.

van den Berghe, Pierre. *Academic Gamesmanship: How to Make a Ph.D. Pay*. New York: Abelard-Schuman, 1970.

Graduate school in criminal justice

Academy of Criminal Justice Sciences. *Guide to Graduate Programs in Criminal Justice and Criminology, 1991-92*. Highland Heights, KY: ACJS, 1991.

Brustman, Mary Jane. "Recruiting Minority Students and Faculty for Graduate and Professional Schools." *Journal of Criminal Justice Education* 2 (1991): 245-254.

Flanagan, Timothy J. "Criminal Justice Doctoral Programs in the United States and Canada: Findings From a National Survey." *Journal of Criminal Justice Education* 1 (1990): 195-214.

McElrath, Karen. "Standing in the Shadows: Academic Mentoring in Criminology." *Journal of Criminal Justice Education* 1 (1990): pp. 135-152.

Nemeth, C. P. *Anderson's Directory of Criminal Justice Education 1990-91*. Cincinnati, OH: Anderson Publishing Co.

Teaching Sociology. "Special Issue of Graduate Education" Volume 19 (No. 3), July 1991.

Federal criminal justice careers

ASA. *How to Join the Federal Workforce and Advance Your Career*. Washington DC: American Sociological Association, nd.

FOCIS (Federal Occupational and Career Information System.)

Phillips, David Atlee. *Careers in Secret Operations: How to be a Federal Intelligence Officer*. University Publications of America, Inc., 1984.

Warner, John W. (Jack). *Federal Jobs in Law Enforcement*. New York: ARCO, Prentice Hall, 1992.

APPENDIX V:

SELECTED JOB OPPORTUNITY LISTINGS

The following is a list of newsletters, magazines and software that carries actual position openings. For information about how much each of these cost, how often they are published and where to obtain them, see the information after the introduction to each section of this book.

General sources of criminal justice job opportunities

American Jails (corrections)

Career Paths Bulletin (human services)

Chronicle of Higher Education (academic criminology/criminal justice and law)

Clearinghouse Review (law)

Criminologist (academic criminology/criminal justice, American Society of Criminology)

Employment Bulletin (academic criminology/criminal justice, from ASA)

Employment Bulletin (academic criminology/criminal justice, from ACJS)

Federal Career Digest

Federal Career Opportunities (Federal Research Services Inc)

Federal Times

Law Enforcement Employment Monthly

National Employment Listing Service (Sam Houston State University)

NASW News (National Association of Social Workers)

Police Career Digest (includes *Express Jobs Newsletter*)

The PSIC (Protective Services Information Center) Listing (police and security)

Social Service Jobs